THE PIONEERS

Images of the Frontier

109 illustrations
selected and introduced by
Joseph Czestochowski

Phaidon

the young country could no longer be considered an extension of Europe, and the assurance of independence precipitated a spirit of immense possibilities. An entirely new phase of civilization seemed imminent. To express this new-found confidence and to emphasize further the permanence of the country, a number of visual images were identified as national symbols, the most propitious of which were those of the pioneer and the frontier wilderness.

As these symbols of progress and possibility emerged, the first wave of artists traveled west and discovered a new American symbol, the North American Indian. More than ten generations after the early pioneers had successfully inhabited the eastern seaboard, the Indian came to be viewed – along with Niagara Falls – as one of the natural wonders of the continent.

To many, and particularly to the English, the creation of a new civilization in the United States clearly necessitated the destruction of another, that of the Indian. This belief in the inevitability of the Indians' fate prompted an active romanticism about them, and although this theme decidedly served contemporary English political purposes, it did, in time, become an essential aspect of the American national identity.

One of England's most widely recognized artists, Joseph Wright, addressed the theme in the last quarter of the eighteenth century. Known for his mastery of dramatic visual effect, Wright – in *The Indian Widow* (Plate 12) – provided for the European community a powerful image of the North American Indian as superior in virtue to America's supposedly civilized society. Almost half a century later, Eugène Delacroix captured a similar feeling in his sensitive portrayal of *Les Natchez* (Plate 13). These pictures, it should be noted, suggest two distinct causes for the demise of the native American. In the former painting we encounter the results of forceful confrontation, whereas in the latter we witness the unintended destruction of the native population through the settlers' introduction of various diseases, such as smallpox and influenza, to which the Indians possessed no immunity.

Although the Indian remained the hero and center of attraction for many Europeans throughout the nineteenth century, the pioneer was never really accepted in Europe as a popular American frontier hero. Nor was the United States pictured, except with derision, as the land of promise. This situation contrasted with the English response to the appealing views of South Africa, Australia and New Zealand. In the viewpoints expressed by the artists Baines (Plate 36 and 37, *top*), Bowler, and Earle (Plates 16 and 19), the pioneers' adventurous exploits were clearly the central attraction.

In America, the Indian was rapidly becoming an anachronism. United States citizens were not without sympathy for the plight of the Indians, but this sympathy bowed before other priorities. Although the pursuit of progress was of primary importance, the theme of the vanishing native race was adopted by a number of American writers, among them James Fenimore Cooper in *The Last of the Mohicans*(see Plate 15) and Henry Wadsworth Longfellow in his *Song of Hiawatha.* William Cullen Bryant echoed this theme in 1824 in his poem 'An Indian at the Burial Place of His Fathers':

They waste us – ay – like April snow
In the warm noon, we shrink away;
And fast they follow, as we go
Toward the setting day –
Till they shall fill the land, and we
Are driven into the Western sea.

The nineteenth-century penchant for scientific inquiry prompted a number of artists to spend periods of time among the native inhabitants of several countries. In the words of George Catlin, these artist-explorers were determined 'to rescue from oblivion so much of their primitive looks and customs'. Among the many artists who attempted to preserve a vital impression of the vanishing natives were the Swiss national Karl Bodmer (Plates 20 and 37, *bottom*), the American Catlin (Plates 28 and 46), the Canadian Paul Kane (Plates 24 and 29, *top*), and the Australian Robert Dowling (Plate 76, *bottom*). Each spent a concentrated period of time among his subjects, and the results are among the most enduring records of these people. Although still interested in preserving customs, the later work of Alfred Jacob Miller (Plates 32 and 33), Charles Deas (Plates 22 and 60, *bottom*), and John Mix Stanley (Plate 29, *bottom*) was more concerned with the dramatic visual possibilities afforded by their unusual activities.

Simultaneously, an active interest in the landscape emerged. Since the wilderness played such a central role in the pioneers' experience, it is not unexpected that one of the earliest iconographies focused on the primordial majesty of nature. Clearly, the uniqueness of a new environment – from the Table Bay Mountains in South Africa to the Buffalo Ranges in Australia (Plate 50) to the Rocky Mountains in America (Plate 49) – first inspired the pioneer artist's imagination.

During the first quarter of the nineteenth century in America, it became evident that the country possessed extraordinary natural wonders. As early as 1820, John Hill, in his *Picturesque Views of American Scenery,* stated, 'The vast regions which are comprised in or subjected to the republic present to the eye every variety of the beautiful and sublime ... Striking, however, and original as the features of nature undoubtedly are in the United States, they have rarely been made the subjects of pictorial delineation ... America only, of all the countries of civilized man, is unsung and undescribed.' Within a short time, however, America's first group of native landscape artists, the Hudson River School, was founded by Thomas Cole and the shortcoming was remedied. A contemporary of John Constable, Cole extolled the virtues of the American landscape with the hope of projecting a unique national identity. Unlike many of the more generalized topographical views of Thomas Baines and Thomas Bowler, Cole sought to isolate and investigate a microcosm of the new land (Plates 15 and 21).

A previously undisturbed natural wilderness, the Hudson River Valley was on the threshold of change. As Cole recognized, the completion of the Erie Canal in 1825 introduced, as had the Conestoga wagon in 1740, a new period of frontier exploration and expansion. The West was now readily accessible through an intricate system of natural and man-made waterways; in a short time, the trade and migratory activity along this waterway surpassed that of any other in the country, and as trade prospered, so too did the urban centers along both the Atlantic coast and this interior network. By the 1840s, periodicals were already lamenting the destruction of America's natural resources for the sake of progress and bidding artists to preserve these attributes on canvas before it was too late. 'The axe of civilization', stated one such article, 'is busy with our old forests, and artisan ingenuity is fast sweeping away the relics of our national infancy ... Yankee enterprise has little sympathy with the picturesque, and it behooves our artists to rescue from its grasp the little that is left, before it is forever too late.'

At about the middle of the nineteenth century, the persuasive writings of John Ruskin swept both England and the United States, eventually influencing the pioneer movement and its art. In advancing Ruskin's ideas, Andrew J. Dowling stated in his 1850 *Architecture of Country Houses,* 'a good house ... is a powerful means of civilization ... there is a moral influence in a country house.' Thomas Cole restated this attitude more eloquently: 'The cultivated scenery must not be forgotten, for it is still more important to man in his social capacity ... it encompasses our homes, and, though devoid of the stern sublimity of the wild, its quieter spirit steals tenderly into our bosoms.' In response to such comments, artists like Cole, Krieghoff (Plates 42 and 43), and Chevalier (Plate 50) adopted this imagery to praise the virtues of the rural pioneer endeavor.

Indirectly, the Industrial Revolution had its impact as well. As the population changed from rural to urban, as the frontier became more of a memory than a reality for most people, artists increasingly idealized nature. The great migrations into the cities, as significant in their own way as the earlier frontier surge, simply failed to capture either the popular or the artistic imagination.

What did, however, attract the public's attention were the plans announced for the first transcontinental railroad. Realizing that the physical remoteness of the newly acquired territories of Oregon (1846) and California (1848) had to be overcome in order to create a unified nation, the public came to view the railroad as a metaphor for the country's destiny and restless spirit. Henry David Thoreau's reaction is apt: 'When I meet the engine with its train of cars moving off with planetary motion ... breathing fire and smoke from its nostrils (what kind of winged horse or fiery dragon they will put into the new mythology I don't know), it seems as if the earth had got a race now worthy to inhabit it.'

Almost immediately, the theme of manifest destiny captured the American imagination. The drama of the winning of the American West was beginning and it quickly found expression in the visual arts through artists such as George Caleb Bingham (Plates 34 and 61, *bottom*), J. H. Beard (Plate 39), Asher B. Durand (Plates 30 and 41), Emanuel Leutze (Plates 45 and 75, *top*), and Thomas P. Rossiter (Plate 25).

This spirit was interrupted by the Civil War, but, contrary to expectations, post-Civil War society was characterized by an enormous sense of vitality. An English observer stated, 'Probably, the parallel of this is not to be found in the world's history ... America ... has shown that the heaviest and most costly civil conflict can be borne not only without exhaustion, but even with an increase of national prosperity.' In the decades that followed, America discovered itself, becoming fully aware, for the first time, of its continental dimensions. The great West was the setting for this adventure, and the completion of the transcontinental railroad in 1869 merely confirmed the reality.

The sprawling nation needed a unifying hero, and the pioneer settler – manifest destiny embodied – fitted the specifications admirably. A hero, of course, required a villain, who was readily available in the person of the Indians. Thus, a series of visual metaphors was established, with the pioneer representing civilization and destiny, and the Indian a savage impediment to that destiny. In contrast to the early nineteenth-century scenes of Bodmer and Catlin, in which the Indian was an object of ethnographic curiosity, the native was now viewed as a very real and dangerous threat.

Undaunted nevertheless, the pioneers embarked upon their quest, confident of the righteousness of their endeavor. Numerous government-sponsored expeditions returned from the West with news of its extraordinary wonders and the geographical vastness that allowed economic progress. The poignant hardships of the journey west were usually ignored by artists in favor of mythic portrayals of the pioneers conquering the frontier. We are rarely made aware of the horrors of Indian retaliation against the intruding settlers, the frequent dissolution of families due to death or an inability to cope with the wilderness, the inevitable economic reversals, and the continued social stratification. In short, the frontier experience, as visually interpreted, served more than anything else to nurture an active American mythology.

While these images of the American West do not realistically reflect the social and cultural history of the times, they do demonstrate how artists responded to the strong popular interest in the frontier and they enable us to chronicle the progression of objects or situations that served as focal points of aesthetic interest.

As did the New World's earliest artist-explorers, a large number of painters sought the wilderness in the company of surveying expeditions. Some were most captivated by the immensity of the Great Plains, and Worthington Whittredge (Plate 58) explained this fascination: 'I have been accustomed to measure grandeur, at the most, by the little hills of Western Virginia; I had never thought it might be measured horizontally as on our great Western plains. In fact, I believe it is the accepted idea that all grandeur must be measured up and down.'

While artists such as Whittredge and Colman (Plate 68) were drawn to this sort of topography, others, including Albert Bierstadt (Plates 49 and 65) and Thomas Moran (Plates 66 and 67), found a greater attraction in the mountains. Inspired by the technical possibilities evident in the luminist works of J. M. W. Turner, these artists favored the dramatic and picturesque qualities of their themes. Moran, in responding to an art critic, stated, 'While I desired to tell truly of Nature, I did not wish to realize the scene literally, but to preserve and to convey its true impression.' Writing about Moran, another individual described his approach: 'While he reverences the local truth of a scene, conscious that it is impossible for man to improve the creations of the Almighty, he so renders it as to give it the unmistakable stamp of his own mind and style, and invests it with the poetic sentiment of a highly-wrought imagination.'

This post-1860 penchant for the picturesque also manifested itself in the splendid works of Verner (Plate 64), O'Brien (Plate 51) and Piguenit (Plate 69). Temporarily, attention turned to the quieter aspects of the surrounding environment, as an active genre tradition emerged, receiving widespread public response. Once again, however, the majority of images created by such artists as Nahl (Plates 54 and 63) and Roberts (Plate 77, *bottom*) were more literary than realistic. Although graphic and convincing in detail and true to the spirit of the events, the paintings are far from a mirror of life.

Clearly, a conclusion to the frontier experience was approaching with the end of the century, yet the popular appetite for adventure and heroes required the maintenance of a frontier imagery. Briefly, a substitute was sought in the mysterious northern lands, as several artists – among them Bierstadt and Bradford (Plate 57) – journeyed to the Arctic regions. However spectacular the scenery of these lands may have been, their very strangeness proved too great an obstacle for widespread acceptance.

Of more enduring interest to people in the East and West alike was the romanticism of the individual on the frontier. In America, at least, the closing decades of the nineteenth century meant the end of a way of life for the settler, the cowboy, the Indian, and others. Especially to the artists closest to the frontier, the closing of the open ranges by the cattle rancher's barbed wire signified the loss of an integral part of the natural wilderness.

At the close of the last century, the historian Frederick Jackson Turner in his *The Significance of the Frontier in American History* (1899) best described the changes that were taking place: 'The United States lies like a huge page in the history of society. Line by line as we read this continental page from West to East we find the record of social evolution. It begins with the Indian and the hunter, it goes on to tell of the disintegration of savagery by the entrance of the trader, the pathfinder of civilization; we read the annals of the pastoral stage in ranch life; the exploitation of the soil by the raising of unrotated crops . . . and finally, the manufacturing organization with city and factory system.'

Industrialization thus signaled the close of the frontier and the completion of an entire age in American history. New symbols arose, and artists quite naturally reflected on matters of contemporary social, political, and economic concern; like their nineteenth-century predecessors, they hoped to influence the public's attitudes. At the same time, certain other artists like Farny (Plate 73) and Berninghaus (Plates 70 and 71) sought to preserve images from the recent past.

In terms of history, mythology, and art, the experience and importance of the frontier cannot be underestimated. As indicated previously, the absence of readily identifiable and commonly held traditions required a number of collective symbols to nourish a sense of national continuity and vitality. The sheer vastness of the continent and its far-flung civilization demanded accessible popular heroes and images whose spirits were capable of unifying the nation in times of stress.

Throughout, this study has examined one such popular hero – the pioneer – as well as the frontier environment as integral parts of a vast human endeavor called Progress. As a body of work, these paintings constitute a lasting monument to the pioneers' accomplishments and capture a quality of civilization during the eighteenth and nineteenth centuries. These images continue to exert an appeal in the present century, as seen in the work of Scholder (Plate 93), Beal (Plate 95), O'Keeffe (Plate 96), Benton (Plate 92), and others.

The frontier may extend now into space and under the ocean, but for most people, the world has been all too thoroughly charted. One wonders if, when viewing these images of the frontier from the perspective of several centuries, our descendants will recognize, or even seek to recognize, the subtle balance between history and legend.

Notes to the Plates

John White (English, *fl.* 1577–93)

1 Indians Fishing

Watercolor touched with white and gold, 14 × 9¼ in. About 1585. London, British Museum.

With hopes of establishing the first permanent English colony in North America, Sir Walter Raleigh dispatched from Plymouth, England, a group of seven ships under the command of Sir Richard Grenville. Among the colonists in the expedition was White, whose purpose was to serve as draughtsman and cartographer. In the collection of the British Museum are fifty-nine drawings from this expedition. As indicated by the frontispiece to the folio, they were intended to present 'the true pictures and fashions of the people . . .' In the words of Thomas Hariot in his accompanying *Brief and true report of the new found land of Virginia,* 'Dowbtless yt is a pleasant sighte to see the people, sometymes wadinge, . . . in their posteritie, content with their state, and livinge friendlye together of those thinges which god in his bountie hath given unto them . . .'

Pedro Reinel (Portuguese, *c.* 1500–40) and Lopo Homen (Portuguese, *fl.* 1517–65)

2 Map of South America

Watercolor on vellum, 16½ × 23¼ in. About 1525. Paris, Bibliothèque Nationale.

In addition to merely indicating the coastal outlines of the newly discovered continents, most cartographers sought to provide some indication of the lands' striking characteristics, such as native flora, fauna or inhabitants. Included in the well-known 'Miller atlas', this map is labeled *Teira Brasilis* – the land of the brazil trees, and bears the following inscription in the upper left corner, 'This is the chart of the region of great Brazil . . . Its people are somewhat dark in color. Savage and very cruel, they feed on human flesh. These same people are most skillful in the use of the bow and arrow. Here are multicolored parrots and innumerable other birds and monstrous wild beasts, . . . and there grows in great quantity the tree called brazil which is considered proper for dying clothes in purple.'

Unidentified Artist

3 The Landing of Christopher Columbus

Title page to Giuliano Dati (d.1524) : La lettera dell isole che ha trovato nuovamente il Re di Spagna. 1493. Florentine woodcut, $4\frac{5}{8} \times 4\frac{1}{2}$ in. London, British Library.

This is quite possibly the earliest attempt by a European artist to depict the landing of Columbus in the West Indies. Although great significance is now placed on this event, the contemporary reaction to the landing was at best neutral. Except for their nudity, the West Indians appeared to be Asiatics. Thus their discovery failed to satisfy the high expectations of most Europeans. As noted by Columbus in 1493, 'They are well-built people of handsome stature ... In these islands I have so far found no human monstrosities, as many expected; on the contrary, among all these people good looks are esteemed; nor are they negroes, as in Guinea, but with flowing hair.' (From S. E. Morison, *Christopher Columbus, Mariner,* London, 1956, p.220)

Cornelius Visscher (Dutch, *c.* 1619–62)

4 America

Engraving, 20 × 26 in. About 1650–60. The New York Historical Society.

This engraving presents a splendid allegorical image of the new fourth continent – America. And the inscription it bears indicates how widely the myth of the Indian as a savage was perpetuated: 'America is by far the strangest continent; / Here people live as lawless savages / . . . The inhabitants of this land take each other's lives / And slaughter each other like cattle in an unheard of manner. / Like mindless and innocent animals, they destroy each other, / Then roast the flesh as their usual fare.'

Dirk Valkenburg (Dutch, 1675–1721)

5 *(left)* A Plantation in Surinam

Oil on canvas, $20\frac{3}{4} \times 18$ in. 1707. Amsterdam, Rijksmuseum.

By 1597 the Dutch had settled parts of the Guiana coast, but it was not until 1621 that the Dutch West India Company founded the colony of Surinam. The introduction of coffee as a crop greatly increased the economic importance of Surinam in the eighteenth century. In February 1706, Valkenburg – a native of Amsterdam – was commissioned by the merchant Jonas Witsen to paint several views of the plantations that he owned in Surinam. He returned to the Netherlands in 1708, after visiting the three Witsen plantations at Surimombo, Palmeneribo and Waterlant on the Surinam River. Precise identification of this plantation is not possible from the available information.

Benjamin West (American, 1738–1820)

(right) The Indians in Conference with Colonel Bouquet

Ink and wash, $10 \times 8\frac{1}{2}$ in. About 1769. New Haven, Connecticut, Yale Center for British Art and British Studies.

The theme of reconciliation or the enactment of a treaty between the English and the Indians was frequently adopted by Benjamin West. His most striking use of it is found in his painting of 1771 entitled *Penn's Treaty with the Indians* (oil on canvas, $75\frac{1}{2} \times 107\frac{1}{2}$ in. Pennsylvania Academy of the Fine Arts). Although minor by comparison, the small ink-and-wash drawing illustrated here offers a more intimate and sensitive account of the human emotions surrounding such an event. It clearly conveys the success of Henry Bouquet in his expedition against the Ohio Indians in 1764.

James Peachey (English, *fl.* 1781–93)

6 *(top)* Loyalists at Jamestown, Lower Canada

Watercolor, $5\frac{1}{2} \times 13\frac{3}{4}$ in. 1784. Ottawa, The Public Archives of Canada.

An important, although overlooked, result of the American Revolution is depicted in this watercolor. It shows a group of British Loyalists who fled from America, perhaps in fear political persecution. These Loyalists worked along the St Lawrence River as early pioneers in an already thriving environment.

Alexander von Humboldt (German, 1769–1859)

(bottom) View of the Gas Volcanoes of Turbaco

Colored engraving, plate 41 from printed book, *Vues des Cordillières et monuments des peuples indigènes de l'Amérique.* 1810. $16 \times 22\frac{1}{2}$ in. New York, The American Museum of Natural History Library.

In the late eighteenth and early nineteenth centuries, as Europeans were beginning to consider America civilized, interest in Central and South America was growing. Although tales abounded about these exotic lands, scientific exploration was not allowed by the Spanish government until Humboldt managed to obtain permission for free access in 1799. A sensitive interpreter, Humboldt was totally fascinated by certain intriguing aspects of this new land. He spent more than eighteen months studying and recording the flora and fauna, which resulted in the publication of more than thirty volumes between 1805 and 1834. Humboldt's striking images of the richness and strangeness of South America prompted the two American artists F. E. Church and M. J. Heade to visit there in the middle of the century.

Charles B. J. F. de Saint-Memin (French, 1770–1852)

7 An Osage Warrior

Watercolor, $7\frac{1}{2} \times 6\frac{3}{4}$ in. About 1804. Courtesy of the Henry Francis du Pont Winterthur Museum, Delaware.

Saint-Memin introduced the 'physiognotrace' and quickly became known in New York, Philadelphia, Washington, Richmond and Charleston for his small medallion portraits produced by this device. It enabled him to produce a near life-size portrait in pencil (usually on red paper), from which he reduced the image to a two-inch miniature on a copper engraving plate. For thirty dollars, the subject would receive the drawing, the copper plate and twelve proofs.

When in 1804 President Jefferson invited a group of twelve Osage chiefs to visit Washington, Saint-Memin was there to produce some of the earliest known portraits of the Plains Indians. As conveyed in this watercolor, he was impressed by the noble dignity of their physical characteristics. Only five of the portraits done by him on this visit have been preserved.

Jan Mostaert (Dutch, *c.* 1475–1555/6)

8 West Indian Landscape

Oil on oak panel, $34\frac{1}{8} \times 60\frac{1}{4}$ in. About 1542. Haarlem, Frans Hals Museum, on deposit from the State-owned Art Collections Department, The Haque.

Discovered in 1909, this is the earliest known painting of the New World. Countless interpretations exist regarding the exact nature of the scene that is depicted. Some possibilities are Cortes in central Mexico, Coronado in the American Southwest, Columbus landing on Goanin, or the Portuguese invading Brazil in 1550. More important, however, than the precise location of this scene is its representation of a perpetual conflict between man and nature. As stated recently by Hugh Honour in his excellent monograph on *The European Vision of America* (Cleveland, Ohio, Cleveland Museum of Art, 1975), 'The painting is perhaps best understood and appreciated as a visual parable on the innocence and peace of unspoilt nature and the destructive urge of civilized man – a secular counterpart to Mostaert's painting of Eve banished from Eden with Cain killing Abel nearby.'

Frans Jansz. Post (Dutch, *c.* 1612–80)

9 São Francisco River and Fort Maurice

Oil on canvas, $24\frac{3}{4} \times 38$ in. 1638. Paris, Musée du Louvre.

By 1628, after a series of territorial reversals, the Dutch possessed a stronghold in Brazil. Within less than ten years, Count Johann Maurits (1604–79) was appointed the first governor general of the colony. Soon after his appointment, Maurits embarked upon the first scientific Dutch survey of the South American continent. From the Netherlands he gathered an impressive group of forty-six scholars, scientists, artists and craftsmen. Among the six professional artists was Post. His painting offers one of the finest early views of Brazil. The eerie strangeness of the new environment is clearly discernible in his tentative handling of the alien flora and fauna.

Charles Bird King (American, 1785–1862)

10 Young Omawhaw, War Eagle, Little Missouri, and Pawnees

Oil on panel, $25\frac{1}{4} \times 27\frac{3}{4}$ in. 1821. Courtesy of the Smithsonian Institution, Washington, D.C.

At the same time that the United States Government was attempting to learn more about its newly acquired frontier, there was a drive to bring distinguished Indian leaders to Washington, D.C., where they might learn more about white civilization. There was also a growing curiosity about the nature of these strange savages. The first of many groups of Indians arrived in late 1821. After a brief stay in Washington, they traveled to Baltimore, Philadelphia and New York, where on 15 December *The New York American* described them as 'fine specimens of the native race of this continent, uncorrupted by all the civilization the Indian has been capable of acquiring – its vices'.

This painting by King is of five of the younger members of this 1821 delegation. It was commissioned by the current Superintendent of Indian Trade, Thomas L. McKenney, and it aptly captures the noble pride of these warriors. As such, it was only fitting that this painting formed the nucleus of the famous National Indian Portrait Gallery, which contained nearly 150 portraits of Indian visitors to Washington until 1837. In time, the Indians were acknowledged as an extraordinary race, but the costs of colonization were foretold when a government official supported such a portrait gallery because 'this race was about to become extinct, and that a faithful resemblance of the most remarkable among them would be full of interest in after times'.

Francisco José de Goya y Lucientes (Spanish, 1746–1828)

11 *(top)* **Cannibals**

Oil on panel, 13 × 18½ in. About 1812. Besançon, Musée des Beaux Arts.

Although the source of the artist's inspiration is unknown, scholars generally agree that this scene is associated with Canada. The strikingly dramatic composition is almost fanciful in terms of the contrast between Goya's Indians and those in real life. The composition, however, is indicative of early nineteenth-century notions about these unknown lands.

Peter Rindisbacher (Swiss-American, 1806–34)

(bottom) **Captain W. Andrew Bulger Saying Farewell, Fort Mackay, Prairie du Chien, Wisconsin, 1815**

Pen and watercolor, 14 × 24 in. About 1823. Fort Worth, Texas, Amon Carter Museum of Western Art.

Rindisbacher and his parents left their native Switzerland under the misconception that they were heading to a region by the Red River in Louisiana. Instead, they arrived in 1821 at Lord Selkirk's Red River Colony in the cold prairie wilderness of southern Manitoba and Saskatchewan. Consequently, the Rindisbachers and the other Swiss colonists were among the most ill-prepared pioneers in history. The young Rindisbacher possessed an affinity for drawing, although he was never formally trained. He profited by his experiences in this new land, eventually augmenting his family's meager income by selling his pictures. As his reputation grew, so too did the demand for his pictures, their prices at times reaching $130. A portfolio of six colored lithographs after his drawings of Hudson's Bay Colony was published in London, which secured the active support of several patrons, including Captain Bulger between 1821 and 1826. Unfortunately, Rindisbacher died as he was beginning to achieve a national reputation. As stated by the *Missouri Republican* (St Louis) shortly after his death, 'Mr. Rindisbacher had talents which gave every assurance of future celebrity . . . He possessed a keen sensibility and the most delicate perception of the beautiful.'

Joseph Wright, called Wright of Derby (English, 1734–97)

12 **The Indian Widow**

Oil on canvas, 39½ × 49½ in. 1785. Derbyshire, Derby Museums and Art Gallery.

English soldiers returning from the Revolutionary War sparked a renewed interest in the manners and customs of the North American Indians. Although the image of the Indians as savages was still widespread, several writers and artists depicted them as the embodiment of virtues superior to those in the civilized world. With his customary interest in atmospheric effects, Wright has created a sensitive and noble image of a mourning Indian woman. When the painting was exhibited in London in the spring of 1785, Wright stated: 'The Widow of an Indian Chief watching the arms of her deceased husband. The picture is founded on a custom which prevails among the savage tribes of America, where the widow of an eminent warrior is used to sit the whole day, . . . without shelter, and perseveres in her mournful duty at the hazard of her own life from the inclemencies of the weather.' The popular appeal of such a scene is attested by the fact that an engraved version of it was published by J. R. Smith in January 1789.

Eugène Delacroix (French, 1798–1863)

13 **Les Natchez**

Oil on canvas, 35½ × 45¾ in. 1824-35. Collection of Lord and Lady Walston, Royston, Hertfordshire.

This painting was inspired by the highly popular epic *Atala* by François René de Chateaubriand (1768–1848). First published in 1801, *Atala* – subtitled 'the loves of two savages in the wilderness' – was recently described as a 'strange *mélange* of barbaric ferocity and soft but chaste amorous dalliance, erotic impulse and Christian piety'. In this poignant depiction of the last survivors of the dying Natchez race, Delacroix illustrated the imagery suggested in the epilogue of *Atala:* 'We were the last survivors of the Natchez tribe. After the massacre of our people by the French, the few survivors found refuge with the Chickasaws, a neighboring tribe. For some time we lived peacefully together. But seven moons ago white men from Virginia took possession of our land, saying it had been given them by a European king. We looked to the heavens and, taking with us the remains of our ancestors, set off across the desert. I gave birth to my child during the journey, and since my milk was bad after all I had suffered, my child died.'

William Havell (English, 1782–1857)

14 **Garden Scene on the Braganza Shore, Harbor of Rio de Janiero**

Gouache, 13½ × 20¼ in. 1827. London, Victoria and Albert Museum.

A founding member of the Royal Society of Painters in Watercolor, Havell was influenced by Joseph M. W. Turner (1775–1851) in his early training.

Thomas Cole (American, 1801–48)

15 **Scene from 'The Last of the Mohicans'**

Oil on canvas, 25 × 35 in. 1827. New York State Historical Association, Cooperstown.

In the 1830s, the hitherto dominant tradition of history painting was superseded by that of landscape painting. Inspired by the spirit of Jacksonian democracy, artists embraced this new tradition, seeking to express the beauty and purity of our native wilderness and to nurture the growing awareness of an American national consciousness and distinctiveness from Europe. Of the many artists who gave rise to the term 'Hudson River School', Thomas Cole was perhaps the most influential. He prospered in an environment that was as much literary as it was artistic, for his close associates included William Cullen Bryant, Washington Irving, and James Fenimore Cooper. This painting shows the dramatic climax of Cooper's novel, when Cora is found kneeling in front of Tamenund, surrounded by the Indian tribe. However, the literary tableau is overshadowed by the magnificent landscape. The viewer is almost immediately impressed by the splendid flood of color contained in the vast and seemingly inaccessible environment. In this painting, Cole embodies his appreciation for the American landscape and his belief in the intimate connection between the beautiful and the good.

Augustus Earle (English, 1793–*c.* 1838)

16 **The Meeting of the Artist with the Wounded Chief Hongi, Bay of Islands, November 1827**

Oil on canvas, 23¼ × 35¼ in. 1827. Wellington, Courtesy of the Alexander Turnbull Library.

Like painters in the American West, Earle was fascinated by the native cultures he encountered, and his paintings of the Maori are the last record of that people before Europeans poured into the land. Earle saw the Maori in romantic, even heroic terms; of this meeting he later wrote: 'To me it almost seemed to realize some of the passages of Homer, where he describes the wanderer Ulysses and his gallant band of warriors.'

James Pattison Cockburn (English, 1778–1847)

17 **Ice Cutting at the Mouth of the St Charles River, Lower Canada, Quebec**

Watercolor, 14½ × 19¼ in. 1831. Ottawa, The Public Archives of Canada.

'Before I saw the breaking up of the vast body of ice, which forms what is here called the bridge, from Quebec to Point Levi, I imgined there could be nothing in it worth attention. But I found the great river, as the savages with much propriety call it, maintain its dignity in this instance, and assert its superiority over those petty streams which we honor with the names of rivers in England. Sublimity is the characteristic of this western world; the loftiness of the mountains, the grandeur of the lakes and rivers, the majesty of the rocks shaded with a picturesque variety of beautiful trees and shrubs, and crowned with the noblest of the offspring of the forest, which form the banks of the latter, are as much beyond the power of fancy as that of description: a landscape-painter might here expand his imagination, and find ideas which he will seek in vain in our comparatively little world. The object of which I am speaking has all the American magnificence.' (As quoted by Frances Brooke in *The History of Emily Montague,* 1769).

John James Audubon (American, 1785–1851)

18 **Trophy of American Game Birds**

Oil on canvas, 42 × 32 in. 1830. Courtesy of Kennedy Galleries, Inc., New York.

His name a household word, Audubon was the finest ornithological artist in American history. Educated in the neoclassicism of Jacques-Louis David, Audubon embarked on his search for new species of birds as early as 1812, when he and his wife were living in Kentucky. The results of his efforts became apparent with the publication of his monumental *Birds of America* folio between 1826 and 1838. Engraved in England by Robert Havell, Jr, the folio consisted of 435 hand-colored plates. This painting was done at the time of Audubon's return to the United States from London, where he had been supervising the publication of these plates between 1826 and 1829. Throughout this time, he was doing very little drawing, preferring to make copies in oil of his earlier watercolor studies.

In the background of this painting is Louisville, Kentucky; however, the important image is that of the passenger pigeon among the other suspended gamebirds. Audubon described a flight of these birds: 'As the birds arrived, and passed over me, I felt a current of air that surprised me. Thousands were soon knocked down by polemen. The current of birds, however, still kept increasing . . . It was a scene of uproar and confusion.' It was Audubon's belief that the reduction of the native forests would seriously endanger the survival of these birds. In 1914 the last survivor of the once numerous flocks died in captivity.

Augustus Earle (English, 1793–*c.* 1838)

19 A Bivouac of Travellers in Australia in a Cabbage Tree Forest, Day Break

Oil on canvas, $41\frac{1}{2} \times 32\frac{3}{4}$ in. About 1838. Canberra, National Library of Australia, Nan Kivell Collection.

A nephew of the well-known American portrait painter Ralph Earle (1751–1801), Augustus remained in Australia for only three years before joining Charles Darwin in 1831 as a topographical artist aboard the *H.M.S. Beagle.* Executed after his return to England and exhibited in 1838 at the Royal Academy, this painting responded to the popular demand of the British imagination for representations of colonial frontier life. It depicts a scene from the Illawarra district of New South Wales and once again advocates the nobility of migration to the new world and the exoticism of a new pastoral land. As stated by Major Mitchell two years earlier: 'As I stood, the first European intruder on the sublime solitude of these verdant plains, as yet untouched by flocks and herds, I felt conscious of being the harbinger of mighty changes there for our steps would soon be followed by the men and the animals for which it seemed to have been prepared.'

Karl Bodmer (Swiss, 1809–93)

20 The Interior of the Hut of a Mandan Chief

Aquatint and etching with stipple, $17\frac{3}{4} \times 24\frac{1}{2}$ in. About 1839. George Lucas Collection, on indefinite loan to the Baltimore Museum of Art, Maryland.

Bodmer arrived in the United States in 1832, with the German naturalist Prince Maximilian of Wied (1782–1867). Their purpose was to explore the Missouri frontier, with Bodmer acting as the draughtsman and the Prince as journalist. In order to prepare themselves, they carefully studied the Peale and Seymour drawings from the 1819 Long Expedition, Rindisbacher's works from the 1820s, and the collection of paintings assembled by Catlin. They then set out from St Louis, traveling up the Missouri River. After seven weeks and a distance of 1500 miles, the expedition arrived at Fort McKenzie in Montana. In the course of their two-year stay, Bodmer was particularly impressed by the Mandan Indians. Once extremely prosperous, the Mandans were being decimated by the outbreak of a smallpox epidemic. Thus, Bodmer's work was the last to record the qualities of this tribe. Upon returning to Europe, Bodmer set to work on engraving his preliminary drawings for Maximilian's two-volume book *Reise in das Innere Nord-Amerika in den Jahren 1832 bis 1834* (Coblenz, 1839-41).

Thomas Cole (American, 1801–48)

21 Pioneer Home in the Woods

Oil on canvas, 44 × 66 in. About 1845-6. Reynolda House, Inc., Winston-Salem, North Carolina.

During his lifetime, Thomas Cole did very few genre scenes. This painting is perhaps his most outstanding. The scene is in New Hampshire, a fact revealed by the presence of Mount Chocorua, which is located near the present-day town of Conway, New Hampshire. Today, we tend to forget that settlers in remote parts of New England were pioneers in a primitive wilderness. The painting gives us an idyllic view of such a family in a realistic pioneer setting.

Charles Deas (American, 1818–67)

22 Death Struggle

Oil on canvas, 30 × 25 in. 1845. Shelburne, Vermont, Shelburne Museum, Inc.

Descended from a distinguished Revolutionary War family, Deas was initially prompted to seek a military career. Failing to gain admittance to West Point, he turned to art and enrolled at the National Academy of Design for the next two years.

After seeing an exhibition of Catlin's Indian paintings in 1837-8 Deas vowed 'to visit the scenes of Nature's own children, to share the repast of the hunter, and taste the wild excitement of frontier life'. In 1840, only ten years after his distinguished predecessor Seth Eastman, he arrived at Fort Crawford, Prairie du Chien, Wisconsin. He remained in the West until 1847, when he returned to New York. There, after two years, he suffered a mental breakdown.

Charles Heaphey (English, 1822–81)

23 Kauri Forest, Wairoa River, Kaipara

Watercolor, $18\frac{3}{4} \times 15$ in. 1827. Wellington, Courtesy of the Alexander Turnbull Library.

The New Zealand Colonisation Company, formed in London in 1838, sent 57 ships and 8600 emigrants to the undeveloped territory in the space of four years. At the age of 17, Charles Heaphey was appointed artist and draughtsman for the Company and sailed on the first ship, the *Tory,* in 1839.

His best work reflects the influence of the British watercolor tradition, moderated by the thoroughly untamed environment of New Zealand. His *Kauri Forest* painting boldly documents the way in which early loggers cleared openings in the densely forested wilderness of the Northland. Paintings such as this and *Lambton Harbor and Wellington* (Plate 26) served both topographic and propagandistic purposes for the Company.

Paul Kane (Canadian, 1810–71)

24 An Indian Encampment on Lake Huron

Oil on canvas, 19 × 29 in. 1845. Toronto, Art Gallery of Ontario.

In the preface to his *Wanderings of an Artist* of 1858, Paul Kane stated, 'The principal object in my undertakings was to sketch pictures of the principal chiefs, and their original costumes, to illustrate their manners and customs, and to represent the scenery of an almost unknown country.' He left Toronto on 17 June, 1845, and throughout his explorations he kept a daily journal in which he made notes concerning his numerous sketches. Kane stated that this painting 'represents an Indian encampment amongst the islands on Lake Huron; the wigwams are made of birch-bark, stripped from the trees in large pieces and sewed together with long fibrous roots; when the birch tree cannot be conveniently had, they weave rushes into mats called Apuckway, for covering, which are stretched round in the same manner as the bark, upon eight or ten poles tied together at the top and stuck in the ground at the required circle of the tent, a hole being left at the top to permit the smoke to go out. Their canoes are also made of birch-bark stretched over a very light frame of split cedar laths; the greatest attention being paid to symmetry and form.'

Thomas Pritchard Rossiter (American, 1818–71)

25 The Opening of the Wilderness

Oil on canvas, $17\frac{3}{4} \times 32\frac{1}{2}$ in. About 1846-50. Boston Museum of Fine Arts, M. and M. Karolik Collection.

Rossiter was closely associated with the Hudson River School as a result of his travels both to England in 1840 with Asher B. Durand and John F. Kensett, and to Rome in 1841 with Thomas Cole. He remained in Rome for five years. Returning to this country in 1846, he set up a studio in New York. This painting was completed during this time, and it is unique among his compositions. Rossiter was usually known for his large figural compositions of important historical events, such as those about Washington's life. In this picture he has created an imaginary view of railroad trains meeting on the frontier. The actual event did not occur until 1869, but the painting does express the optimism voiced by many people that the completion of the transcontinental railroad would at last fulfill America's destiny by finally connecting the country and penetrating the wilderness frontier. The progress made possible by the railroad was observed with some remorse. As stated in an 1870s issue of *Leslie's Weekly,* 'The Railway has so bridged time and space, that the continent is rapidly losing its romance and becoming prosaic . . . We have almost ceased to speak of the frontier.'

Charles Heaphey (English, 1822–81)

26 Lambton Harbor and Wellington

Watercolor, $17\frac{1}{2} \times 28\frac{1}{4}$ in. 1814. Wellington, Courtesy of the Alexander Turnbull Library.

John William Hill (American, 1812–79)

27 Erie Canal

Watercolor, $9\frac{1}{2} \times 13\frac{1}{2}$ in. 1831. The New York Historical Society.

In the early years of the republic, there was great demand to improve the avenues of communication among the widely settled inhabitants. Before this could be accomplished, an easier mode of travel was necessary. In the 1810s, a proposed solution to this problem was the canal. Unlike the numerous rivers with their rapids, floods and sandbars, the canal was a relatively comfortable, safe way to travel. The grandest of these new waterways was the Erie Canal, which was begun in 1817 in an area of upstate New York that Jefferson referred to as a wilderness.

By October 1825, the canal was complete, resulting in the greatest impetus for westward travel in the history of the United States. This canal literally opened up the West by connecting New York City to Lake Erie, and thus to the other Great Lakes and the Mississippi River. At times over 50 boats a day left Albany for the West, and by

1847 the trade and activity in this one city was greater than that along the entire Mississippi River.

George Catlin (American, 1796–1872)
28 Pigeon's Egg Head Going to and Returning from Washington

Oil on canvas, $27\frac{3}{4} \times 23$ in. 1832. Courtesy of the Smithsonian Institution, Washington, D.C.

During the nineteenth century, George Catlin was among the most impressive and prolific artists painting pictures of Indian life. The beginning of the 1830s witnessed both the passing of the Indian Removal Act and the describing of the North American Indian by Washington Irving as the 'Adonis of the frontier'. Within two years, Catlin made the first of several expeditions up the Missouri River. His purpose was, 'to use my art and so much of the labor of my future life as might be required in rescuing from oblivion the looks and customs of the vanishing race of native men in America'. Paying close attention to detail and color, Catlin produced over seven hundred paintings in addition to his important two-volume ethnographic record of 1841, *The Manners, Customs, and Condition of the North American Indian.* At the expense of great personal and economic sacrifice, Catlin conceived of himself as a spokesman for the Indians in the white man's world. Perhaps the best evidence of his country's reaction to his efforts at preserving a visual record of the native American was Congress's refusal to purchase his Indian Gallery, which in 1837 consisted of 494 paintings. Today, we are fortunate that a large number of his works are preserved in both the National Collection of Fine Arts and the National Gallery of Art.

Paul Kane (Canadian, 1810–71)
29 *(top)* The Man that Always Rides

Oil on canvas, $24 \times 18\frac{1}{4}$ in. 1846. Toronto, Royal Ontario Museum.

Kane arrived at Fort Carlton on the North Saskatchewan River on 4 September, 1846. He stated, 'There were some Cree Indians about the fort, which is one of the trading ports of that nation who extend along the Saskatchewan to the Rocky Mountains, and is one of the largest tribes of Indians in the Hudson's Bay Company's dominions. This tribe has been from time immemorial at war with the Blackfeet, whom they at one time conquered and held in subjection . . . These wars are kept up with unremitting perseverance from year to year; and were they as destructive in proportion to the numbers engaged as the wars of civilized nations, the continent would soon be depopulated of the whole Indian race; but, luckily, Indians are satisfied with small victories, and a few scalps and horses taken from the enemy are quite sufficient to entitle the warriors to return to their friends in triumph and glory.'

John Mix Stanley (American, 1814–72)
(bottom) The Osage Scalp Dance

Oil on canvas, $40\frac{1}{2} \times 60\frac{1}{2}$ in. 1845. Courtesy of the Smithsonian Institution, Washington, D.C.

Stanley was among the most prolific and widely traveled artists of the early West. He embarked on his career as an artist in 1842, with a goal in mind somewhat similar to that of George Catlin – to create a gallery of Indian paintings. Operating from a studio in Fort Gibson, Oklahoma, over the next ten years Stanley attended the 1843 council of chiefs of the Cherokee tribe at Tahlequah, visited New Mexico in 1845, joined the Stephen Kearney expedition to California in 1846, and traveled to Oregon in 1847 and to Hawaii in 1848/9. Finally, in 1852, his 150 paintings were exhibited at the Smithsonian Institution. The painting illustrated was included in the exhibition and was subsequently one of five that survived a devastating fire in 1865. It cannot be said that Stanley's paintings in any way mirrored the scientific realism found in works by Bodmer; rather, they recreate a highly dramatic and popularly appealing image of the Indian.

Asher B. Durand (American, 1796–1886)
30 Kindred Spirits

Oil on canvas, 44×36 in. 1849. New York Public Library, Gift of Miss Julia S. Bryant.

Upon the unexpected death of Thomas Cole in 1848, the leadership of the Hudson River School passed to his close friend Asher B. Durand. Apprenticed at an early age to a New Jersey wood engraver, Durand was interested in the visual qualities of line, detail and tonal contrasts. These technical preferences were common to the work of Cole and Durand, although Durand's meticulous draughtsmanship differed from Cole's more generalized approach to nature. This painting was commissioned by the art patron Jonathan Sturgis in appreciation of W. C. Bryant's splendid oration at Cole's funeral. It depicts Cole and Bryant contemplating the great truths to be learned from nature. Less than ten years after this masterpiece was completed, Durand in his important 'Letters to Young Painters' of 1855 succinctly expressed the sentiments embodied in his *Kindred Spirits:* 'Go not abroad then in search of material for the exercise of your pencil, while the virgin charms of our native land have claims on your deepest affections. Many are the flowers in our untrodden wilds that have blushed too long unseen . . . The 'lone and tranquil' lakes embosomed in ancient forests, that abound in our wild districts, the unshorn mountains surrounding them with their richly-textured covering, the ocean prairies of the West, and the many other forms of Nature yet spared from the pollutions of civilization, afford a guarantee for a reputation of originality that you may elsewhere long seek and find not.'

François Régis Gignoux (French-American, 1816–82)
31 Niagara Falls in Winter

Oil on canvas, 52×36 in. 1848. Washington, D.C., United States Capitol Collection.

A native of Lyons, France, Gignoux received his earliest training at the École des Beaux-Arts in Paris. After marrying an American girl in Paris, he went to the United States in about 1840, where he was immediately taken with the bold beauty of the natural scenery. He specialized in landscapes, perhaps becoming best known for the winter scenes in which he rendered the effects on nature of the changing seasons. In the 1840s Gignoux taught a young landscapist from Newburgh, New York named George Inness, who became one of America's greatest artists. The natural splendors of Niagara Falls were strongly praised by Thomas Cole in his *Essay on American Scenery* (1835): 'And Niagara, that wonder of the world! – where the sublime and beautiful are bound together in an indissoluble chain . . . At our feet the floods of a thousand rivers are poured out – the contents of vast inland seas. In its volume we conceived immensity; in its course, everlasting duration; in its impetuosity, uncontrollable power.' (From McCoubrey, *American Art, 1700-1960, Sources and Documents*, 1965, p. 105)

Alfred J. Miller (American, 1810–74)
32 The Lost Greenhorn

Oil on canvas, 16×20 in. 1852. Courtesy of Kennedy Galleries, Inc., New York.

This subject was evidently one of Miller's most popular, judging by the number of versions that he recorded having painted, and that have survived. The inspiration for the painting was the misfortune that befell one of Captain Drummond Stewart's party during the tour to the Rocky Mountains on which Miller served as expedition artist. After a morning wasted in futile chasing after game, the 'greenhorn' spent an anxious afternoon trying to locate his party and himself on the featureless prairie. At the time Miller did this painting, 'greenhorn' referred generally to someone of little experience and judgment; in later years, it was particularly applied to emigrants fresh from the old world and new to the ways of America.

33 Sioux Camp Scene

Oil on canvas, $17\frac{1}{2} \times 23$ in. Courtesy of Kennedy Galleries, Inc., New York.

During the months in 1837/8 that he accompanied Captain William Drummond Stewart on his expeditions to the Rocky Mountains, A. J. Miller collected enough impressions of the people and landscape to keep him busy in his studio for the remainder of his career. The more than one hundred drawings completed during this expedition are readily distinguished by their small size and their unfinished quality.

Stewart was particularly impressed with the Sioux Indians, and with the opportunities they offered a painter with a taste for the romantic to depict their magnificant physical appearance, their fine horses, and gaudy, picturesque finery. Another feature that made the Sioux stand out among other Plains tribes was their practice of shaving the entire head, leaving only the scalp lock waving in the breeze.

George Caleb Bingham (American, 1811–79)
34 Daniel Boone Escorting a Band of Pioneers into the Western Country *(detail)*

Oil on canvas, $26\frac{1}{2} \times 50$ in. 1851. St Louis, Washington University Gallery of Art.

Among the frontier personalities that capture the American imagination, Daniel Boone (1734–1820) is by far the best known. He epitomized the spirit of the frontiersman who fled the confines of society in order to establish a more democratic civilization. Boone's exploits were so famous that his reputation as a folk hero almost approached that of a mythical figure. He was portrayed by several artists, including William Ranney, but this painting by Bingham is the finest. As the personification of a contemporary Moses leading his people to the promised land, Boone stands at the Cumberland Gap, a fissure in the eastern Tennessee mountains near the Kentucky border. As a famous passage for travelers heading west, it was best described by Frederick J. Turner when he said, 'Stand at the Cumberland Gap and watch the procession of civilization, marching single file – the buffalo following the trail to the salt springs, the Indian, the fur-trader and hunter, the cattleraiser, the pioneer farmer – and the frontier has passed by.' (From *Frontier and Section: Selected Essays of Frederic Jackson Turner,* Prentice-Hall, Inc., 1961, p.38.)

As in Bingham's other paintings, the figures have been placed facing the spectator, in an ascending pyramidal design. Bingham frequently used classical copy books to assist in his painting and in placement of figures within the composition. This use of copy books as well as the prevalence of soft, misty colors to suggest the expanding horizon are both seen clearly here. Finally, the connection between the figure of Boone leading the woman on the horse and Leutze's *Westward the Course of Empire Takes Its Way* of 1861 (Plate 45) is unmistakable. Leutze probably knew this composition well, as he hosted Bingham and his family when they visited Dusseldorf during the late 1850s.

C. J. Grant (English *fl.* 1832–3)

35 Emigration: Detailing the Progress and Vicissitudes of an Emigrant

Lithograph, 18 × 14 in. 1833. Library of Congress, Prints and Photographs Division.

The years following the American Revolution witnessed a tremendous increase in the number of Europeans coming to the United States. Their social and economic situations varied greatly, but inevitably they sought 'a better life'. As the realities of the new land emerged and many of their preconceived notions were discarded, some emigrants decided to return home and publish accounts of their experiences. In fact, a vast literature was developed, in large part by the English, who were still convinced of the merits of their own country. The lithograph reproduced here provides an interesting and humorous account of both the realistic and romantic conceptions of the American frontier in the nineteenth century.

Thomas Baines (South African, 1820–75)

36 *(top)* Surfboats off the Jetty, Algoa Bay

Oil on paper, 18 × 25¾ in. About 1848. Courtesy of Sotheby Parke Bernet South Africa (Proprietary), Ltd., Johannesburg.

An extremely prolific artist, Baines arrived at Cape Town in 1842. Along with his contemporaries Thomas Bowler (1813-69) and George Angas (1822-86), he produced an interesting record of British South Africa, depicting the shipping patterns, wild animals, inhabitants, customs and adventures of the early pioneers. More often than not, the paintings were made to send back to England to satisfy the curiosity of the public there as to what the 'Barbaric South' was like. Many of the pictures were subsequently engraved for publication in the *Illustrated London News.*

(bottom) Ferry Boat on the Orange River

Oil on paper, 18 × 26 in. 1848? Courtesy of Sotheby Parke Bernet South Africa (Proprietary), Ltd., Johannesburg.

Thomas Baines (South African, 1820–75)

37 *(top)* A South African Boer Chasing Wildebeest

Watercolor, 6 × 10 inches, Courtesy of Sotheby Parke Bernet South Africa (Proprietary), Ltd., Johannesburg.

Karl Bodmer (Swiss, 1809–93)

(bottom) The Steamer Yellowstone on 19 April 1833

Watercolor. 1833. Northern Natural Gas Company Collection, Joslyn Art Museum, Omaha, Nebraska.

Bodmer made eighty-two engravings illustrating his experiences on the Missouri frontier (see Plate 20). These engravings, as well as his numerous watercolors, provide our most complete insight into the life of the Plains Indians. Unlike Catlin, who sought to preserve the momentary impression of a situation, Bodmer sought with almost ethnological accuracy to depict all aspects of the environment and way of life of his subjects. Many of these works appeared recently in *People of the First Man* (1976).

Dennis Malone Carter (Irish-American, 1827–81)

38 Arrival in the New World

Oil on canvas, 34 × 47 in. 1861. Courtesy of Kennedy Galleries, Inc., New York.

Many a story of Western adventure actually began beyond the Atlantic Ocean, and some of them were concluded abruptly at the eastern edge of the continent. Dennis Carter's rather sentimental painting shows a group of colonial emigrants forsaking the tranquillity of an English village for the uncertainties of a New World log cabin, complete with a welcoming Indian ambush. The motives that induced people to emigrate to the new continent were many and various: hopes of religious or political freedom, freedom from military conscription and the dangers of war, opportunities to seek wealth or to own land – all of these reasons played their part in settling America. For many of the earlier emigrants, however, there was virtually no other choice. Throughout the nineteenth century, the English countryside was being turned to crops or products more rewarding than the traditional subsistence farming that had been part of the feudal rights of tenants for centuries, and the frontiers of America seemed no more menacing to the dispossessed cottagers than the crowded slums of burgeoning industrial cities in England, probably their only alternative.

James Henry Beard (American, 1812–93)

39 Westward Ho!

Oil on canvas, 63 × 79½ in. 1850. Courtesy of Kennedy Galleries, Inc., New York.

Born in the northern Ohio wilderness at Painesville, Beard was an itinerant portrait painter in the frontier cities of Pittsburgh, Louisville, Cincinnati and New Orleans. Despite his lack of formal art training, Beard managed to do quite well, returning to his trade as a riverboat master when his portrait commissions were few. By the late 1830s, he was acknowledged for his strikingly realistic portrayals of politicians and young children. This limited success prompted him to move to New York City, where there was a great popular demand for paintings with the theme of westward migration. In 1846 Beard exhibited a painting similar in subject-matter – although smaller – to the one illustrated here. It sold almost immediately, receiving the highest price thus far paid for such a picture. *Westward Ho!* is the largest and most important work of its type that Beard produced.

William T. Ranney (American, 1813–57)

40 Advice on the Prairie

Oil on canvas, 40 ×54 in. 1853. Mr and Mrs J. Maxwell Moran, Paoli, Pennsylvania.

Ranney's experience in the West was limited to a short tour of duty in the Texan Army during 1836. The sketches he made as a soldier and his recollections of this experience provided him with a lifetime of subject-matter. Ranney's point of view was quite different from that of the majority of his contemporaries. Unlike, for instance, the German-born artist Wimar, he was not concerned with picturing the Indian. Ranney was impressed most by the pioneering exploits of trappers and settlers on the vast plains. Technically well trained, he strove for a simple, well-ordered composition, with a minimum of detail. In this regard, he is often compared to Bingham, who shared a similar predilection for defining forms through the effects of light over generalized surfaces.

Asher B. Durand (American, 1796–1886)

41 Progress

Oil on canvas, 48 × 72 in. 1853. From the Warner Collection of the Gulf States Paper Corporation, Tuscaloosa, Alabama.

This painting has also been called *The Advance of Civilization* and *A Pioneer Settlement.* It was one of seven exhibited by Durand in the National Academy of Design exhibition of 1853, and it was described by a reviewer for the *Knickerbocker* (Vol. XLII, July 1853, pl. 95) as follows, 'We observe a higher degree of perfection than this fine artist has ever previously attained. It is purely American. It tells an American story out of American facts, portrayed with true American feeling, by a devoted and earnest student of Nature.' In 1894, John Durand, the artist's son, described this painting as 'a large landscape composition ... showing on American soil the use of the canal, steamboat, and railway, and that of the telegraph, then recently perfected'.

Cornelius Krieghoff (Canadian, 1815–72)

42 A Settler's Log House

Oil on canvas, 24½ x 36½ in. 1856. Toronto, Art Gallery of Ontario. Gift of Wells Leonard Estate, 1937.

Krieghoff is generally considered the pioneer painter of Canada. After many years of wandering through Europe as an itinerant artist and musician, and after serving with the United States Army in the Seminole War, Krieghoff settled in Quebec in 1853. The picture illustrated is characteristic of the more than seven hundred scenes of Canadian genre that Krieghoff painted for visitors to the province and the officers in the local garrison.

43 Habitants Sleighing

Oil on canvas, 12⅛ × 18 in. About 1855. Toronto, Art Gallery of Ontario. Bequest of Mrs H. M. Mowat, 1939.

Charles F. Wimar (German-American, 1828–62)

44 Attack on an Emigrant Train

Oil on canvas, 55¼ × 79 in. 1856. Ann Arbor, University of Michigan Museum of Art. Bequest of Henry C. Lewis.

Born near Dusseldorf, Wimar arrived at St Louis in 1844, where evidence of pioneer life was still pronounced. Apprenticed to the painter. Louis Pomarede, Wimar ventured up the Mississippi River in

1849 to research a panoramic river commission. This experience provided Wimar with his first view of the vast countryside with its roving bands of Indians. Desiring to become a 'proper' artist, in the spring of 1852 Wimar returned to Dusseldorf to enter Emanuel Leutze's studio. Strangely enough, he concentrated on paintings representing Indians and frontier life, which fascinated the Germans. Less than half a century before Wimar, two native American artists – John Vanderlyn and Benjamin West – had also appealed to the European penchant for paintings portraying the drama of the frontier confrontation between settlers and Indians.

Emanuel Leutze (German-American, 1816–68)
45 Westward the Course of Empire Takes Its Way

Oil on canvas, 33 × 43 in. 1861. Washington D.C., National Collection of Fine Arts, Smithsonian Institution.

Early in the eighteenth century, an Irish bishop named George Berkeley wrote a poem that expressed the thoughts of his contemporaries on a new Golden Age. Entitled 'Verses on the Prospect of Planting Arts and Learning in America', this modest effort voiced what was to become the resounding chorus of the nineteenth century. In the final stanza of Berkeley's poem, America is proclaimed the grand culmination of the progress of civilization:

Westward the course of empire takes it way;
The first four Acts already past,
A fifth shall close the Drama with the day;
Time's noblest offspring is the last.

In the midst of the social and political confusion wrought by the first stages of the Civil War, Emanuel Leutze was awarded a $20,000 commission to complete his painting *Westward the Course of Empire Takes Its Way* (also known as *Westward Ho!*) for the new United States Capitol building. At about the same time, Congress passed the Homestead Act, which granted a settler 160 acres of public land after five years of residence and the payment of a nominal fee. Incorporated into Leutze's final composition were thematic representations of the following: Moses leading the Israelites, Columbus, Arion on a dolphin, Jason and the Golden Fleece, Hebrews bringing fruits from Eschol, and numerous incidents dealing with settlement – the hunter, farmer, missionary, and the displaced Indian. Taken together, these various elements clearly indicate that Leutze not only sought to celebrate the emigrant's settling in the West, but also, and perhaps more importantly, to create a contemporary characterization of the New World Eden. Also, the dominant foreground placement of the black man was meant to convey Leutze's personal vision of the new land. Leutze was asked, 'Did you mean this group to teach a new gospel to this continent, a new truth which this part of the world is to accept – that the Emigrant and the Freedman are the two great elements which are to be reconciled and worked with? The young, beautiful Irish woman, too, is she not your new Madonna? The artist's face glowed and . . . in the first flush of his pleasure he told me that I was the first American that had understood his picture.' (Quoted in Anne Brewster, 'Emanuel Leutze, the Artist', *Lippincott's Magazine,* 2, 1868, p. 536).

In addition to the sense of optimism expressed by the pioneers heading west, Leutze has clearly expressed the realities of such an arduous journey. The sun-drenched bones and burial scene in the foreground recall the victims of emigration. Almost one hundred years later, Georgia O'Keeffe was to take a similar scene and convey its intense imagery in a more spiritual manner (Plate 96).

George Catlin (American, 1796–1872)
46 Ambush for Flamingoes

Oil on canvas, 19 × 26½ in. About 1857. Pittsburgh, Pennsylvania, Museum of Art, Carnegie Institute.

A precise date cannot be assigned to Catlin's first interest in South America; however, his acquaintance with Alexander von Humboldt since the 1845 Paris showing of the Indian Gallery probably kept the lure of South America active in his mind. A firm decision to travel there was not made until the early 1850s, when Catlin learned of the lost gold mines in the Crystal Mountains of Brazil. He departed almost immediately and, after a short time spent seeking gold, decided to create a record of the South American Indians similar to that which he had done in North America. From 1852 to 1856, he visited the entire coastal region of South America and journeyed up the Amazon River across the jungle interior of Brazil. Stylistically, the images created on this trip are similar to those made in North America; the technical facility is present, as well as the emphasis on color and design. The location of this scene is the Grand Saline marshes on the Rio Salado, south of Buenos Aires. A companion piece entitled *Shooting Flamingoes* is in the Memorial Art Gallery of the University of Rochester. Both paintings were done after Catlin had left South America. The paintings he did while actually there in 1855-6 are in the collection of Paul Mellon, Upperville, Virginia.

Winslow Homer (American, 1836–1910)
47 Veteran in a New Field

Oil on canvas, 24 × 38 in. 1865. New York, Metropolitan Museum of Art, Bequest of Miss Adelaide Milton de Groot, 1967.

In the years between 1862 and 1881, Winslow Homer transformed the conception of American genre painting from a rather unimaginative basis to one of monumental proportions. Like Bingham, he translated the commonplace into a form of contemporary history painting. In 1875, reacting to paintings such as the one illustrated here, Henry James stated, 'Mr Homer goes in, as the phrase is, for perfect realism . . . He is a genuine painter; that is, to see, and to reproduce what he sees, is his only case . . . He has chosen the least pictorial features of the least pictorial range of scenery and civilization; he has resolutely treated them as if they *were* pictorial, as if they were every inch as good as Capri or Tangiers; and to reward his audacity, he has incontestably succeeded.'

Frederick Edwin Church (American, 1826–1900)
48 Cotopaxi

Oil on canvas, 47 × 84¼ in. 1862. The Chrysler Museum at Norfolk, Virginia, Gift of Walter P. Chrysler, Jr.

From the artist's viewpoint, an important aspect of the frontier experience was the search for a native and heroic subject-matter that possessed a timeless and cosmic meaning. As the nineteenth century progressed, this search began to focus on the vivid drama of nature found in South America and the Arctic. Encouraged by his earlier success as a painter of Niagara Falls, Church set off for South America in 1853. This was his first trip in search of an exotic landscape that might convey a fresh view of God-in-nature. Compelled by the thrill of undiscovered frontiers and the exhilarating writings of the German naturalist Alexander von Humboldt, Church visited South America again in 1857. He executed numerous pencil and oil sketches, which were later worked into finished paintings. The most persistent image from these trips was that of Cotopaxi, a still active volcano in north central Ecuador. Placing the spectator almost over the foreground precipice, Church – with botanical exactitude – presents a vast panorama of a spectacular geography. In its curious mingling of atmospheric effects, both real and imagined, the painting provides the spectator with an escape from reality. When exhibited, these large paintings created a sensation. Depiction of such an exotic landscape was new to American painting. So convincing was the imagery that spectators often spent hours examining each portion of it through opera glasses.

Albert Bierstadt (American, 1830–1902)
49 The Rocky Mountains

Oil on canvas, 73½ × 120¾ in. 1863. New York, Metropolitan Museum of Art.

After completing more than three years of intensive study in Dusseldorf and one year in Rome, Bierstadt returned to the United States in 1857, fully trained in the techniques of sketching from nature in oil, pencil and charcoal. Two years later, at his own expense, he joined the famous Lander expedition of 1859, which was to survey the wagon trail to the Pacific coast. By June of that year, Bierstadt had left the group and, accompanied by one friend, had set out to explore on his own. The exhilaration he experienced is expressed in a letter dated 10 July to the *Crayon:* 'I am delighted with the scenery. The mountains are very fine . . . [they] present a scene which every lover of landscape would gaze upon with unqualified delight . . . the figures of the Indians are so enticing, traveling about with their long poles trailing along the ground, and their picturesque dress . . . and now is the time to paint them, for they are rapidly passing away . . .'

In 1863 Bierstadt made a second trip to the Rocky Mountains, this time accompanied by F. H. Ludlow, who in describing the scene in this painting, said that it was like going to the original site of Eden. Like both F. E. Church and T. Moran, Bierstadt was a painter of popular showpieces. All of these individuals shared a common interest in exotic scenery; however, Bierstadt demonstrated a disposition for conveying the picturesque qualities of a scene rather than its accurate detail. As stated by John Wilmerding, 'Here was a consummate emblem of national celebration, geology and metaphysics joined in common service.' (*American Art,* 1976, p.127)

Nicholas Chevalier (Australian, 1828–1902)
50 The Buffalo Ranges, Victoria

Oil on canvas, 51 × 71 in. 1864. Melbourne, National Gallery of Victoria.

Chevalier immediately captured public attention with this celebration of the dignity of pioneering labor set in local scenery.

Lucius Richard O'Brien (Canadian, 1832–99)
51 Sunrise on the Saguenay

Oil on canvas, 34½ × 49½ in. 1880. Ottawa, National Gallery of Canada.

The son of a founding member of the settlement on Lake Simcoe (Ontario), O'Brien was by trade both an artist and a civil engineer. In 1880 he became the first president of the newly organized Royal Canadian Academy of Arts.

The view in this painting is of Cape Trinité on the Saguenay River.

O'Brien's interest in the mystic qualities of light clearly indicates the influence of both Bingham and Church. Church, in fact, had visited Canada at the invitation of two of O'Brien's close associates, Lady Dufferin and Lord Lorne. Also, during his tenure as president of the Royal Canadian Academy, O'Brien acted as the picture editor for G. M. Grant's publication *Picturesque Canada* (1882).

Jean-Francois Millet (French, 1814–75)
52 *(top)* **The American Mazeppa**

Lithograph, $14\frac{1}{2} \times 20\frac{3}{4}$ in. 1852. New York, Metropolitan Museum of Art, Gift of the Museum of the American Indian, Heye Foundation.

Inspired by Byron's popular poem recounting an incident in seventeenth-century Poland, this lithograph actually portrays an event from the American Revolution – the capture of Simon Butler, a Kentucky pioneer, by the Indians.

The picture belongs to a group of four prints published in 1852 by Goupil as *Annals of the United States Illustrated – The Pioneers.* The original commission for the set went to Karl Bodmer. Unable to complete the work himself, Bodmer asked Millet to assist on several stones, including the one illustrated.

Charles F. Wimar (German-American, 1828–62)
(bottom) **Indians Pursued by American Dragoons**

Oil on canvas, 33 × 46 in. 1853. Courtesy of Sotheby Parke Bernet Inc., New York.

Like the other work by Wimar illustrated in this survey (Plate 44), this painting was done while the artist was studying in Dusseldorf. These rare paintings are among only twelve works known to have been done by Wimar during 1853-56. After his return to St Louis in 1856, Wimar continued to paint the Indians of the Great Plains. However, he shed many of the theatrical mannerisms characteristic of the Dusseldorf paintings.

Samuel Thomas Gill (Australian, 1818–80)
53 *(top)* **Overlanders**

Watercolor, $13\frac{1}{4} \times 23$ in. About 1865. Sydney, Art Gallery of New South Wales.

As the nineteenth century progressed, so too did the frontiers of settlement in Australia from the coastal areas to the inland regions. The earlier topographical scenes of John Eyre (*c.* 1771-1812) and Conrad Martens (1801-78) gradually yielded in popularity to new themes depicting stockmen and drovers. Pictures such as this one by Gill, as well as his many lithographs, did much to popularize the image of the frontiersman in both Australia and England. Gill's interests were echoed by the first Australian poet to receive acclaim in England, Adam Lindsay Gordon (1833-70) ''Twas merry in the glowing morn, among the gleaming grass, / To wander as we've wandered many a mile / . . . Setting loosely in the saddle all the while.' (*The Sick Stockrider*).

William G. R. Hind (Canadian, 1833–88)
(bottom) **Foot of the Rocky Mountains**

Watercolor, $8\frac{3}{4} \times 12\frac{1}{4}$ in. 1862. Montreal, McGill University, McCord Museum.

Of the several early pioneer artist-explorers from Canada, Hind is perhaps the most important and interesting. During his career, he visited practically every Canadian province, faithfully recording its peculiarities in a distinctly Pre-Raphaelite style. His watercolors are so detailed as to include carefully rendered blades of grass. In 1862, inspired by the discovery of gold, Hind joined a band of twenty-four young men from Toronto and Eastern Canada and traveled to the Cariboo Mountains by way of Fort Garry. This scene represents one of the numerous pictures that he sketched after leaving Fort Garry, heading west on the old fur-traders' trails. It was painted near Yellowhead Pass on the present boundary between Alberta and British Columbia, where Hind and the 'Overlanders of '62' entered the Rocky Mountains.

Charles Christian Nahl (American, 1818–78)
54 Crossing the Isthmus of Panama by Way of the Chagres River

Oil on canvas. 1850. University of California, Bancroft Library.

In 1850, shortly after the news of the discovery of gold spread through Europe, Charles Nahl and his brother set sail for California. At that time, there were two ways to reach California. The first was to spend at least five months sailing round Cape Horn at the southern tip of South America to San Francisco. The second and considerably shorter route was to cross the Isthmus of Panama. It is fortunate that Nahl chose the latter method, for it indicates not only some of the practical difficulties of traveling, but also the lush and exotic landscape of this geographical region.

Martin Johnson Heade (American, 1819–1904)
55 The Harbor at Rio de Janeiro

Oil on canvas, $18\frac{1}{2} \times 33\frac{1}{2}$ in. 1864. Reynolda House, Inc., Winston-Salem, North Carolina.

Heade was one of the few American artists who visited this beautiful harbor. This painting was one of two that he completed in 1864, and it is unique in his oeuvre. It is very picturesque, combining several elements in one composition – a foreground genre scene, a panoramic view of the harbor, and a delicate rendering of color conveyed through an almost transparent mist. The painting was subsequently used as an engraved frontispiece for an article on Brazil in the April 1876 issue of *Frank Leslie's Popular Monthly.*

Seth Eastman (American, 1808–75)
56 Spearing Fish in Winter

Oil on canvas, 31 × 44 in. About 1867-9. Washington D.C., United States Capitol Collection.

A graduate of West Point, Eastman served at various military posts on the western frontier. Initially at Fort Snelling (Minneapolis), he returned east briefly to study with Robert W. Weir (1803-89) in 1833, before returning to Fort Snelling by 1841. In the 1850s he was stationed in Texas and Utah. His extensive experience with the frontier and his accomplishment as a draughtsman made him a logical candidate for commissions picturing the West. After his retirement as a Brigadier General, Eastman was commissioned by Congress to provide nine works of Indian scenes. This painting was one of the nine works completed for the commission, and it hung in the room of the Capitol used by the House Indian Affairs Committee.

William Bradford (American, 1823–92)
57 An Arctic Summer, Boring Through the Pack in Melville Bay

Oil on canvas, 52 × 78 in. 1871. Courtesy of Hirschl & Adler Galleries, Inc., New York.

William Bradford first ventured to the Arctic in 1859. In the course of his lifetime he returned there ten times. Although initially fascinated by the stories surrounding the numerous trips in search of Sir John Franklin, once there Bradford was captivated by the rugged beauty of the ice formations, and the strange colors and lights that characterized this wilderness. Supported by the enthusiasm of F. E. Church for the painterly possibilities of the Arctic (Church sailed the Newfoundland coast in 1859), Bradford made another trip in 1869, which resulted in the publication of his *The Arctic Regions, Illustrated with Photographs taken on an Art Expedition to Greenland* . . . (London, 1873). In his accompanying text, Bradford stated: 'The wild rugged shapes, indescribable and ever-changing, baffle all description . . . Nor were the colors wanting to carry out the illusion, from dead white to glossy glistening satin, from the deepest green to the lightest shades; and even from faint blue to deepest lapis lazuli again as some lofty berg passed between us and the sun, its crest would be bordered with an orange-colored halo in which sometimes prismatic shades appeared.'

Worthington Whittredge (American, 1820–1910)
58 Crossing the Ford, Platte River, Colorado

Oil on canvas, 40 × 68 in. 1868-70. New York, The Century Association.

A practitioner of the Dusseldorf style, Whittredge was a close friend of Albert Bierstadt and Emanuel Leutze. At one point he shared a studio with Leutze in the famous Tenth Street Building in New York City. This building later received widespread attention when it was used by William M. Chase (1849-1906) in his splendid paintings of studio interiors. In the years following the conclusion of the Civil War, Whittredge was one of several important landscape painters who traveled west in search of picturesque scenery. Although the painting would appear to be an accurate transcription of those qualities that characterize the vast Plains, Whittredge freely interchanged various geographical and picturesque elements in order to improve the overall visual effect.

Frank Buchser (Swiss, 1828–90)
59 Chippewas on the Warpath

Oil on canvas, $13 \times 27\frac{1}{4}$ in. About 1868. Zurich, Museum der Stadt Solothurn, Besitz des Kunstvereins.

A native of Switzerland, Buchser went to the United States in 1866 and remained there until May 1871. He visited the Great Lakes in 1868 in search of Indian subjects, but was apparently discouraged by what he found: '. . . all the stories of Indians in these quarters are when seen close, nothing at all. The full blood if found is utterly spoiled by the imitation of the whites, their costumes are more like the tasteless makserada of a beggar than an Indian . . . let us make for the south.' He subsequently encountered a group of Chippewas on a reservation near Sault Ste. Marie. He made numerous sketches, and completed this painting at a later date in Detroit.

Arthur F. Tait (American, 1819–1905)
60 *(top)* **American Frontier Life**

Oil on canvas, $24\frac{3}{8} \times 26\frac{1}{4}$ in. 1852. New Haven, Connecticut, Yale University Art Gallery, Whitney Collection of Sporting Art.

Throughout the countless lithographs after his paintings published by Currier and Ives, Tait became one of the best-known artists of his time. Educated in England, he emigrated in 1850 to New York, where he set up his studio. Surprisingly, Tait never visited the West. It is known that before he left England he assisted Catlin with the exhibition of his Indian Gallery and that once in the United States, he studied the paintings of William Ranney and the illustrations of Bodmer, but apparently this was the total extent of his visual resources. In spite of this, Tait was a good painter and storyteller who created believable scenes of frontier life. It was this type of frontier scene that encouraged people to travel west in search of adventure.

Charles Deas (American, 1818–67)
(bottom) **The Prairie Fire**

Oil on canvas, 29 × 36 in. 1847. The Brooklyn Museum, Gift of Mr and Mrs A. B. Martin.

Inspired by the highly popular writings of Washington Irving, Deas frequently employed the theme of pursuit or conflict in his paintings. As in his *Death Struggle* of 1845 (Plate 22), Deas demonstrates a strong interest in the confrontation of opposing forces, be they man and Indian or, as in this case, man and nature. In their realistic detail, Deas's works provide a fascinating insight into the characteristics of the frontier environment.

Frank Blackwell Mayer (American, 1827–99)
61 *(top)* **Independence, Portrait of Squire Jack Potter**

Oil on paper board, $12\frac{1}{2} \times 16$ in. 1858. Washington, D.C., National Collection of Fine Arts, Smithsonian Institution.

In the late 1850s, the most evocative image of the American was that of a unique individual who sprang from the native environment. In both literature and the fine arts, the popular character of the 'Yankee' emerged. Of the numerous artistic attempts to portray this character, this painting is the most interesting. For Europeans as well as Americans, it was the self-confident and shrewdly independent Yankee farmer or frontiersman who was most readily identified with America. Paintings such as this one did much to project the persistent American myth of native simplicity and goodness.

George Caleb Bingham (American, 1811–79)
(bottom) **The Squatters**

Oil on canvas, 25 × 30 in. 1850. Boston Museum of Fine Arts, Future Donation.

As a poet of both the people and the landscape, Bingham preserves in his paintings a unique image of mid-nineteenth-century Missouri as the crossroads of an expanding nation. An integral part of this image was the position of the squatter, or early pioneer, who settled on the public domain. Politically, these people were in a questionable position, with many individuals, including Bingham, opposing the extension of suffrage to them. In a letter from Bingham to the American Art-Union dated 18 November 1850, he stated: 'The Squatters as a class, are not fond of the toil of agriculture, but erect their rude Cabins upon those remote portions of the National domain, where abundant game supplies their phisical (*sic*) wants. When this source of subsistence becomes diminished, in consequence of increasing settlement around, they usually sell out their slight improvement, with their 'pre-emption title' to the land, and again follow the receding footsteps of [the] Savage.'

Erastus Salisbury Field (American, 1805–1900)
62 **The Garden of Eden**

Oil on canvas, $34\frac{3}{4} \times 46$ in. About 1860-70. Boston Museum of Fine Arts, M. and M. Karolik Collection.

In spite of the overt religious connotations of this composition, the allegorical comparisons to America as the new Eden in post-Civil War society are obvious. The painting reflects in large part the atmosphere of hope and reconciliation that prevailed there at that time. It also parallels the type of composition popularized by Edward Hicks (1780-1849) in more than a hundred versions of *The Peaceable Kingdom.*

Charles C. Nahl (American, 1818–78)
63 **Sunday Morning in the Mines**

Oil on canvas, 72 × 108 in. 1872. Sacramento, E. B. Crocker Art Gallery.

On 24 January 1848, James Marshall discovered gold at a sawmill owned by John Sutter on the American River in California. This event was to change the course of westward expansion. By the next year, the population of San Francisco had increased from about 800 to nearly 35,000. Nahl arrived in San Francisco in 1851 and immediately joined in the feverish spirit of the gold miners. In exchange for gold dust he executed portraits, quickly earning a reputation for his precise and vivid sketches of this colorful life. *Sunday Morning in the Mines* is his masterpiece. In this painting, he captured the essence of this environment in all its realistic diversity: men racing horses, miners trying to restrain one of their fellows from losing his gold, one man writing a letter, several others reading and still others doing their washing. At the time of his death, Nahl was hailed as having created the finest scenes of the miners ever done. They were accurate in detail, executed with technical skill, and exuberant in their Western frontier spirit.

Frederick Arthur Verner (Canadian, 1836–1928)
64 **Indian Camp**

Oil on canvas, $32\frac{1}{2} \times 60$ in. 1876. Ontario, Hamilton Art Gallery.

The work pictured is a characteristic example of Verner's art, depicting a prairie scene in Manitoba with several Indians.

Albert Bierstadt (American, 1830–1902)
65 **Seal Rock**

Oil on canvas, 37 × 58 in. 1872. Courtesy of Kennedy Galleries, Inc., New York.

The vast herds of aquatic mammals living along the shores and islands of the North Pacific drew treasure hunters to the California coast long before the first flake of gold was taken from one of her streams. These animals were hunted both for their pelts and for their oil; the latter, in fact, provided one of the property values on the potlatch circuit of the Northwest Coast tribes. Once white intruders joined the hunting of the herds, the seals' teeming numbers were reduced almost to extinction by the end of the nineteenth century. Seal Rock, in the Farallon Islands in the Golden Gate harbor near San Francisco, was a standard tourist attraction when Bierstadt painted this work.

Thomas Moran (American, 1837–1926)
66 **Grand Canyon of the Yellowstone**

Oil on canvas, 86 × 141 in. 1872. Washington, D.C., U.S. Department of the Interior, Courtesy of the National Collection of Fine Arts.

The spectacular beauty of the Rocky Mountains provided one of the most persistent images of the American West. As early as the Lewis and Clark expedition of 1805-6, the American imagination was captivated by numerous stories of towering mountain formations, geysers, waterfalls, and other natural wonders.

Many artists made the arduous journey to record these breathtaking sights. Among them Thomas Moran is considered to have made the most important contribution to our awareness of this region. Inspired by both the technical possibilities found in the luminous works of Joseph M. W. Turner and the popular success of Bierstadt, Moran – at the age of 34 – set out in 1871 with the geologist F. V. Hayden on a government surveying expedition to the Grand Canyon of the Yellowstone. The powerful impression created by his numerous on-the-spot watercolors was perhaps the most important factor in pursuading Congress to preserve this national asset by establishing Yellowstone as a National Park. In the following year, Moran incorporated many of his watercolors into a painting in the large panoramic tradition of Church and Bierstadt. Having taken two months to complete, it received great public acclaim and quickly established his reputation as the finest interpreter of the American West. Unlike his predecessors, Moran was not interested in the topographical accuracy of his landscapes. Instead, he sought to convey a measure of the emotional response that the scene prompted in his mind: 'I place no value upon literal transcripts from Nature. My general scope is not realistic but my tendencies are toward idealization.'

67 **Hot Springs of Gardner's River, Yellowstone**

Watercolor, $20\frac{1}{4} \times 25\frac{5}{8}$ in. 1872. Reynolda House, Inc., Winston-Salem, North Carolina.

The third quarter of the nineteenth century witnessed an increased acceptance of watercolor as a 'respectable' medium among American artists. Inspired by the work of Joseph M. W. Turner in England, in 1866 American artists formed the basis of the American Watercolor Society, which was officially organized in 1877. In the intervening years, Moran emerged as one of the media's most skillful proponents. This watercolor was appropriately described recently by Theodore E. Stebbins when he stated, 'The vision is a perfect one; using a rather dry touch and a limited range of hue ... Moran creates an otherworldly scene with no sign of the artist's intrusion. Moonlike rocks and hot pools of water are brushed in with infinite care, the tinted paper now being used to great advantage, with astonishing, fluid lines of red ink leading one into the composition and off into the distance.' (From *American Master Drawings and Watercolors,* New York, 1976, p. 166)

Samuel Colman (American, 1832–1920)

68 Emigrant Train, Colorado

Oil on canvas, $19\frac{1}{2} \times 40$ in. 1872. Vermont, St Johnsbury Athenaeum, Library and Art Gallery.

A pupil of Asher B. Durand, Colman also studied in Paris and Spain between 1860 and 1862. A large number of works from 1870 indicate a trip to Yosemite Valley; however, from 1871 to 1875, Colman was traveling in England, France, Holland and Switzerland, pursuing his avid interest in the collection of objects of decorative art.

William Charles Piguenit (Australian, 1836–1914)

69 Flood in the Darling, 1890

Oil on canvas, $48\frac{1}{4} \times 78\frac{1}{2}$ in. About 1895. Sydney, Art Gallery of New South Wales.

A native Tasmanian of French descent, Piguenit was an artist-explorer who surveyed the frontiers in America, New Zealand and Australia. Not until 1872 did he abandon his surveying career to pursue his art full-time. In the following years his enthusiasm for the dramatic and sublime in nature prompted numerous journeys into little-known regions. A romantic, Piguenit was similar in temperament to his American counterpart F. E. Church. In capturing a simple seasonal flood across a vast river-flat in the interior of New South Wales, Piguenit demonstrated his preoccupation with natural scenery in its primeval state. The largeness of the canvas emphasizes the feeling of dramatic isolation.

Oscar Berninghaus (American, 1874–1952)

70 Watching the Wagon Train

Oil on canvas, 22×36 in. Courtesy of Kennedy Galleries, Inc., New York.

A lithographer by training, Berninghaus first visited Taos in 1899. Intrigued by the unspoiled beauty of a certain Pueblo village nearby, he returned to Taos each summer until he moved there permanently in 1925. Painting out-of-doors, Berninghaus employed a style that was direct and objective. He sought to show the Pueblo Indians as they are, rather than in a posed or nostalgic fashion.

71 Winter Hunt

Oil on canvas, 22×28 in. Denver, Colorado, Anschutz Collection.

Frederic Remington (American, 1861–1909)

72 A Dash for the Timber

Oil on canvas, $48\frac{1}{2} \times 84\frac{1}{8}$ in. 1889. Fort Worth, Amon Carter Museum of Western Art.

This painting is acclaimed by critics as the masterpiece of Remington's career. It was his first major commission, and followed the receipt of a silver medal in the 1889 Paris Exposition. Remington was given a great deal of freedom in satisfying the demands of the commission, the only real stipulation being that he create a monumental canvas portraying a life struggle on the frontier.

To frontiersmen in the Arizona Territory, the greatest danger was the Apache Indians, in whose domain they were considered intruders. While executing the painting, Remington very carefully considered each aspect of such a situation, striving for accurate fidelity to the nuances of the landscape and the garments of his characters. His efforts were successful, for when the painting was exhibited at the National Academy of Design in 1889, a critic with the *New York Herald* stated on 16 November: 'This work marks an advance on the part of one of the strongest of our young artists, who is one of the best illustrators we have. The drawing is true and strong, the figures of men and horses are in fine action, tearing along at full gallop, the sunshine effect is realistic and the color is good.'

Henry Farny (American, 1847–1916)

73 Indian Encampment

Gouache, 10×14 in. 1901. Denver, Colorado, Anschutz Collection.

Henry Farny was born in Alsace and taken to the United States as a child. He grew up in Cincinnati at a time when that city was an important cultural center. Farny traveled a great deal in the West and was particularly fond of Indian subjects. He enjoyed a fine reputation as an artist in his day, counting Theodore Roosevelt among his admirers.

After his death, Farny's work sank into almost complete oblivion; only in the past twenty years or so has it again won the admiration it so obviously deserves, and his paintings can now be seen in most of the leading museums in the United States. Farny's works command prices equal to and sometimes even surpassing those currently paid for Remingtons and Russells.

This painting is a typical Farny subject. The Indians are probably Crow; Farny loved the rich ornamentation of their robes and horse gear. He preferred to paint the Indians at peace, although he was of course aware of the uprising that took place during his lifetime.

Jules Tavernier (French, 1844–89)

74 White Man's Weapon

Oil on canvas, 28×22 in. 1880. Courtesy of Kennedy Galleries, Inc., New York.

French born and educated, Jules Tavernier traveled to the West in the early 1870s with his fellow-artist and fellow-countryman Paul Frenzeny, for *Harper's Weekly*. Together they wrote and illustrated a number of articles on the new states and territories of the West. Tavernier was so taken with the life in California that he remained in San Francisco until shortly before his death. This painting is one of the finest of his oil paintings known today, an extremely effective symbolic representation of the effect on the Indian and his culture of the introduction of white man's trade goods, especially the highly coveted guns.

Emanuel Leutze (German-American, 1818–68)

75 *(top)* **Prairie Bluffs at Julesburg, South Platte, Storm at Sunset**

Oil on canvas, 18×48 in. About 1863. Department of State, Diplomatic Reception Rooms.

This picture was painted after Leutze's trip west in late 1861. Primarily a painter of grand historical themes such as *Westward Ho!* (Plate 45), Leutze rarely painted aspects of Indian life.

G. B. Gardner

(bottom) **The Mountain Meadow Massacre**

Oil on canvas, $37\frac{1}{2} \times 48\frac{1}{2}$ in. 1875. Courtesy of Kennedy Galleries, Inc., New York.

Most of the emigrant trains heading west in the middle of the nineteenth century passed through Mormon-controlled Utah, and relations between Mormons and visitors were often strained. The Mormons could not forget 'Gentile' persecutions before they had left the States, and they feared the result of the ever-increasing influx of settlers from the East. In 1857, a wagon train from Arkansas and Missouri, both settings of some notable past persecutions of Mormons, was attacked by a party of Mormons disguised as Indians, and all but a few children were massacred. The painting by Gardner, although not fully accurate in its presentation, is expressive of the American reactions to the massacre.

William Strutt (Australian, 1825–1915)

76 *(top)* **Black Thursday**

Oil on canvas, 42×135 in. 1862-4. Melbourne, State Library of Victoria, La Trobe Collection.

Strutt is among the finest proponents of the tradition of history painting in Australia. An able and precise draughtsman, Strutt received his training in Paris, in the atelier of Michel Drolling (1786-1851) and at the École des Beaux-Arts. After some preliminary work as a lithographer and illustrator, he left for Melbourne, where he remained for eleven years. *Black Thursday* is his largest and perhaps most impressive painting. It depicts a well known event in colonial life that occurred in February 1851, shortly after his arrival. In that month, a tremendous bushfire swept the entire state, the temperatures rising to over 117 degrees. After the vast devastation, Strutt prepared an extensive series of sketches that evolved into this painting over a three-year period.

Robert Dowling (Australian, 1827–86)

(bottom) **Group of Natives of Tasmania**

Oil on canvas, 60×120 in. 1859. Launceston, Australia, Queen Victoria Museum and Art Gallery.

Dowling was taken to Tasmania as a young boy in 1831, but returned to London in 1856 to pursue his art. Despite this fact, his many years in Tasmania left a lasting impression on him. Like the countless American and Canadian artists who sought to preserve, at least on their canvases, the rapidly vanishing tribes of the native land, Dowling chose the tragedy of the Tasmanian aborigines as the subject of this painting. When he painted them on Flinders Island in Bass Strait, there were only a few natives left – the result of confinement by the expanding colonists. Devoid of sentimentality, the picture conveys the nobility of these native residents as they contemplate their unreasonable, yet inevitable, fate in the face of civilization's progress.

Carl Gutherz (American, 1844–1907)

77 *(top)* **Ploughing in Dakota**

Oil on canvas, 30×70 in. About 1884-5. Present location unknown, Photograph courtesy of Mr and Mrs Marshall F. Goodheart, Memphis, Tennessee.

Carl Gutherz is among a number of late nineteenth and early

twentieth-century American artists whose works are steadily gaining importance. During his lifetime, Gutherz enjoyed considerable success. His art was regularly exhibited at the Paris Salon and in numerous other shows where it received enthusiastic response from the critics. Gutherz was an integral part of art movements in America and in Europe, but he was one of many victims of the abrupt and inevitable changes in lifestyle and popular taste at the turn of the century.

Characterized by sound drawing and a sensitivity to color, this painting dates from Gutherz's period of exceptional creative growth between 1885 and 1896 in Paris. The earliest sketches for the painting date from 1881 to 1883, when Gutherz and Halsey Ives were establishing the St Louis School of Fine Arts.

The painting's location was the state line of Minnesota near the Dakota Territory, illustrating the heroic settlement of this frontier territory. Purchased by the Department of the Interior in 1887, this painting was described by Gutherz as follows: 'I saw an army of plows moving in measured tread over the vast plains . . . there . . . were men from all nations gathered in contented toil drawing from the earth its fullness. Whilst in Europe, their brothers were being forcibly drilled in modes of warfare . . .' In the 1890s, Gutherz contributed a series of murals to the new Library of Congress building in Washington, D.C.

Tom Roberts (Australian, 1856–1931)

(bottom) Shearing the Rams

Oil on canvas, 47 × 71 in. 1889-90. Melbourne, National Gallery of Victoria.

Prompted by a frequent event at Brocklesby station in New South Wales, Roberts has captured an essential aspect of country life in Australia. The scene renders with striking realism both the shearing shed and the spirit of the men at their task.

Unidentified Artist

78 Buffalo Bill's Wild West, Earl's Court, London

Color lithograph, $24\frac{1}{2} \times 39\frac{1}{2}$ in. About 1887. Fort Worth, Texas, Amon Carter Museum of Western Art.

To both Americans and Europeans, the greatest idol of the West was Buffalo Bill. As stated by Dixon Wecter in his *The Hero in America – A Chronicle of Hero-Worship,* 'Being a hero, in fact, grew to be the prime vocation of his life; he professionalized the role more than any other American in history.'

Born in 1846 as William Frederick Cody, Buffalo Bill spent the better part of fifty years, until his death in 1917, as the popular embodiment of the greatest scout, soldier and gun-fighter of the plains. In truth, he was none of these, but his looks and mannerisms enabled him simply to assume the part. It was not until 1882 that plans were begun for his great Wild West Show. By the mid-1890s, it was to become the greatest attraction on two continents.

Charles M. Russell (American, 1864–1926)

79 The Buffalo Hunt No. 26 – When Buffalo were Plentiful

Oil on canvas, $30\frac{1}{8} \times 48\frac{1}{4}$ in. 1899. Fort Worth, Texas, Amon Carter Museum of Western Art.

Of all the American artists who pictured the West, Russell was perhaps the most intimately acquainted with the realities of the frontier. Beginning in 1879, he spent the next eleven years in Montana actually working as a cowboy. He was considered a friend by the Indians remaining there, and was thus a first-hand witness to the closing of the open range. This of course meant not only the demise of the cowboy, but also of the Indians who depended upon the roaming buffalo herds for their subsistence. Russell had his first one-man exhibition in 1911. It is curious to note that until this date Russell's best patrons and supporters were saloon-keepers.

Frederic Remington (American, 1861–1909)

80 The Vision *or* How Order Number Six Went Through

Oil on board, 27 × 40 in. About 1899. Courtesy of The '21' Club Collection, Peter Kriendler, President, New York.

Charles Schreyvogel (American, 1861–1912)

81 My Bunkie

Oil on canvas, $25\frac{1}{4} \times 34$ in. 1899. New York, Metropolitan Museum of Art.

Charles Schreyvogel executed very few major works. This painting is generally considered to be his masterpiece. It was the result of five months spent sketching numerous scenes in Colorado and Arizona in 1893. At the time of the painting's completion, Schreyvogel was unable to enlist any sort of popular response either to the painting or to the lithograph from it. This situation changed dramatically in 1900, when the painting was included in the annual National Academy of Design exhibition and received the first prize. With these funds, the artist was able to return to the West, where he painted both troopers and Indians.

82 The Dispatch Bearers

Oil on canvas, $27\frac{3}{4} \times 25$ in. 1900. Courtesy of Kennedy Galleries, Inc., New York.

In making his pictorial history of the exploits of the United States cavalry in the Indian wars of the nineteenth century, Charles Schreyvogel painted not only specific historical incidents such as Custer's demand to Sitting Bull, but also incidents typical of countless unrecorded exploits, such as the ambush of military couriers by a band of hostiles.

Frederic Remington (American, 1861–1909)

83 The Bronco Buster

Bronze (Roman Works Cast), $23\frac{1}{2}$ in. high. 1895. Fort Worth, Texas, Amon Carter Museum of Western Art.

This was Remington's first and most popular bronze. It translated into three dimensions the dramatic qualities found in his paintings and thus was a unique contribution to the history of American sculpture. Before the casting was completed, about 300 bronzes were made. They are as popular today, and as highly prized by collectors, as they were during the 1890s.

84 The Fall of the Cowboy

Oil on canvas, 25 × 35 in. 1895. Fort Worth, Texas, Amon Carter Museum of Western Art.

In the thirty years following the Civil War, life on the vast western cattle frontier was on its way to becoming a legend of the past. Successful entrepreneurs had settled the open ranges so quickly that the cowboy was put out of work. Once a necessary ingredient in driving the cattle to market, he suddenly found himself no longer needed, and his way of life obsolete. This poignant painting succinctly expressed this fact. It was done to illustrate an article by Owen Wister on 'The Evolution of the Cow-Puncher,' for *Harper's Monthly* (Vol. XCI, September 1895). In that article Wister stated, 'And what has become of them? Except where he lingers in the mountains of New Mexico he has been dispersed. Three things swept him away – the exhausting of the virgin pastures, the coming of the iron fence, and Mr Armour of Chicago, who set the price to suit himself. But all this may be summed up in the word Progress.'

Anton Van Wouw (South African, 1862–1945)

85 Bad News

Bronze, 19 in. high. 1907. Courtesy of Sotheby Parke Bernet South Africa (Proprietary) Ltd., Johannesburg.

Anton van Wouw was affectionately regarded as 'the artist of the Transvaal Boers'. He was such a realist that he is sometimes dismissed as little more than a copyist. In spite of this criticism, he created sensitive pictures of monumental scale, as well as small, parlor-room works. His smaller works depicted the regional genre of Afrikaner soldiers, Voortrekker girls, and Bantu working in the mines, drinking beer or hunting game. In this particular work, the two Boer soldiers have just received news that the Anglo-Boer War is lost and that the Peace Treaty of Vereeniging has been signed.

Leonard Baskin (American, born 1922)

86 Moving West

Watercolor and ink, $27\frac{1}{4} \times 40$ in. 1974. Courtesy of Kennedy Galleries, Inc., New York.

Strongly influenced by the German expressionist Kaethe Kollwitz (1867-1945), Baskin has studied successively at New York University, Yale University and the Académie de La Grande Chaumière in Paris. His earliest success came in the 1950s as a printmaker and graphic designer, specializing in figurative imagery during a time in which abstract expressionism was preferred. At one time, Baskin stated that the most important subject-matter for him was 'anxiety-ridden man, imprisoned in his ungainly self'. A humanity pervades his work, perhaps reaching its apogee in his sensitive drawings of the American Indian. Since 1953, Baskin has been associated with Smith College as a professor of graphics and sculpture.

Newell Converse Wyeth (American, 1882–1945)

87 Blue Lock, the Queen

Oil on canvas, 32 × 40 in. 1916. Denver, Colorado, Anschutz Collection.

Wyeth was the most successful pupil of Howard Pyle and the founder of what has turned out to be a dynasty of painters, the best known of whom is undoubtedly his son Andrew. Many remember his famous illustrations for *Robinson Crusoe, Treasure Island* and *The Last of the Mohicans.* This painting, an illustration for a story, appeared in *Collier's Weekly Magazine* on 21 October 1916.

John Sloan (American, 1871–1951)

88 Southwest Art (Julius Rolshoven Painting an Indian)

Oil on canvas, 21 × 25 in. 1920. Denver, Colorado, Anschutz Collection.

'Sloan's keen powers of observation and faculty for incisive characterization no doubt developed from his early training as a newspaper illustrator. He had the ability to produce telling visual images from memory. On occasion, the sharp, satiric wit that marked his etchings cropped up in his paintings, as in this work where Sloan pokes fun at the artist Rolshoven, who has had his Pueblo Indian model don a Plains feather bonnet and assume a "heroic" pose.' (From the Denver Art Museum publication, *Picturesque Images From Taos and Santa Fe,* 1974.)

Charles M. Russell (American, 1864–1926)

89 The Wagons

Oil on canvas, 36 × 48 in. 1921. Courtesy of Kennedy Galleries, Inc., New York.

It would have been impossible for the tribes of the West to ignore the great emigrant trains that crossed their territory on the way to Oregon or California, and with experience the attitude of most of the tribes changed from friendly or merely curious to actively hostile. One source of trouble was the slaughter of herds of buffalo by travelers who killed them for delicacies or merely for sport; thus endangering the Indians, for whom the bison herds furnished virtually all the staples of their life. Not every wagon train that crossed the plains suffered attacks by hostile tribes, but every member of every train traveled with a continual awareness of the possibility of such a danger. Russell was a complete partisan of the Indians in their struggles with white invaders, and he has shown this incident from the Indian point of view.

Rockwell Kent (American, 1882–1971)

90 Neither Snow, Nor Rain, Nor Ice

Oil on canvas, 40 × 64 in. 1932. Courtesy of Hammer Galleries, New York.

Throughout his lifetime, Kent frequently traveled to out-of-the-way places in search of undiscovered wilderness. From his early experiences on Monhegan Island, Maine, he ventured to Fox Island, Alaska, Newfoundland, South America, and Greenland. Like William Bradford almost a century before, Kent was completely captivated by the rugged beauty of the austere and monumental far north.

Jackson Pollock (American, 1912–56)

91 Going West

Oil on fiberboard, $15\frac{1}{8} \times 20\frac{3}{4}$ in. About 1934-5. Washington, D.C., National Collection of Fine Arts, Smithsonian Institution.

As this painting clearly shows, Pollock was strongly influenced by his teacher Thomas Hart Benton. While at the Art Students League, Pollock also studied with John Sloan.

In 1967, Thomas Hess commented about Pollock as follows: 'A good deal has been written about Pollock – some of it at his own urging: Pollock the cowboy, the ragged noisy Westerner; some of it at the urging of his exegetes: Pollock, the link between the School of Paris and contemporary formalist abstraction. Both approaches ignore Pollock's own life-long effort which was to find in himself the mythical and symbolic elements that seemed most important (the essences of his feelings) and to express them in paint. He took big banal ideas; discovered what they meant to him as shapes; translated them into visual ideas; and then made them into paintings, with all the intensity and intellectual invention at his command. For a time, the pictures were abstract. The images disappeared behind materializations of the action with which he had found them.'

Thomas Hart Benton (American, 1889–1975)

92 Independence and the Opening of the West

Acrylic polymer on linen mounted on panel, 19 × 32 feet. 1959-62. Independence, Missouri, Museum of the Harry S. Truman Library.

Throughout his long and distinguished career, Thomas Hart Benton sought to express the essential American experience in his paintings. In a statement prepared for the 1957 publication *New Art in America: Fifty Painters of the Twentieth Century,* Benton describes this desire: 'I believe I have wanted, more than anything else, to make pictures, the imagery of which would carry unmistakably American meanings for Americans and for as many of them as possible.' To achieve this end, Benton perceived the archetypal qualities of the commonplace and elevated them in his paintings to almost mythic proportions.

Although this mural deals with the role of Independence, Missouri, in the opening of the West, Benton does not dwell on the subject. Instead, he uses the theme as a basis to present a pulsating drama about westward expansion. The composition is dominated by the settler who stands atop a hill symbolizing the fulfillment of his manifest destiny. On the right, we see the community of Independence readying a group of wagons for the Oregon Trail. On the left, there is the inevitable meeting with the Indians, dominated by the Santa Fe trail and the Rocky Mountains of southern Colorado in the background. Benton's technique and his attention to detail are exquisite. The painting, completed less than twenty years ago, demonstrates the persistent vitality of the frontier experience as an integral image in American art and mythology.

Fritz Scholder (American, born 1937)

93 Indian, Dog with Friend

Acrylic on canvas, 60 × 80 in. 1973. Collection of Mr and Mrs Taylor Nickles French, Memphis, Tennessee.

In many ways, Fritz Scholder is an intriguing successor to George Catlin, whose Indian paintings reflect such urgency and enthusiasm for his subject-matter. Although only just into his forties, he has an impressive list of exhibitions, appointments, commissions, and museum holdings; in 1974 his works were the subject of a major retrospective at the Brooks Memorial Art Gallery in Memphis, Tennessee.

By directing our attention to the physical and mental environment of a small group in a large society, Scholder transforms their joys and sorrows into a provocative statement on the nature of twentieth-century consciousness, Indian and non-Indian. His commentary is a sensitive evocation of a state of being, a candid view of a people.

In some ways, the boldness of Scholder's style and the intensity of his own Indian self-awareness make his work more meaningful than Catlin's. Says the artist, 'I have painted the Indian real, not red. Taboos set by the dominant culture are my target . . . I see in the Indian consciousness the hope of the country.'

John Clymer (American, born 1907)

94 Night Guard

Oil on canvas, 20 × 40 in. 1976. Courtesy of Fenn Galleries Ltd., Santa Fe, New Mexico.

Clymer, a native of the northwest part of America, has put his knowledge of fur trappers and northern Plains Indians to good use as subject-matter for his paintings, which document the pioneers' struggles and triumphs.

Jack Beal (American, born 1932)

95 Colonization

Oil on canvas, 146 × 150 in. 1976-7. Photograph Courtesy of Allan Frumkin Gallery, New York, Department of Labor Building, Washington, D.C., General Services Administration, Art-in-Architecture Program.

This painting is one of a series of four works commissioned by the United States Government. The overall theme of the series is the History of Labor in America; the other paintings are appropriately titled: *Settlement, Industry* and *Technology.*

As a definitive contribution to the history of American mural painting, this series continues in a tradition popularized in the 1930s by Work Projects Administration artists such as Thomas Hart Benton. In the first painting we encounter an early morning scene in the coastal wilderness of seventeenth-century America. Incorporated in the design are seven figures, each of which represents an integral participant in the frontier drama – the trapper, the pioneer family and the Indian. In contrast to Carter's *Arrival in the New World* (Plate 38), Beal has omitted the log cabin, feeling that its presence would have rendered the impression of colonization too safe and settled. Thus a quality of this panel, as well as of the other three, is the element of heroism projected upon his characters.

In describing this project, Beal stated, 'In commissioning this suite of murals on the History of Labor in America, the government offered a challenge unmatched for figurative painters in our time. Three assistants and I painted nearly every day for 15 months, concentrating on the areas of aesthetics and composition, on history, message, and purpose, but mostly on representing the people we know who work hard and are proud of their work.'

Georgia O'Keeffe (American, *b.* 1887)

96 Summer Days

Oil on canvas, 36 × 30 in. 1936. Collection of Miss Georgia O'Keeffe.

The artist writes: 'I have picked flowers where I found them – have picked up sea shells and rocks and pieces of wood where there were sea shells and rocks and pieces of wood that I liked . . . When I found the beautiful white bones in the desert I picked them up and took them home . . . I have used these things to say what is to me the wildness and wonder of the world as I live in it.'

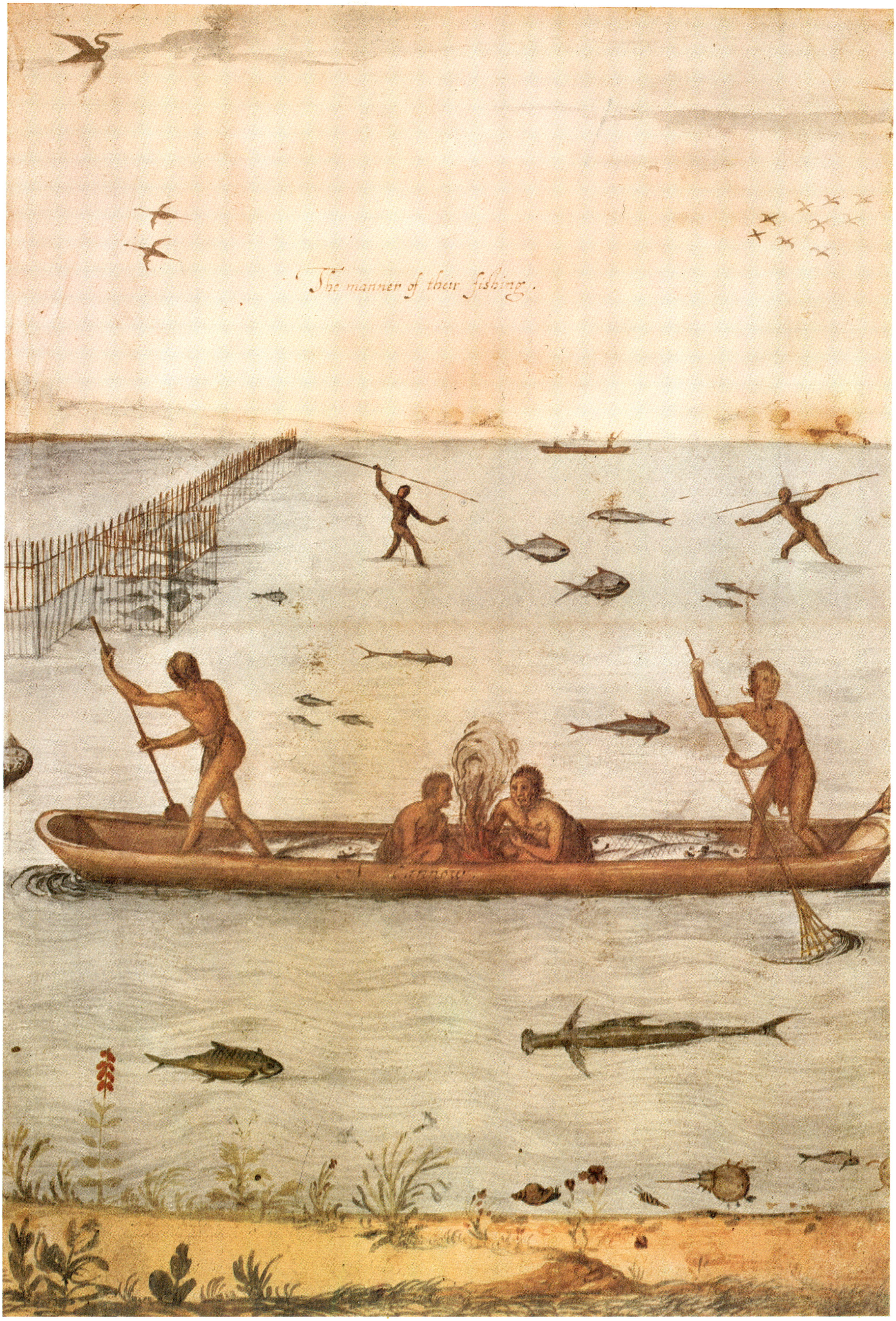
The manner of their fishing.

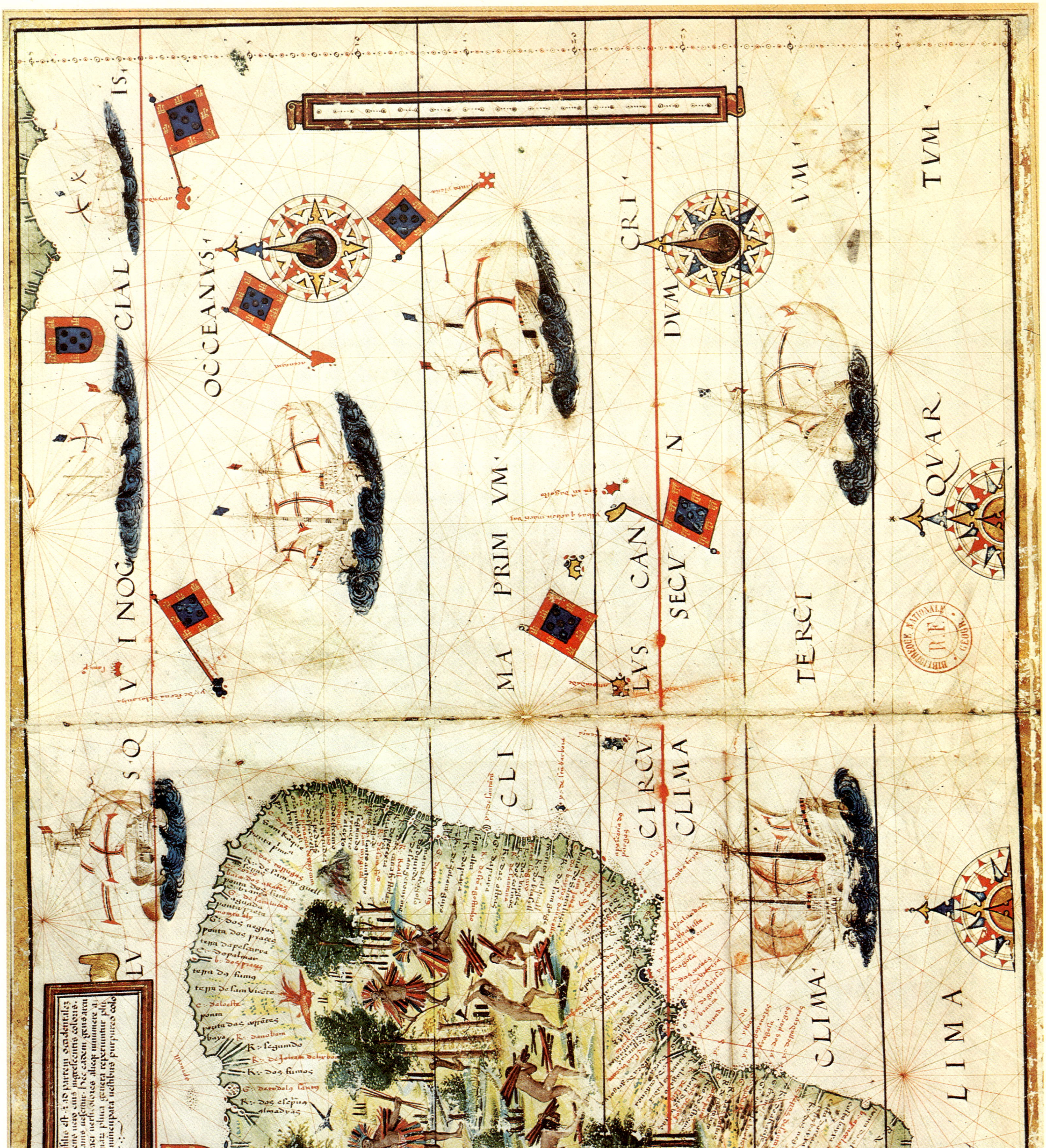
OCCEANVS
TERRA BRASILIS

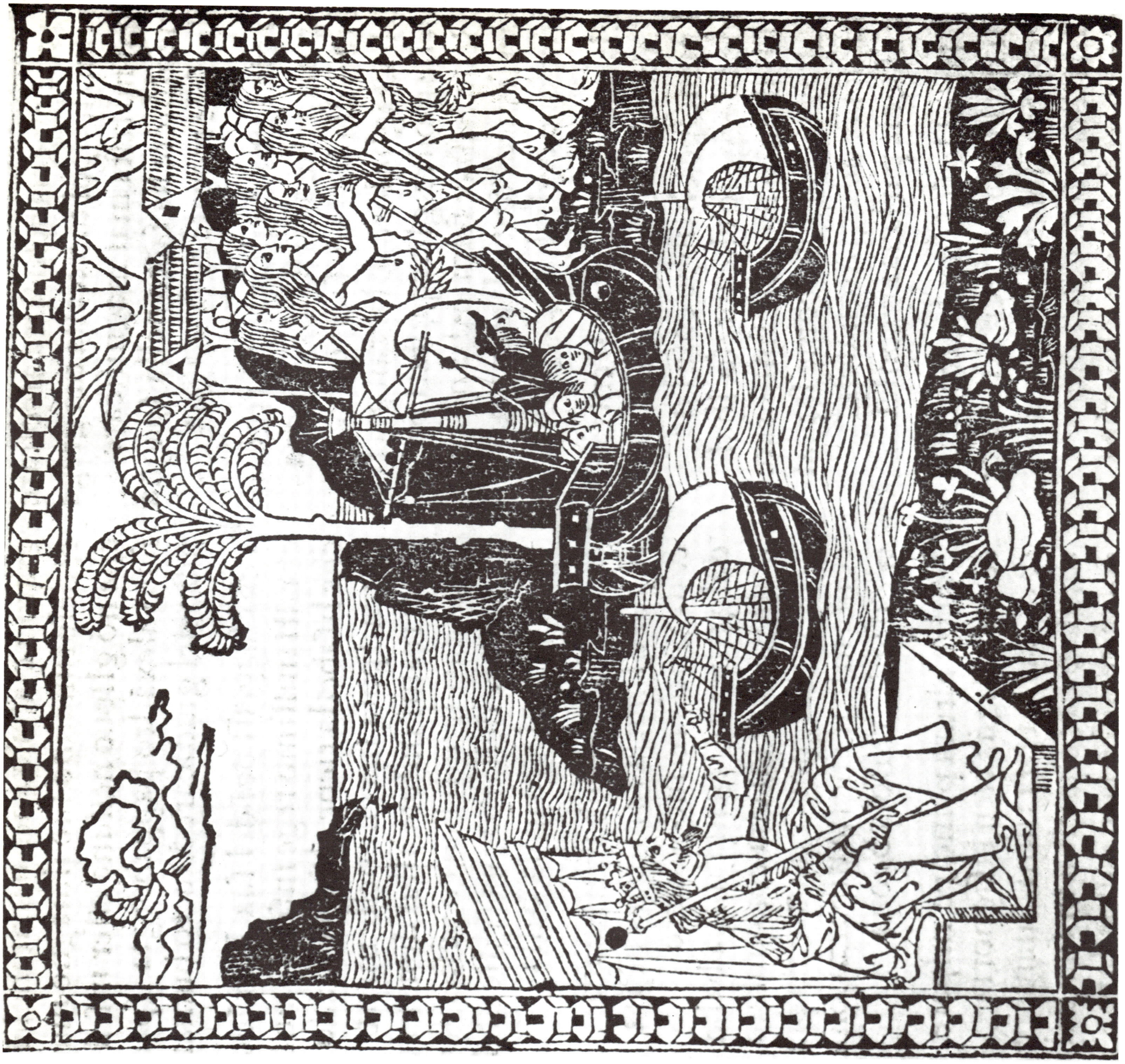

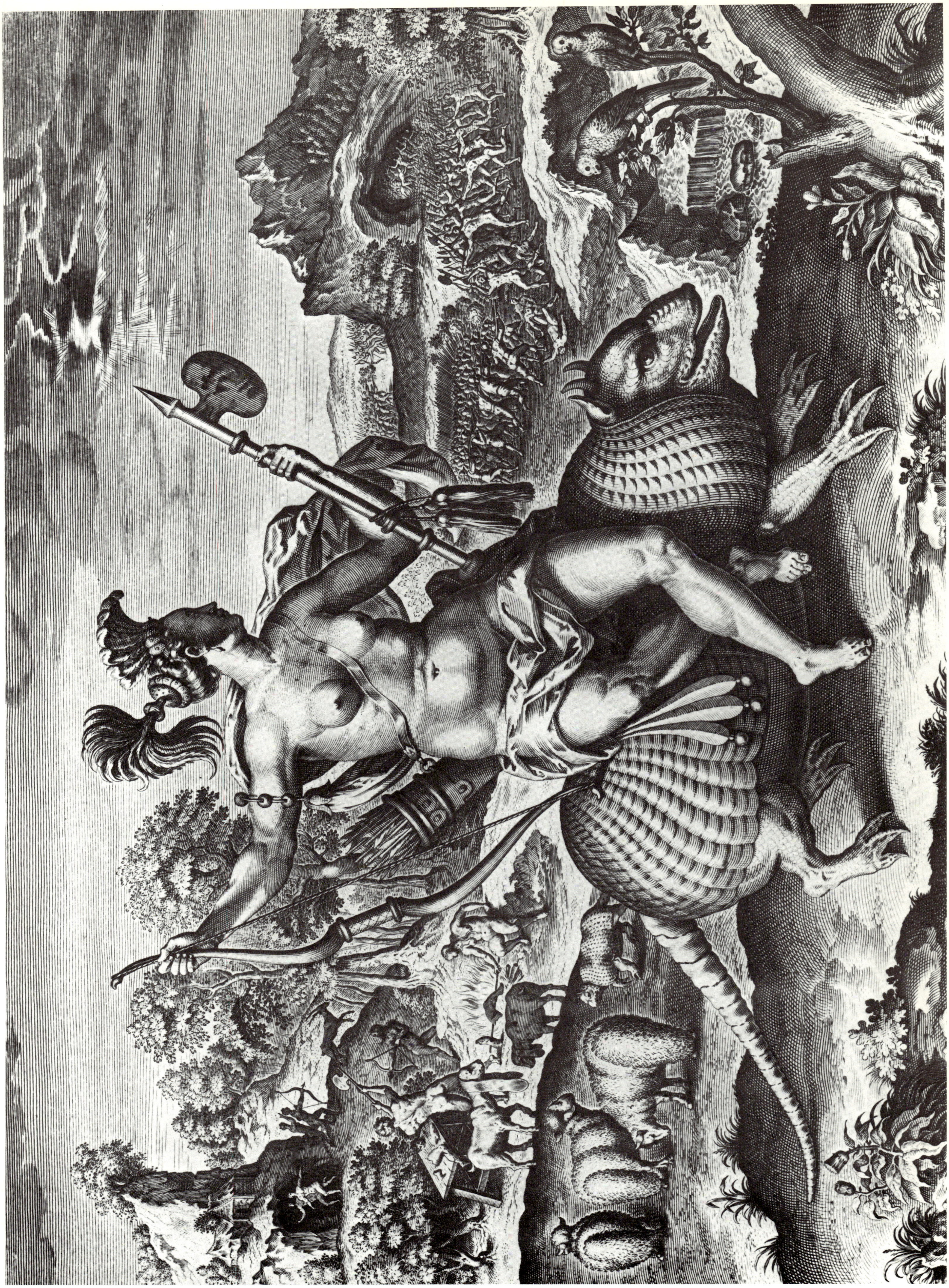

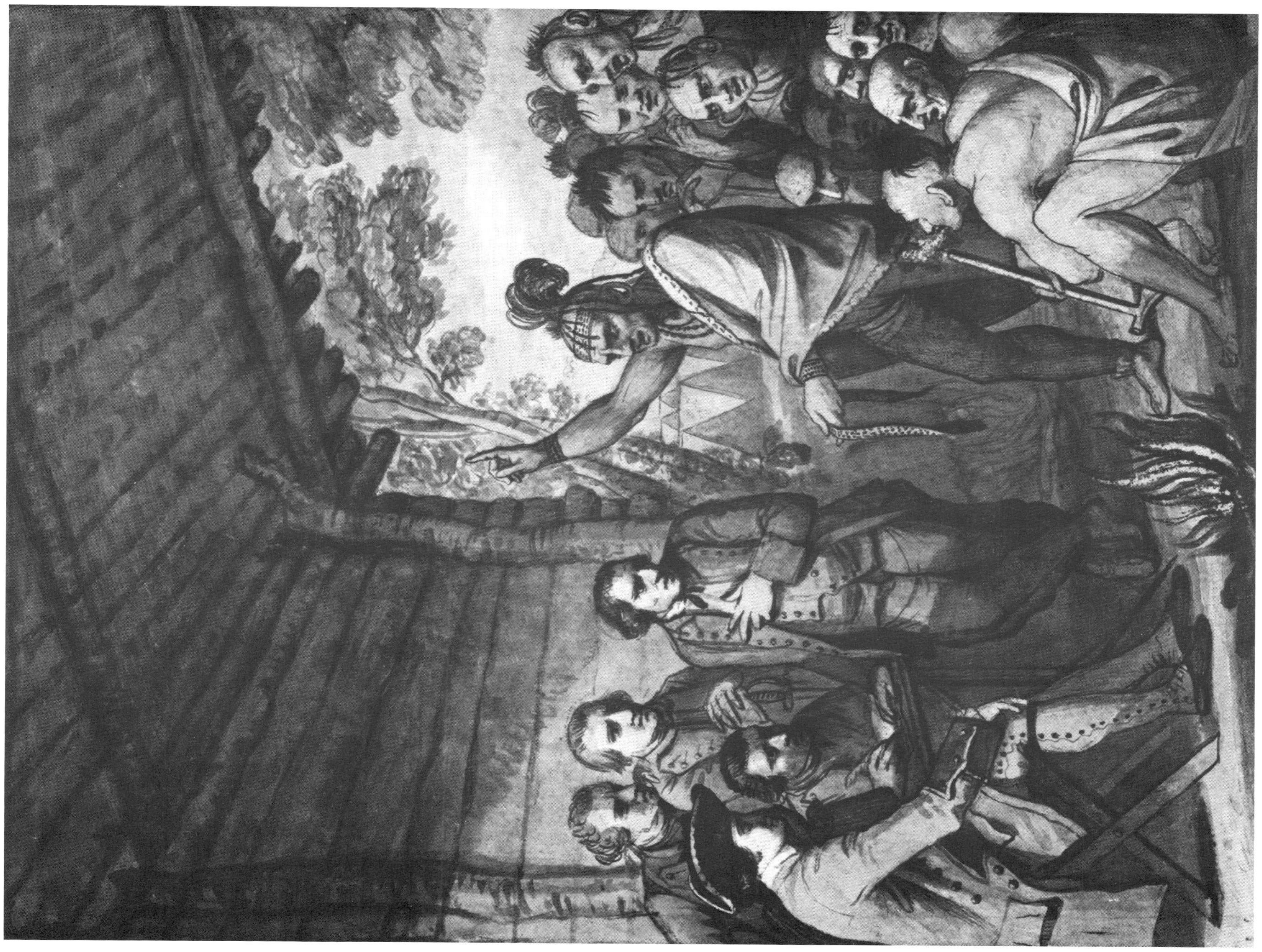

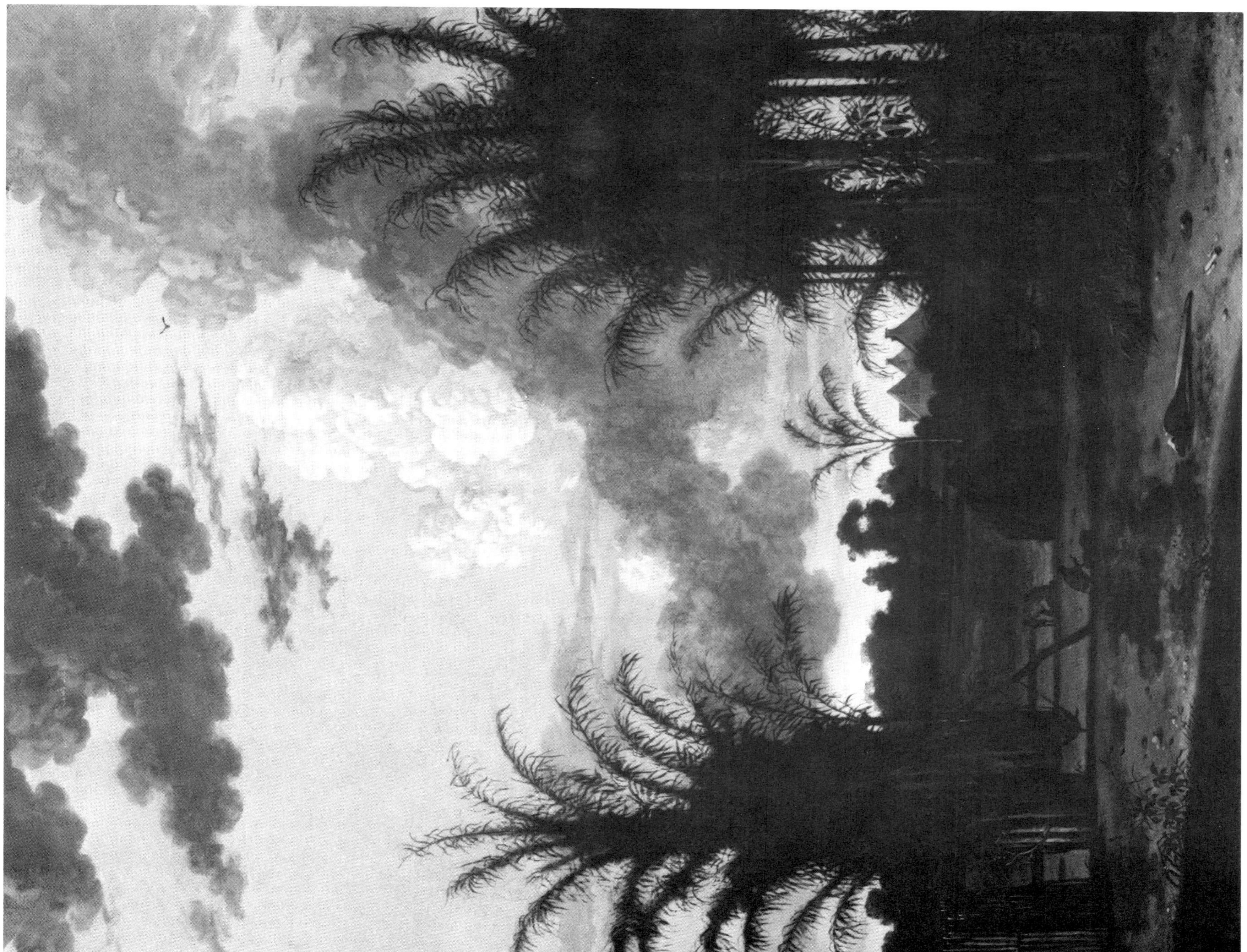

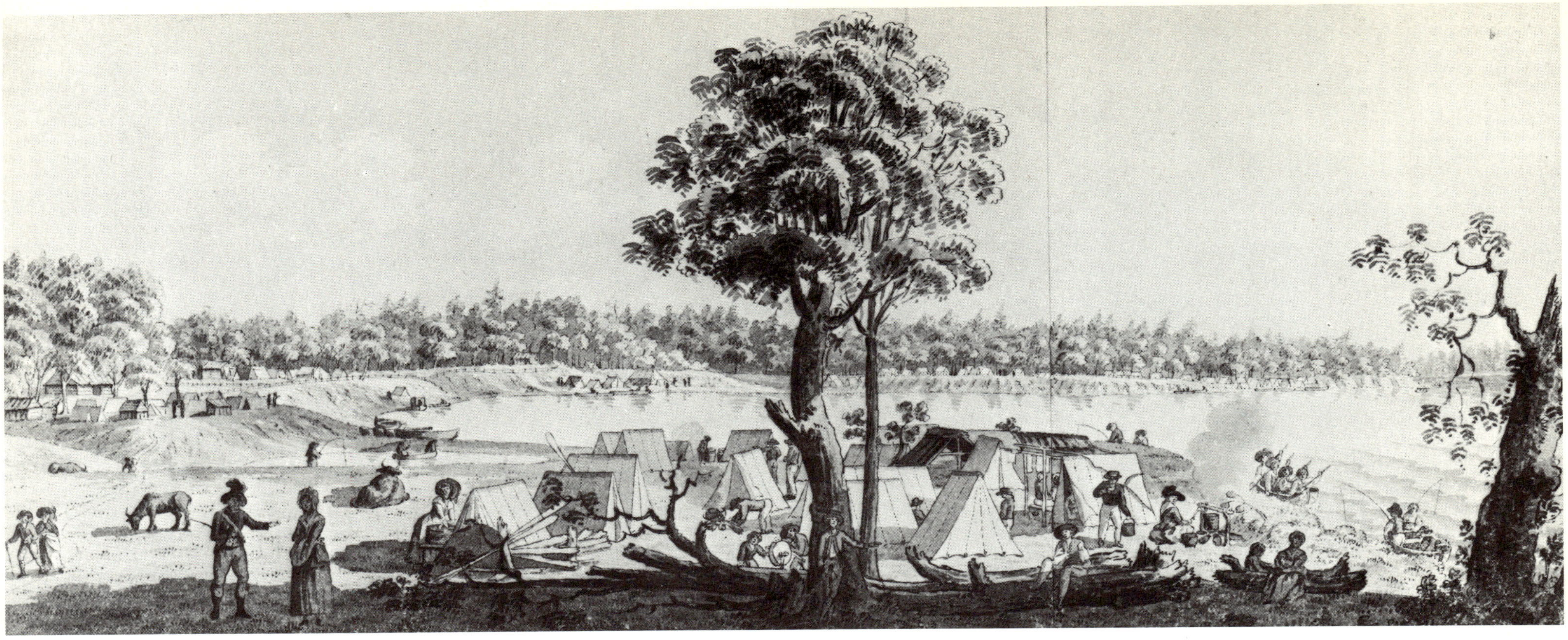

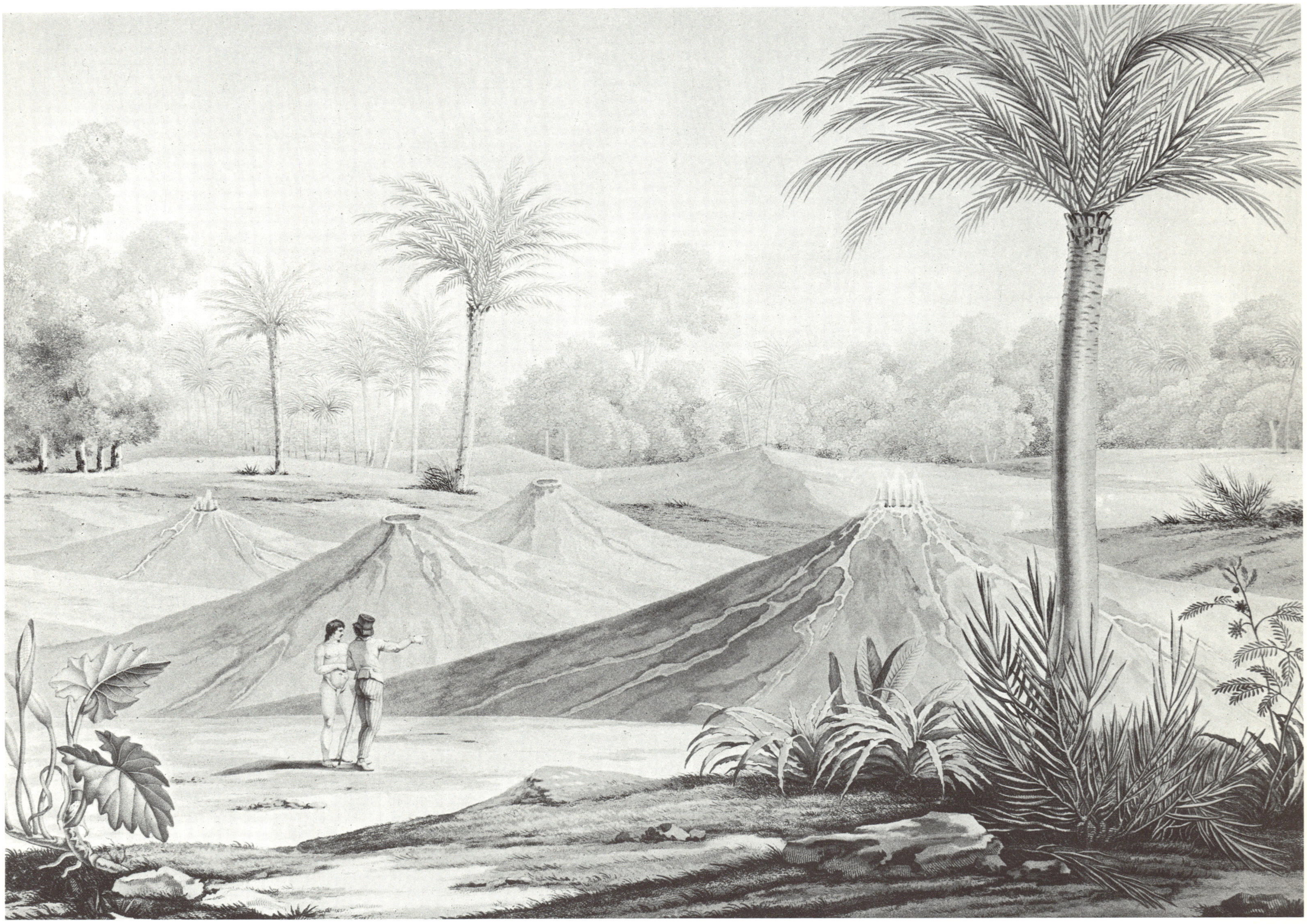

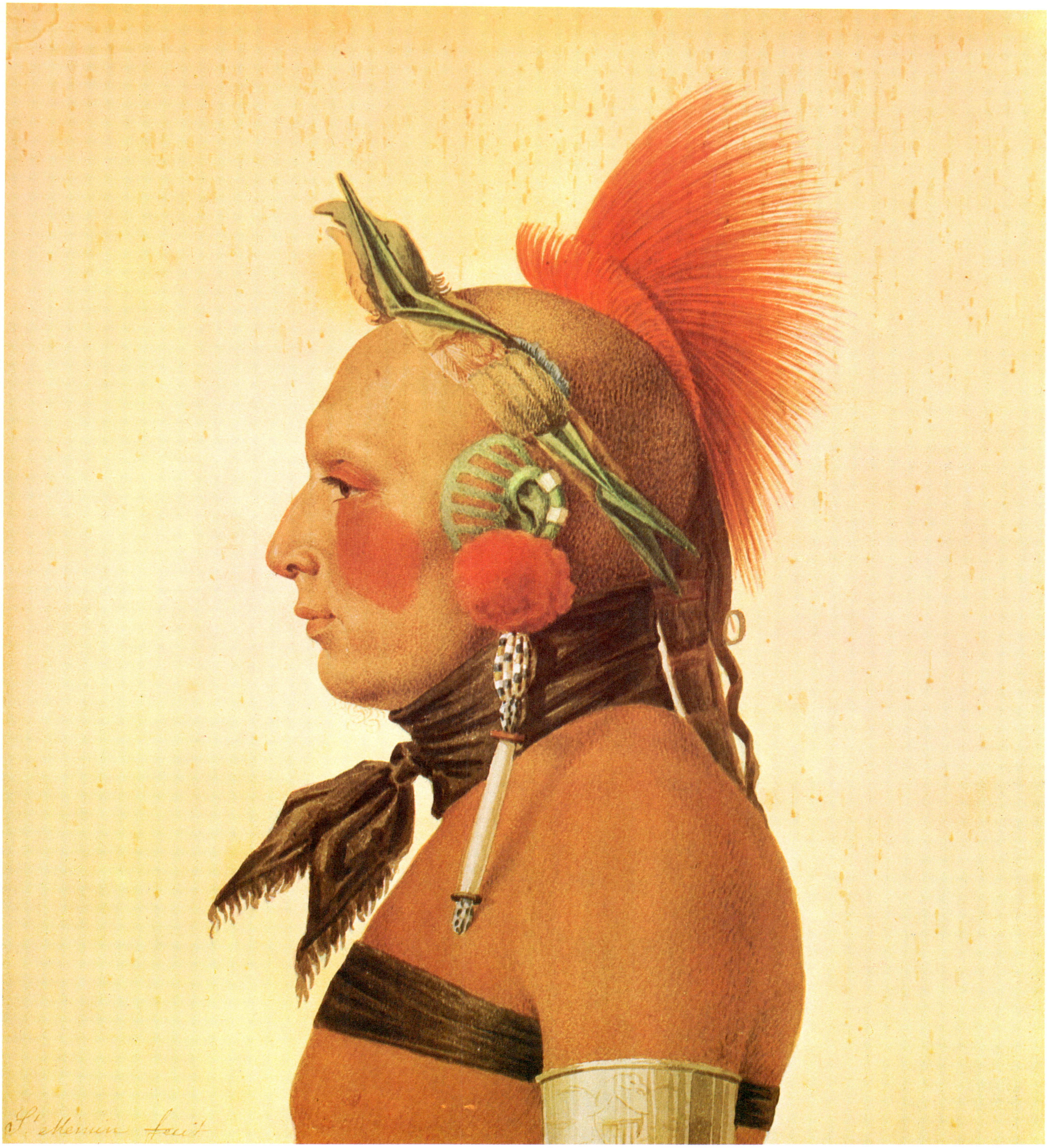
St Mémin fecit

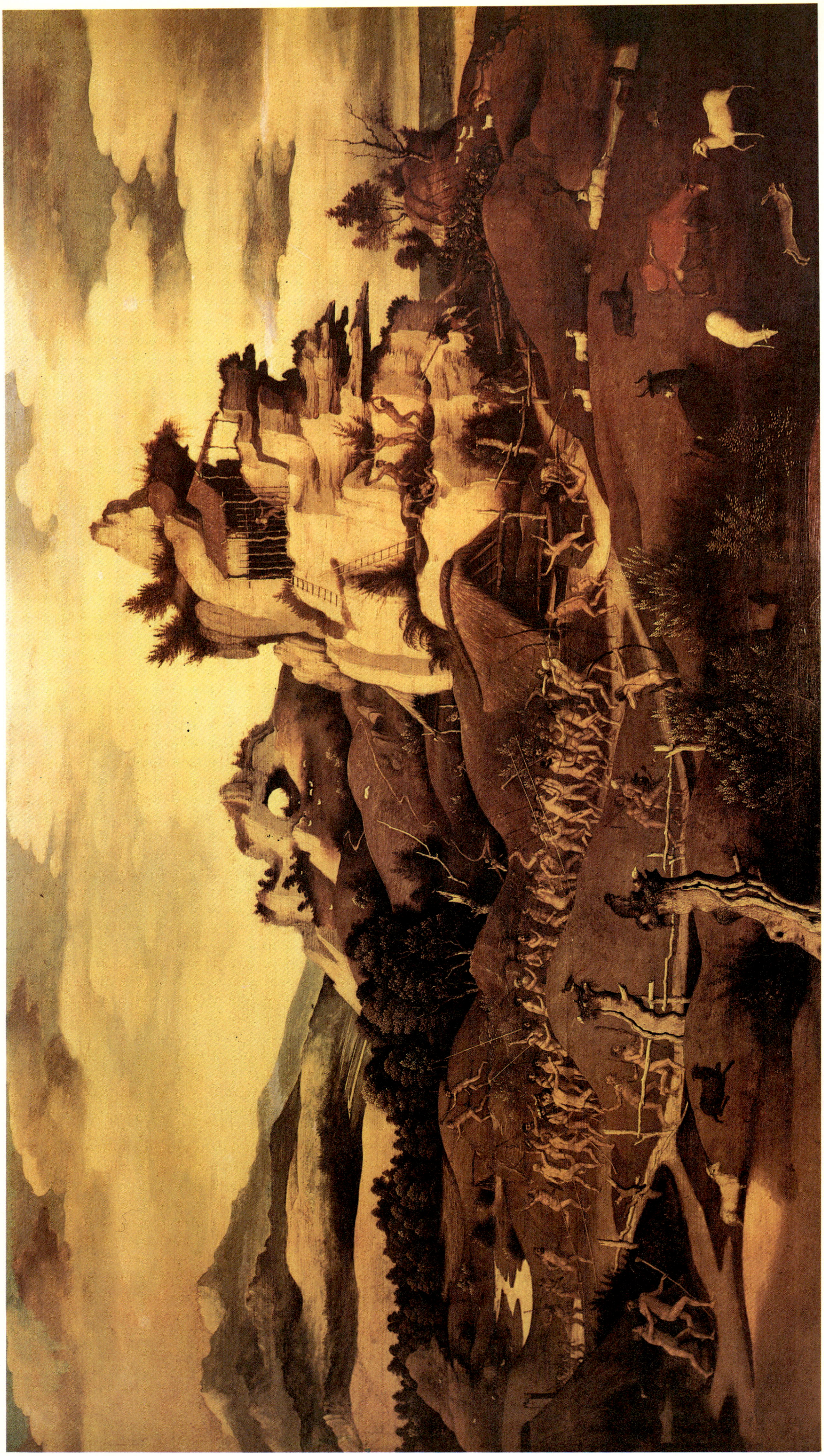

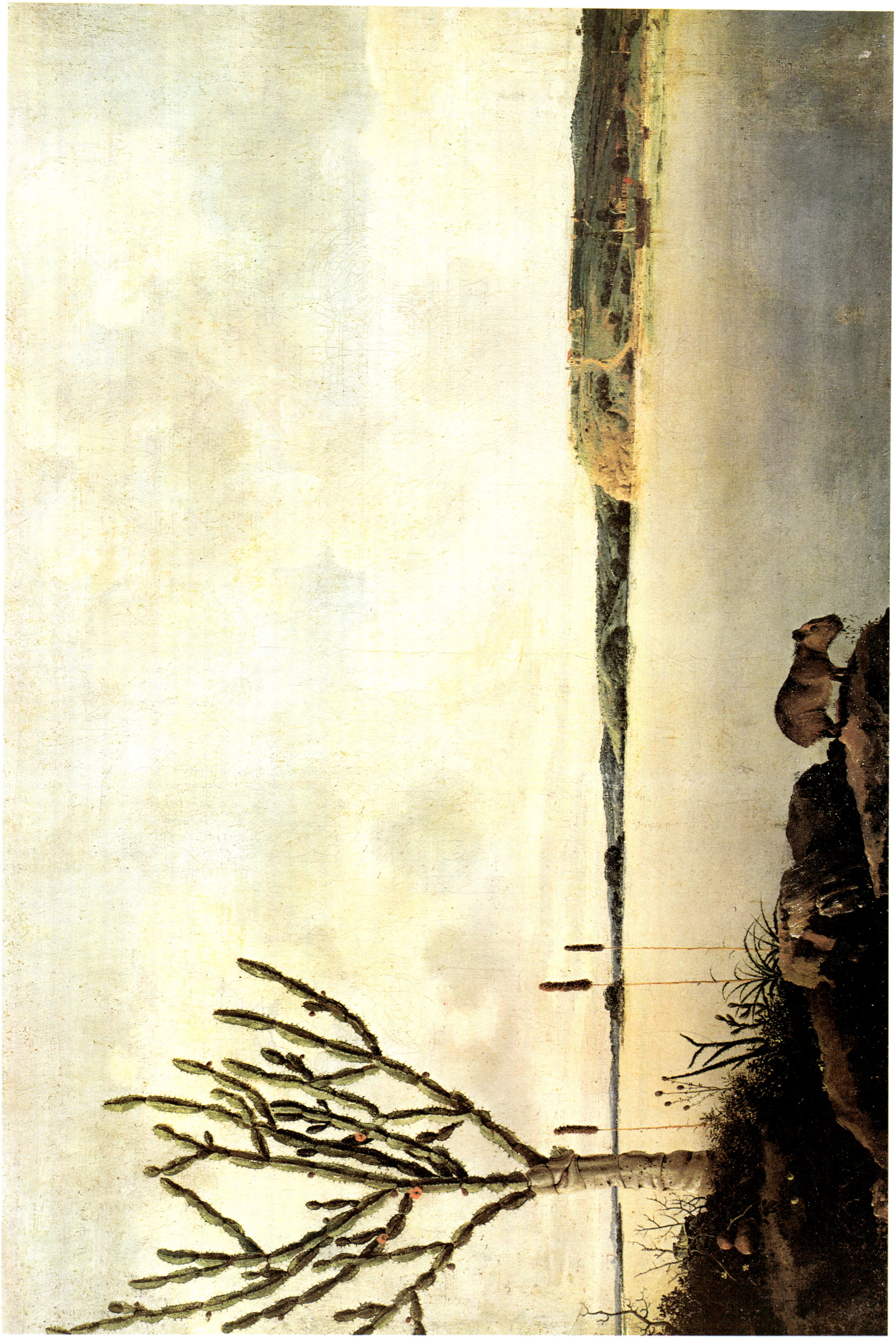

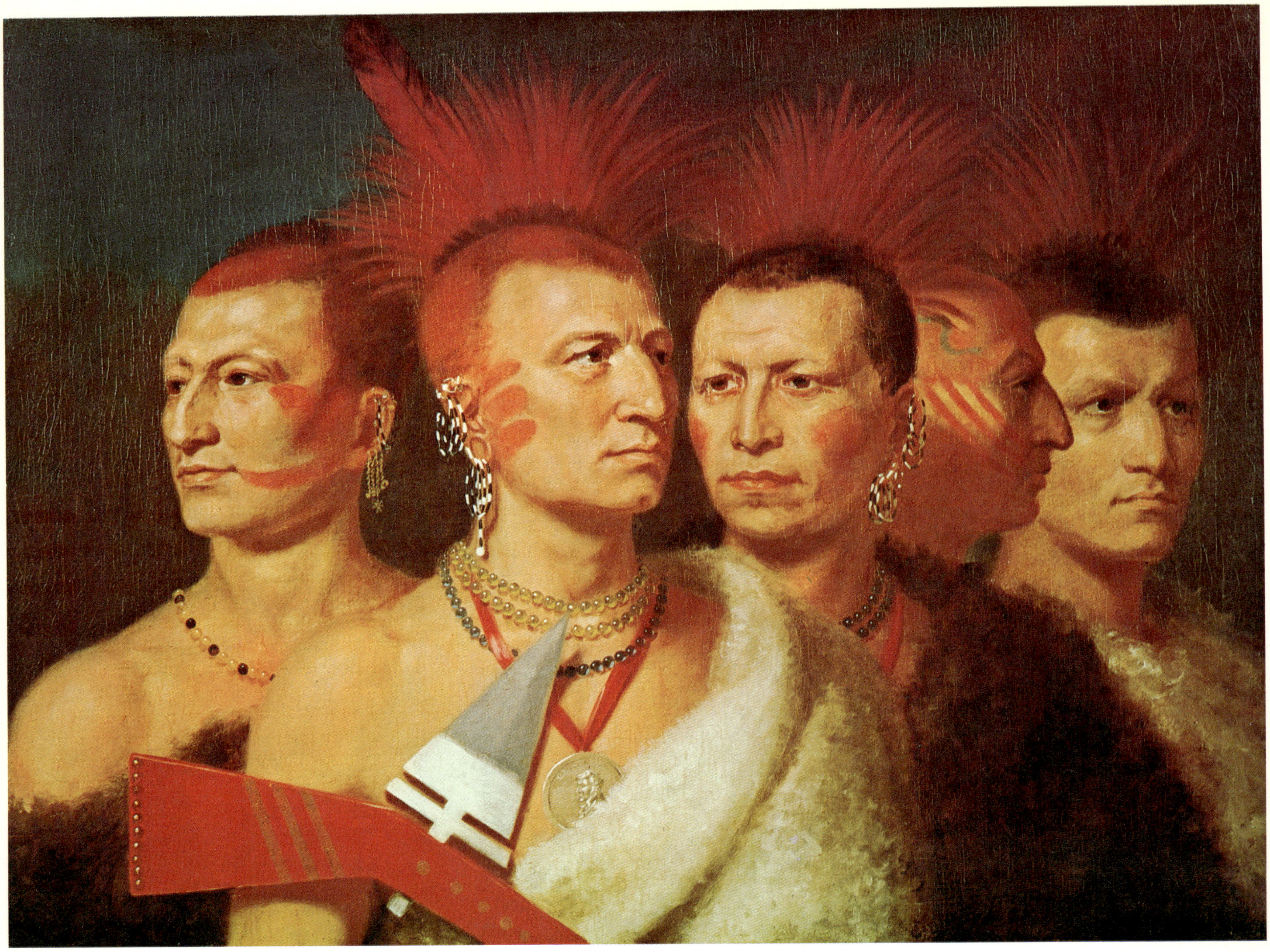

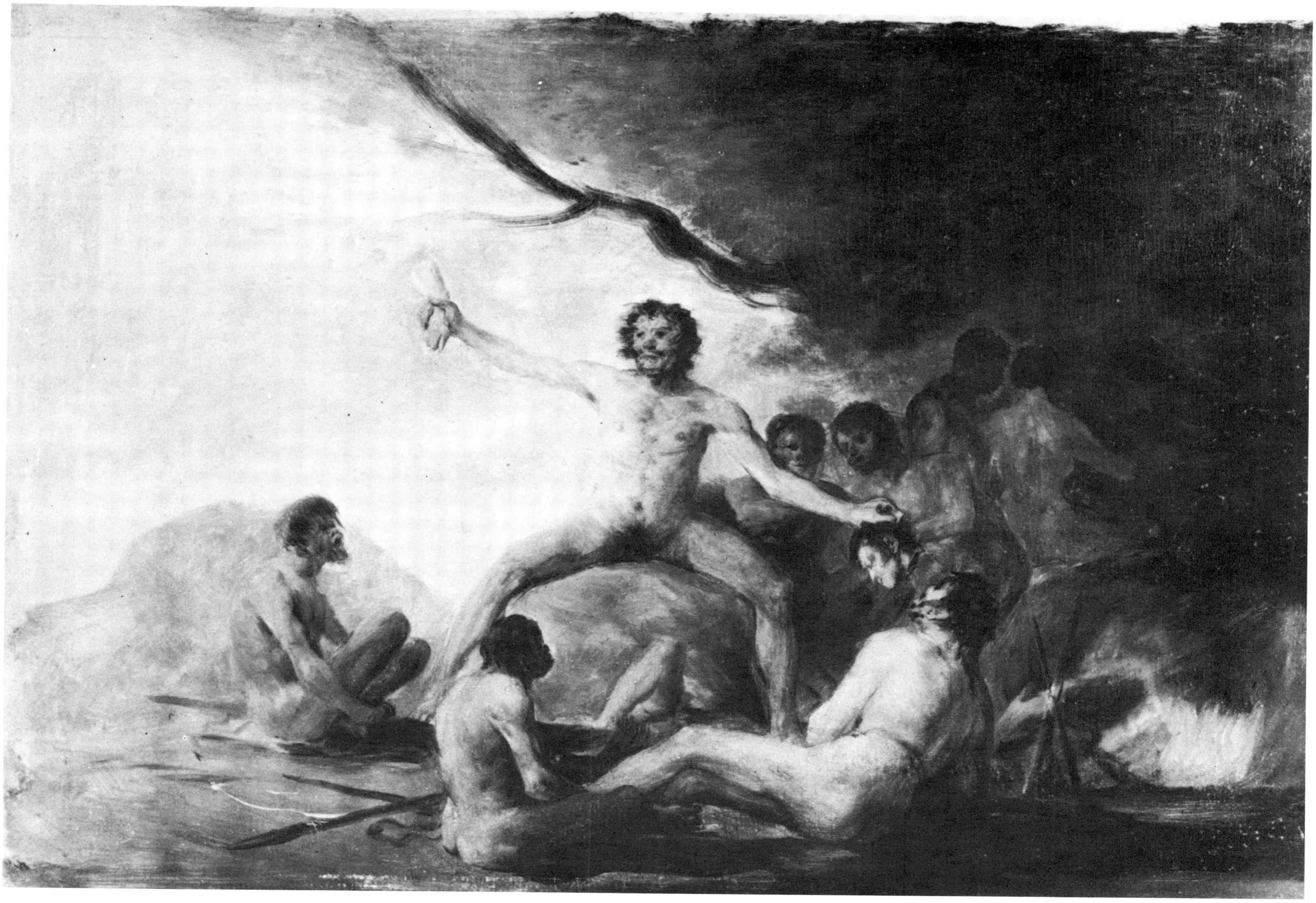

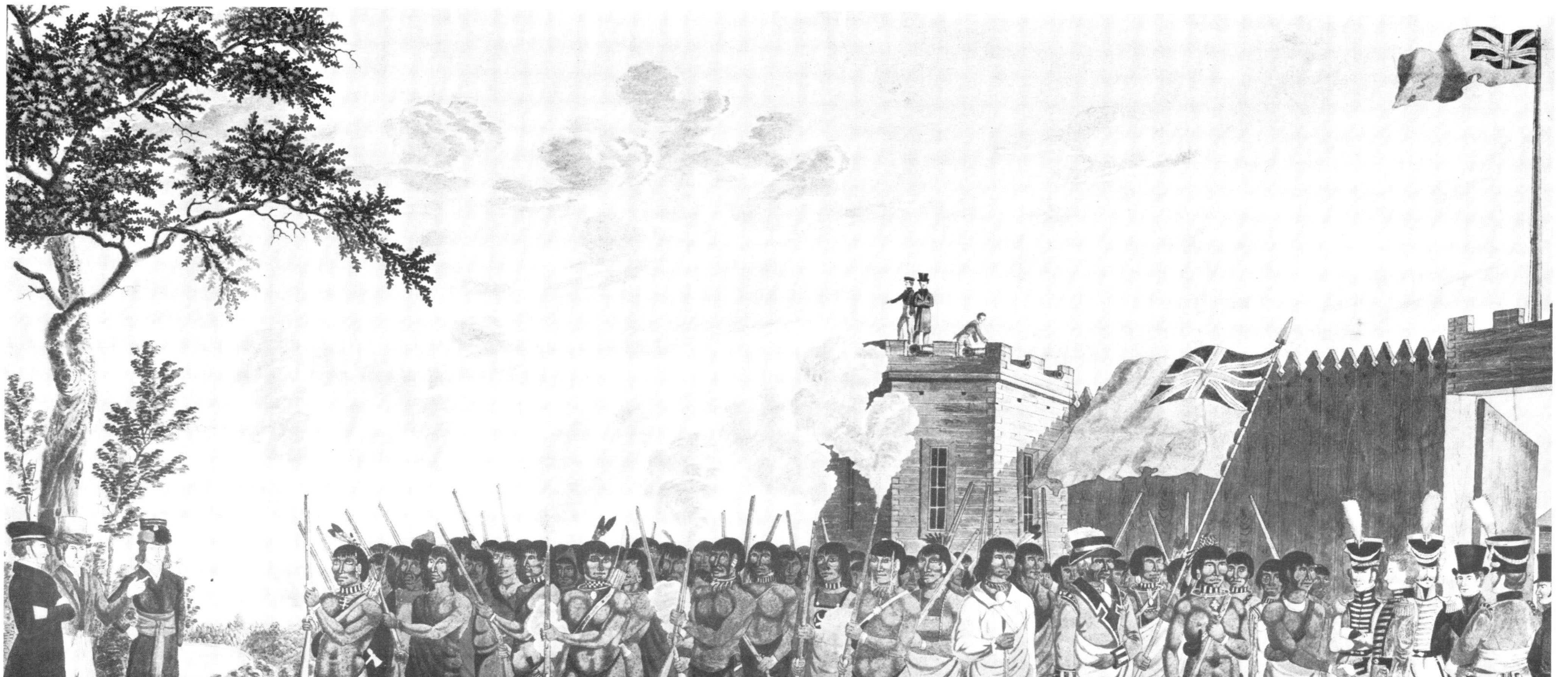

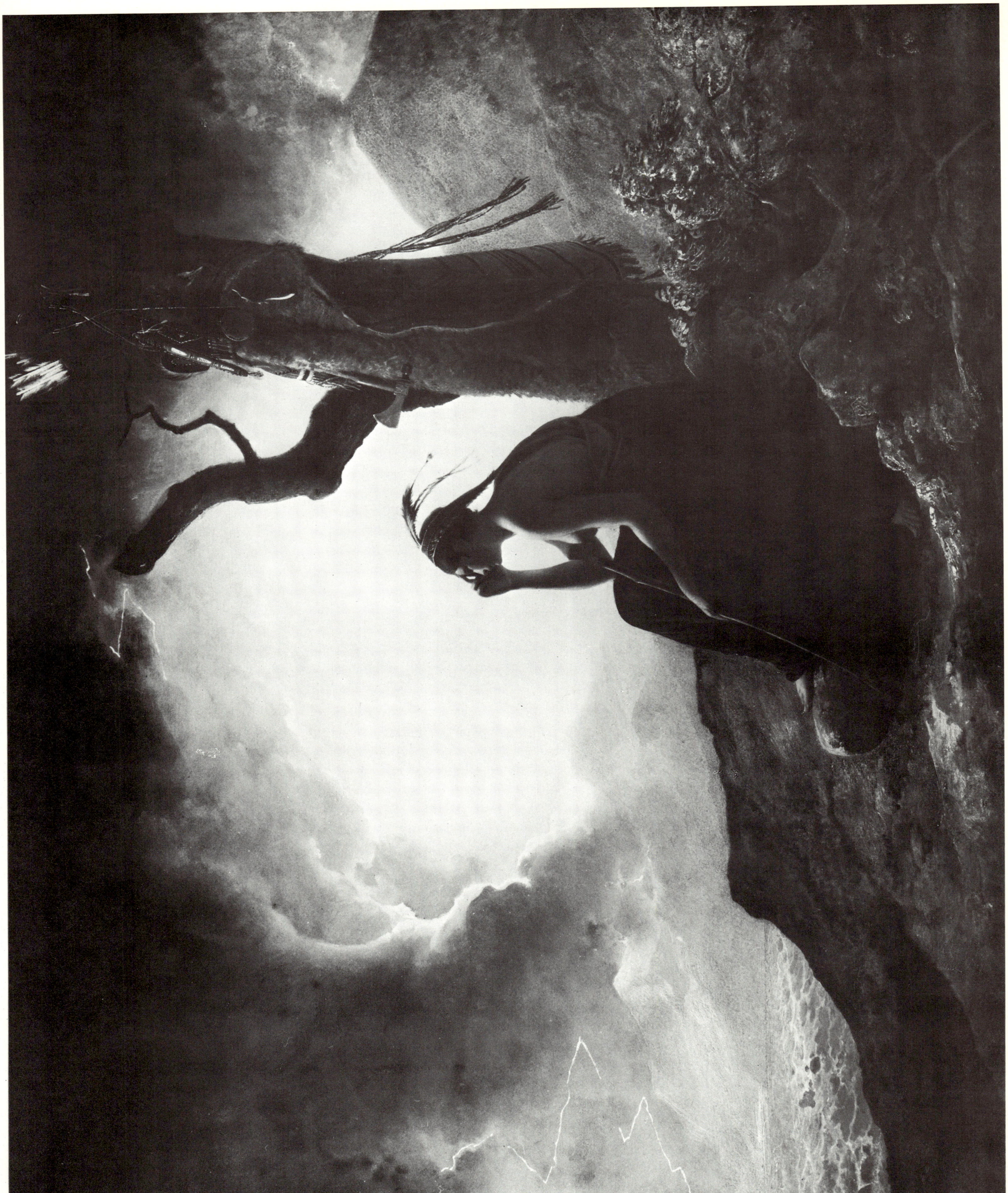

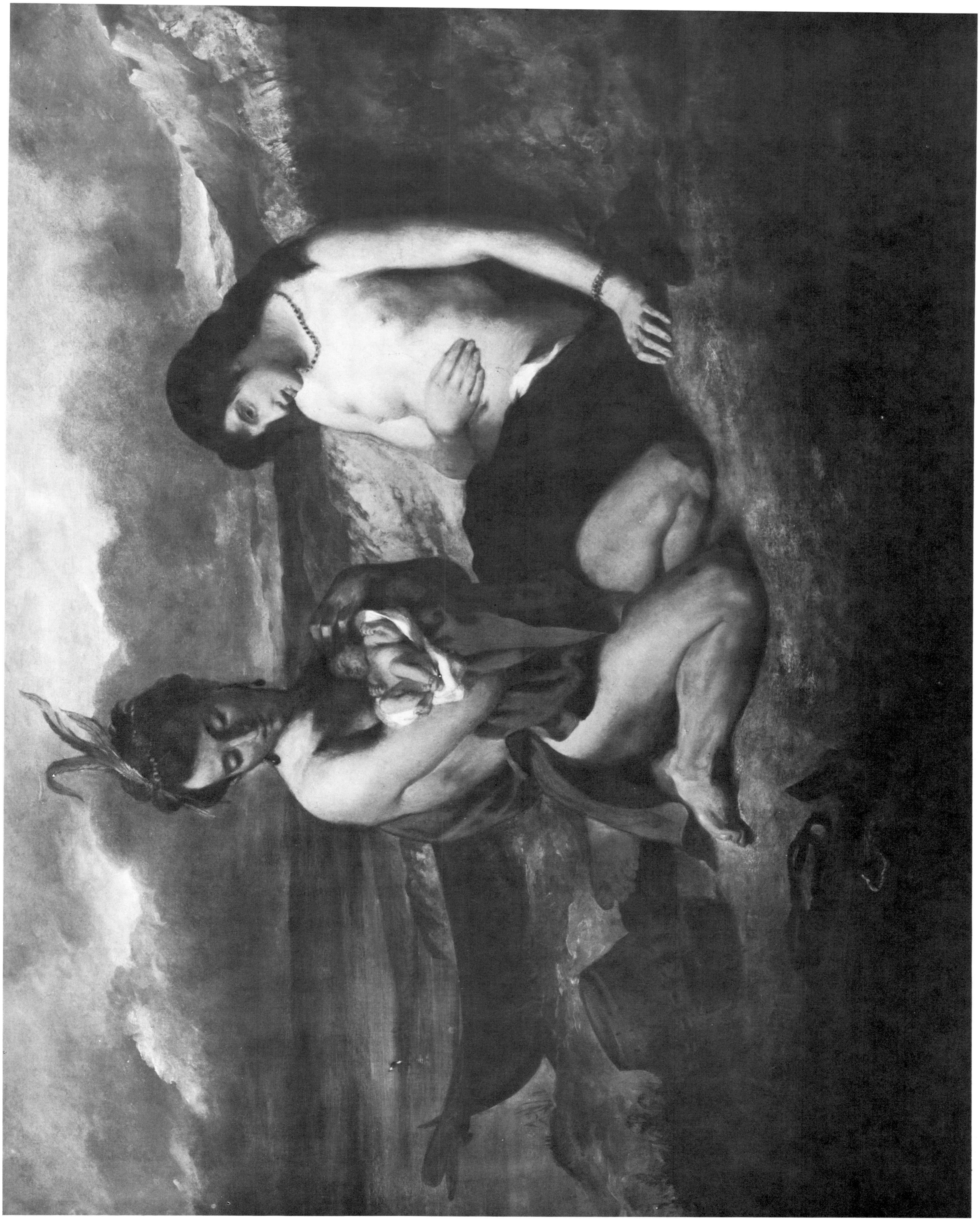

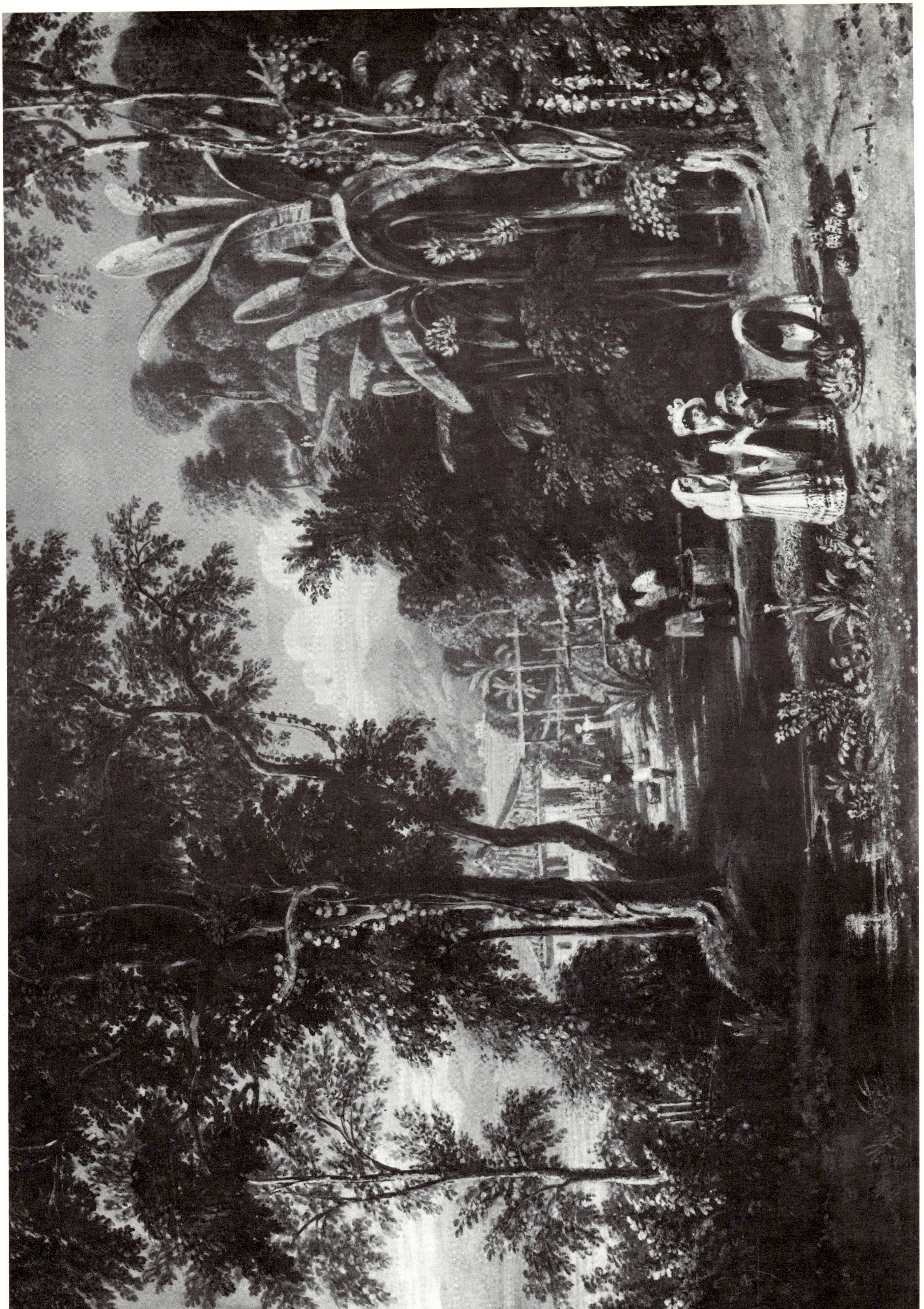

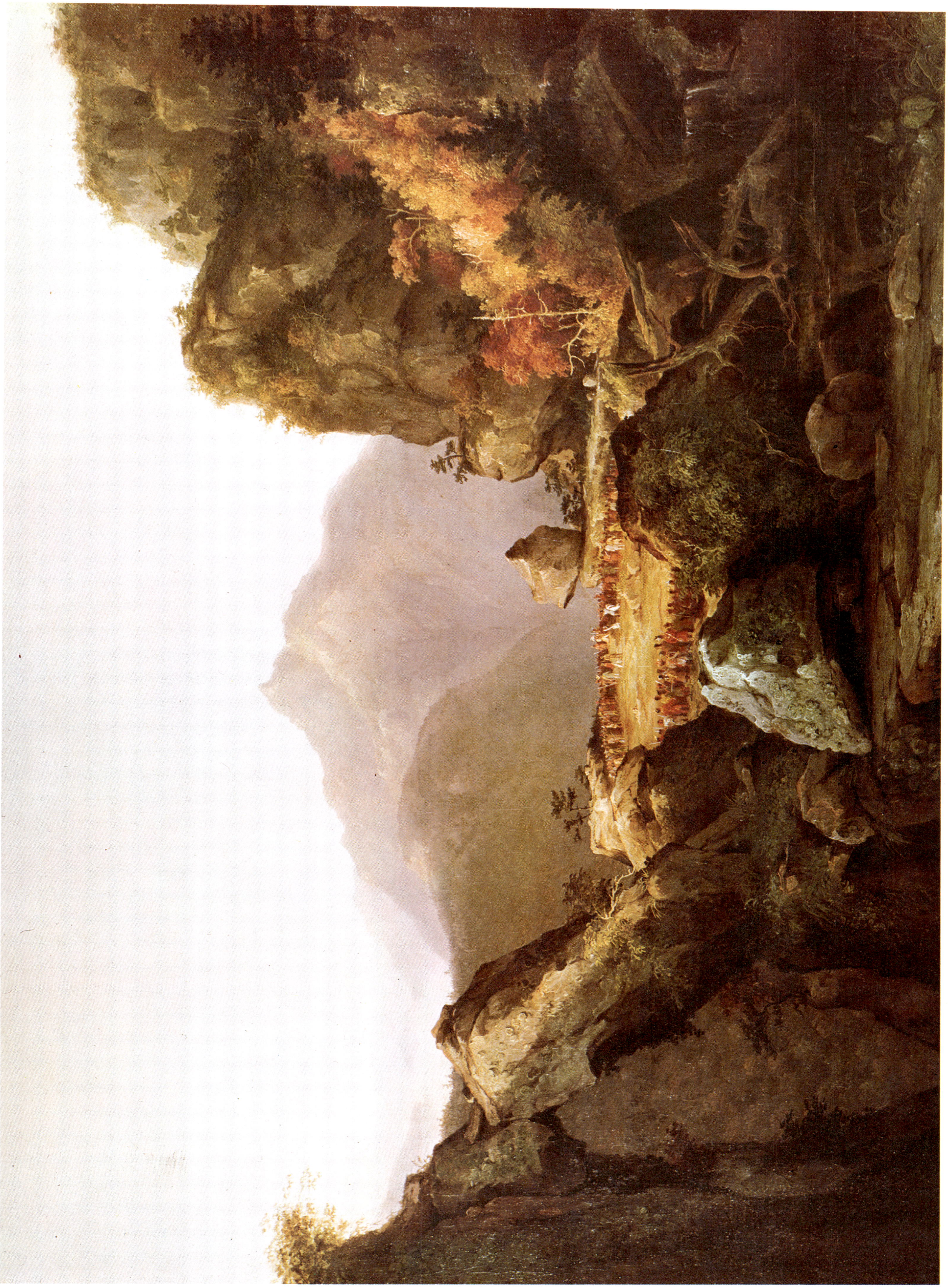

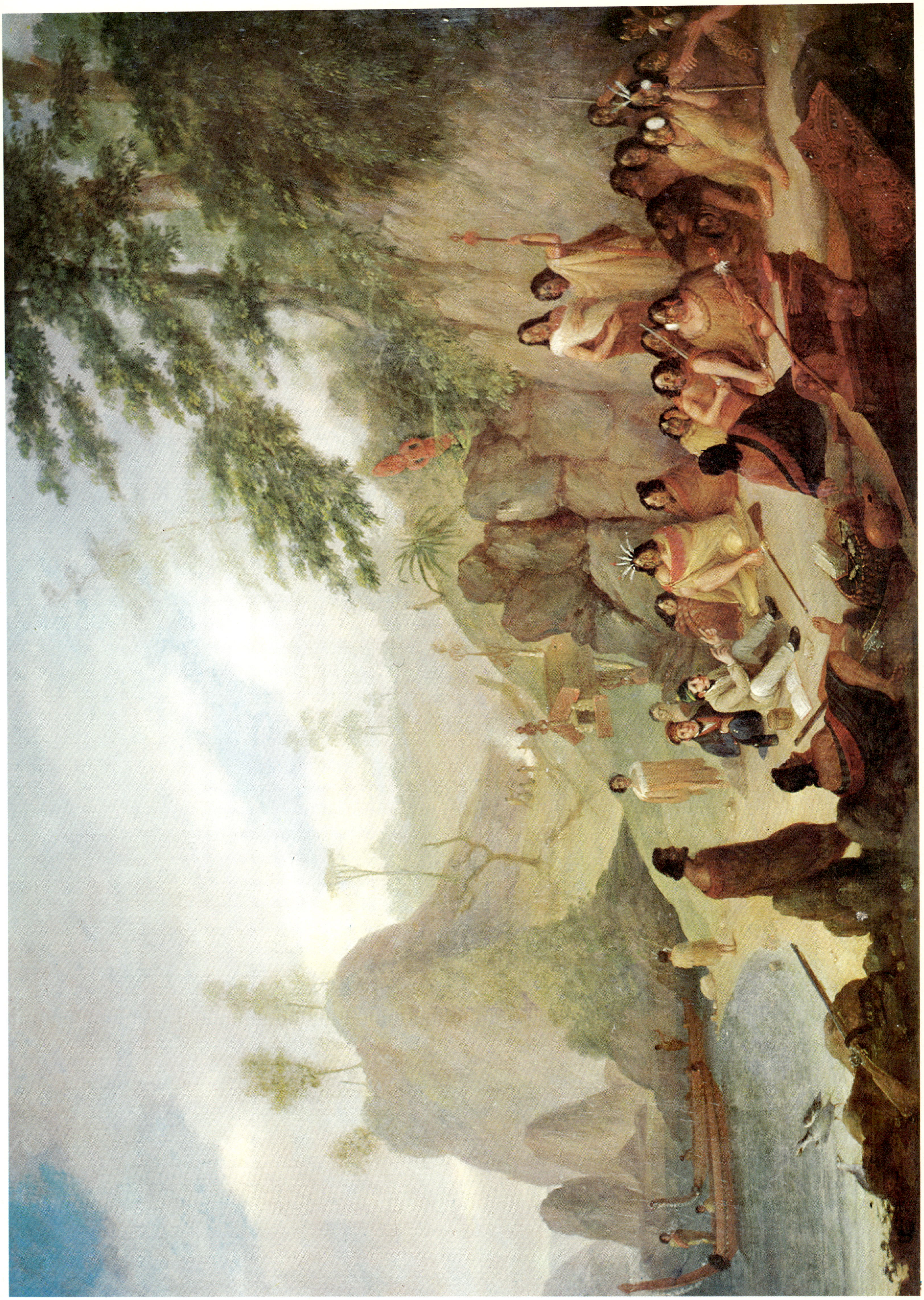

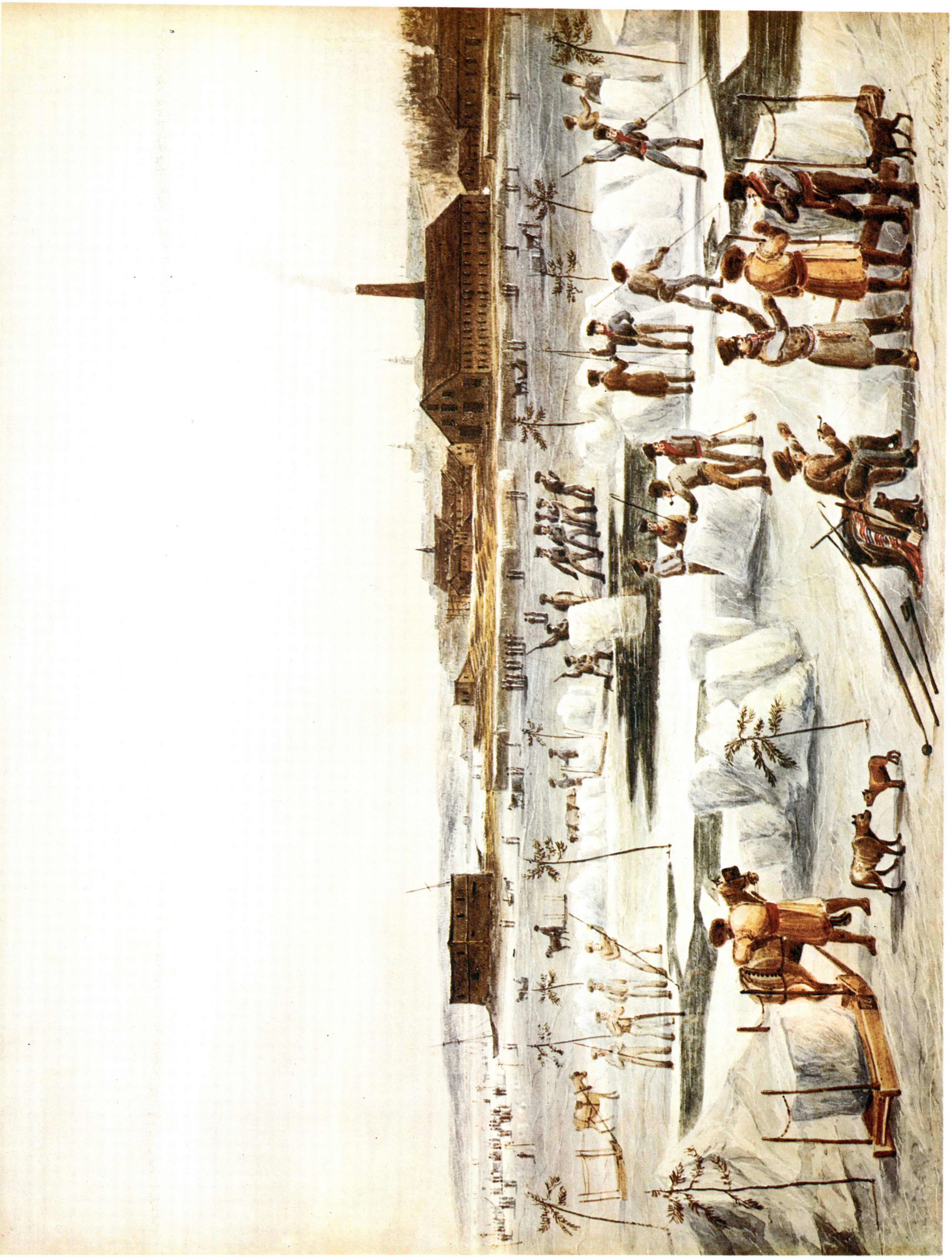

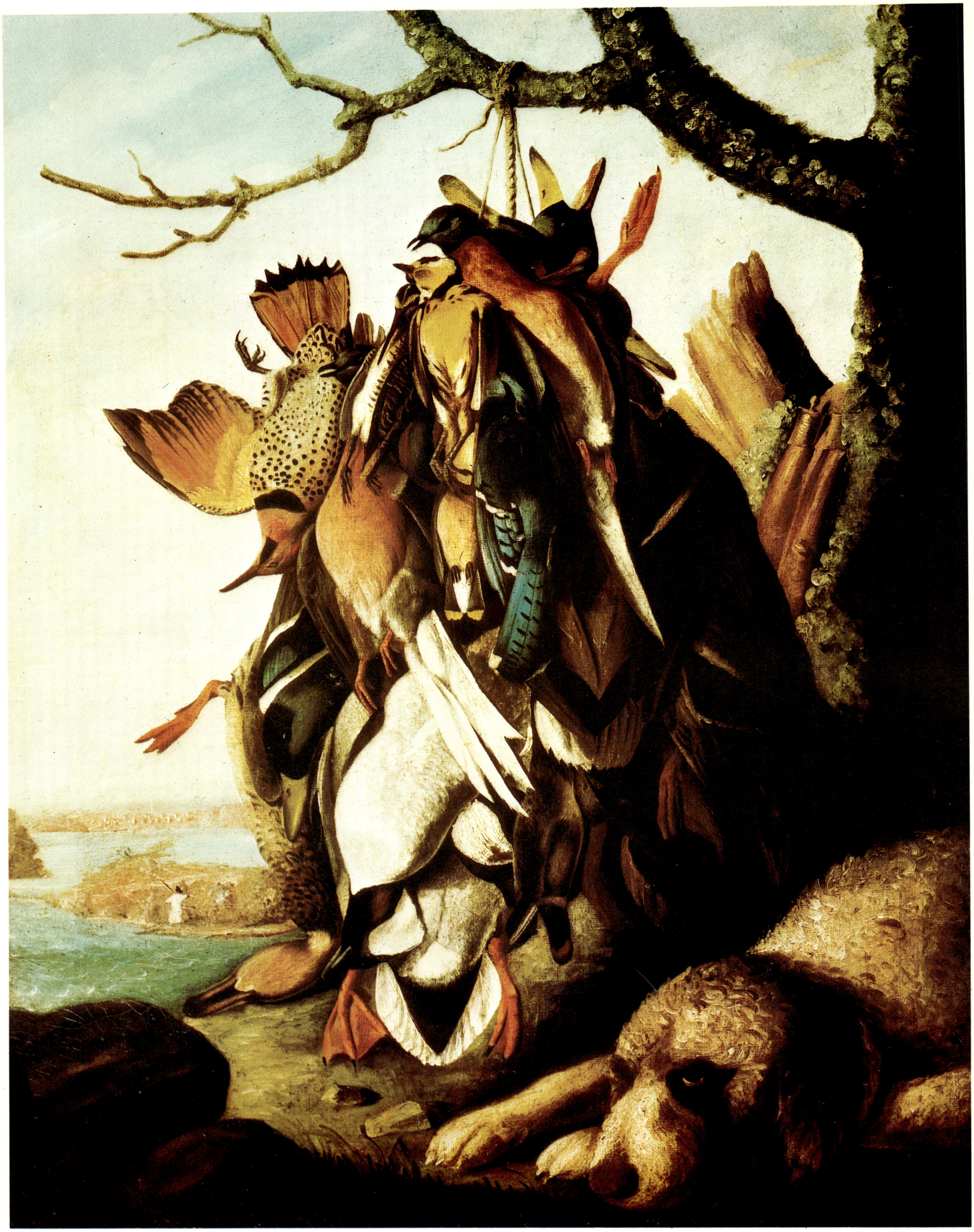

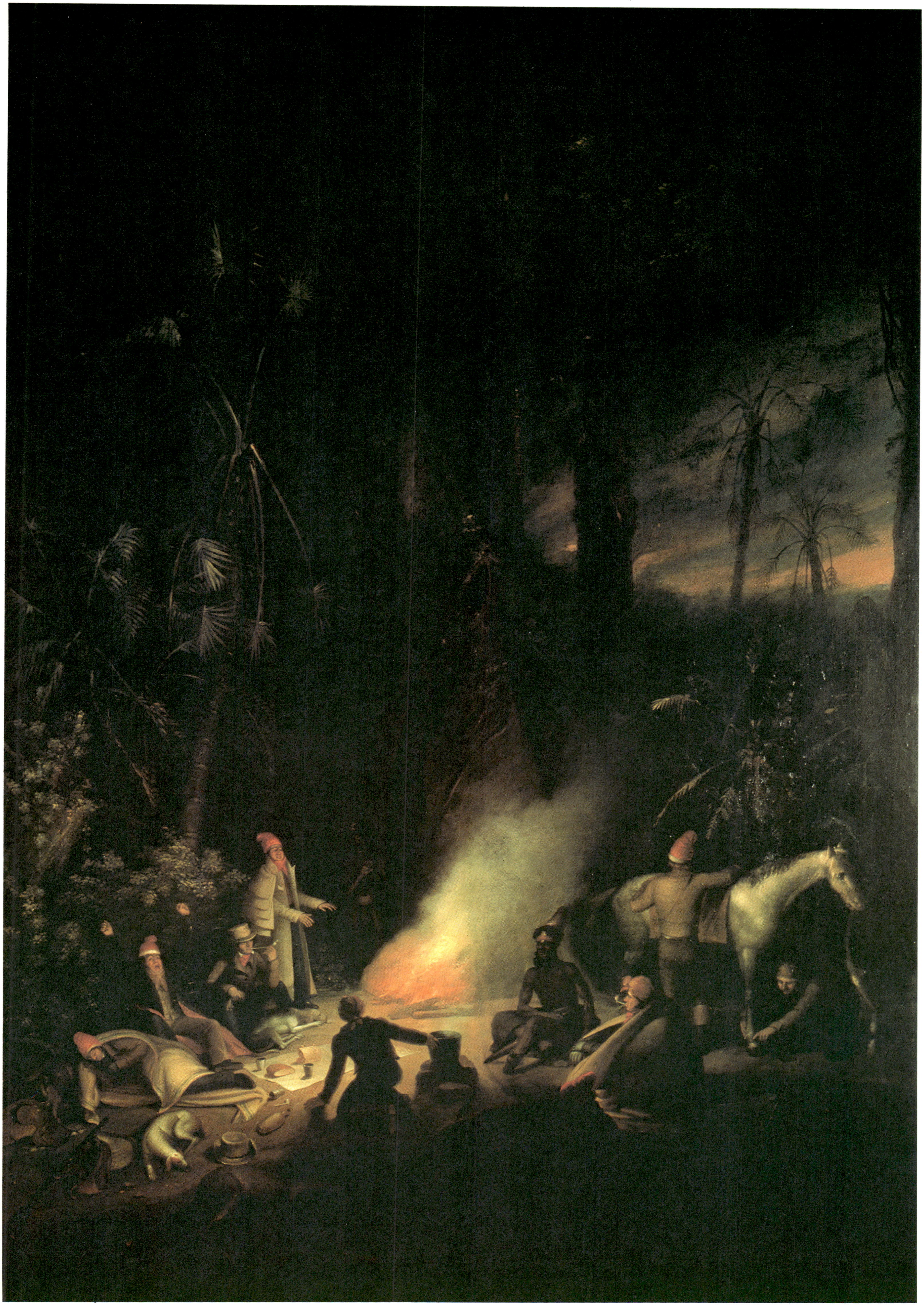

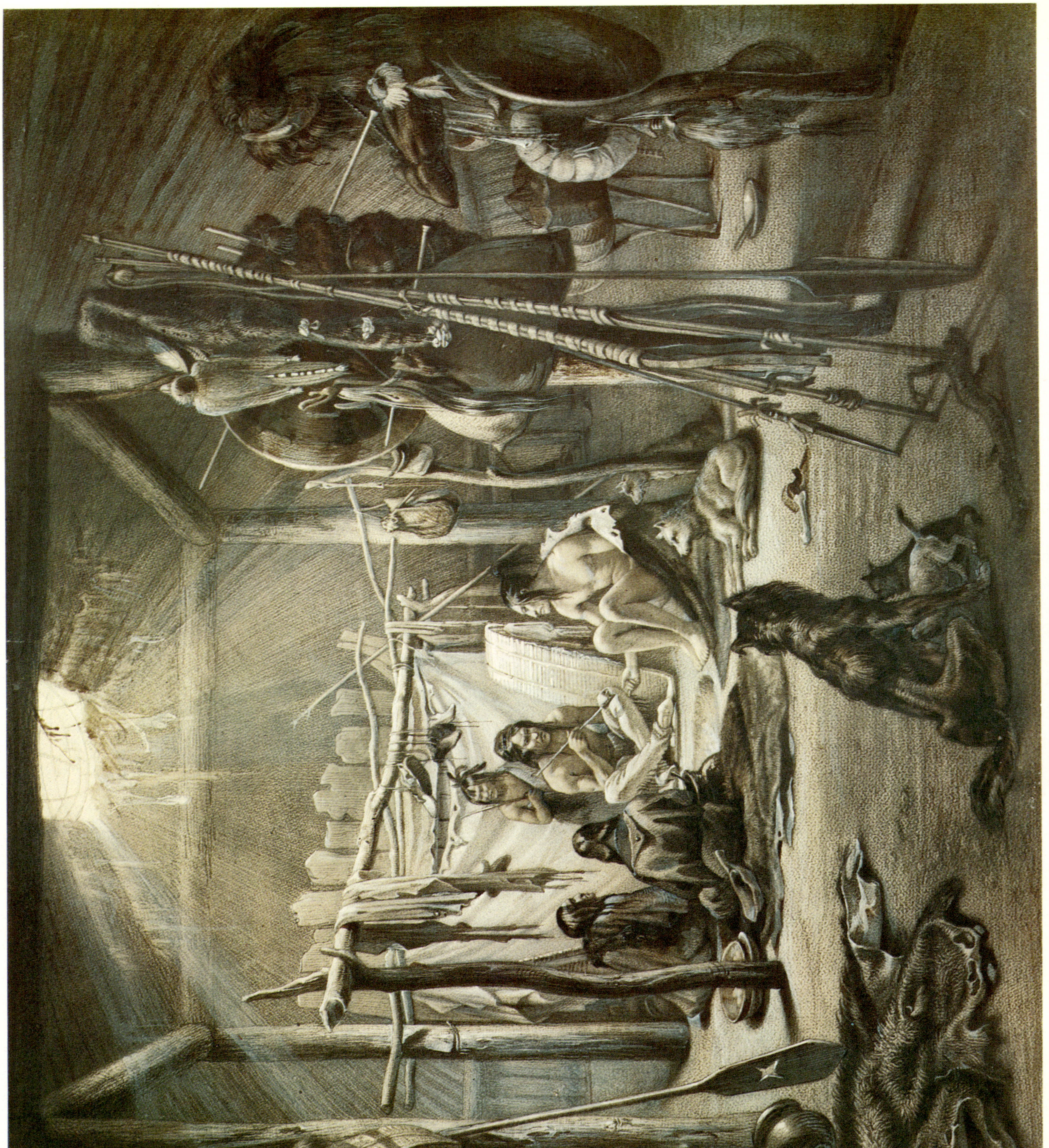

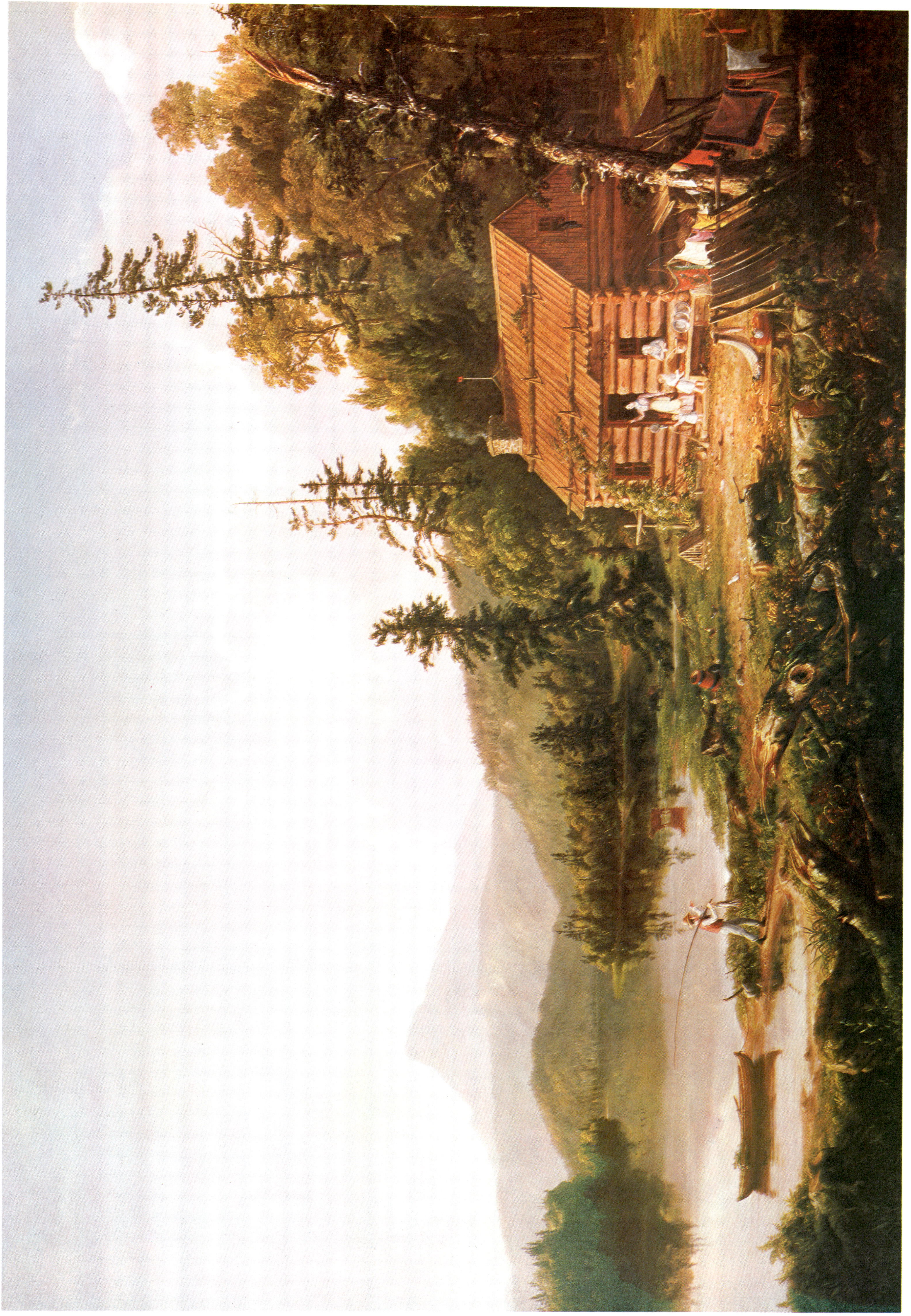

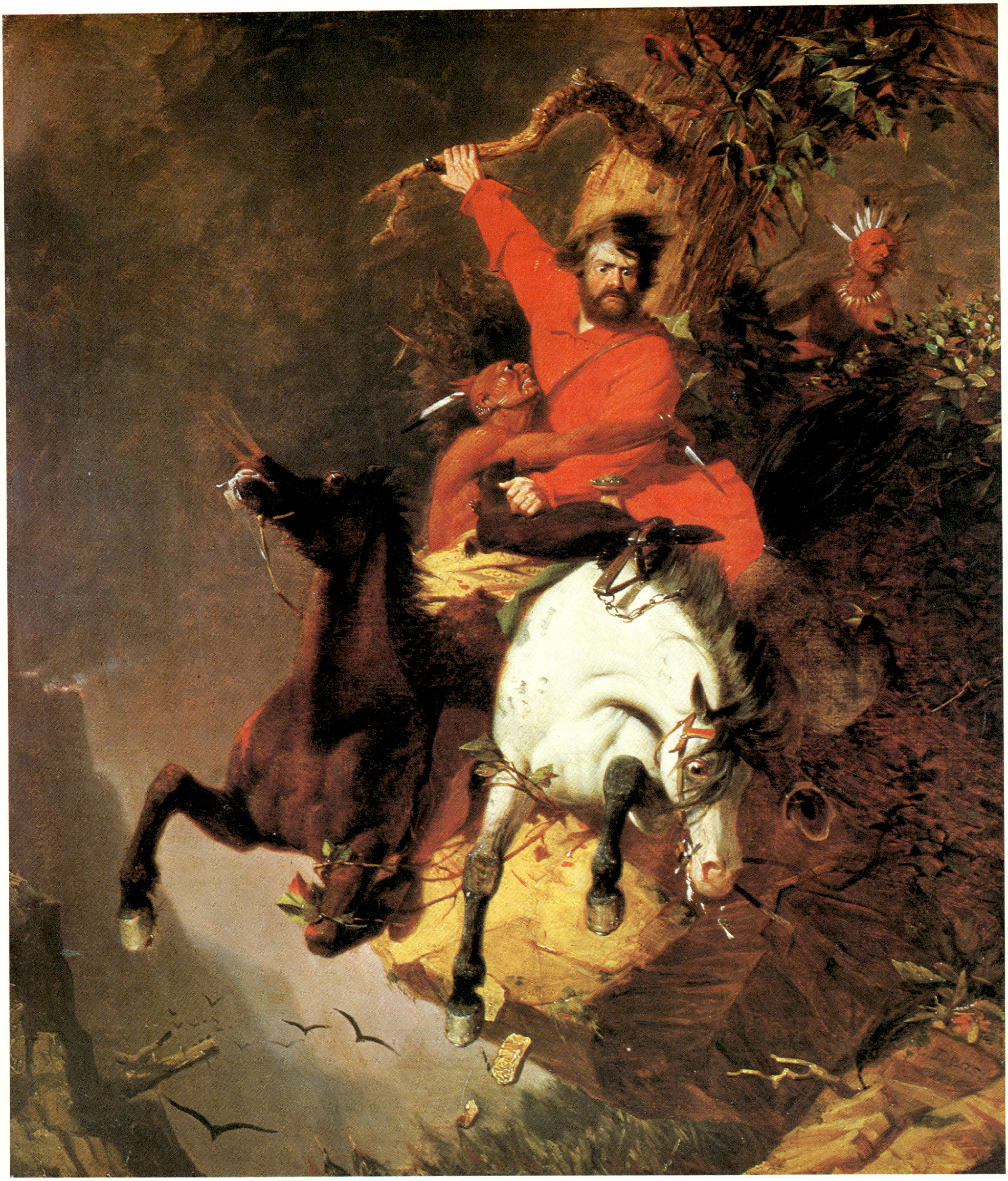

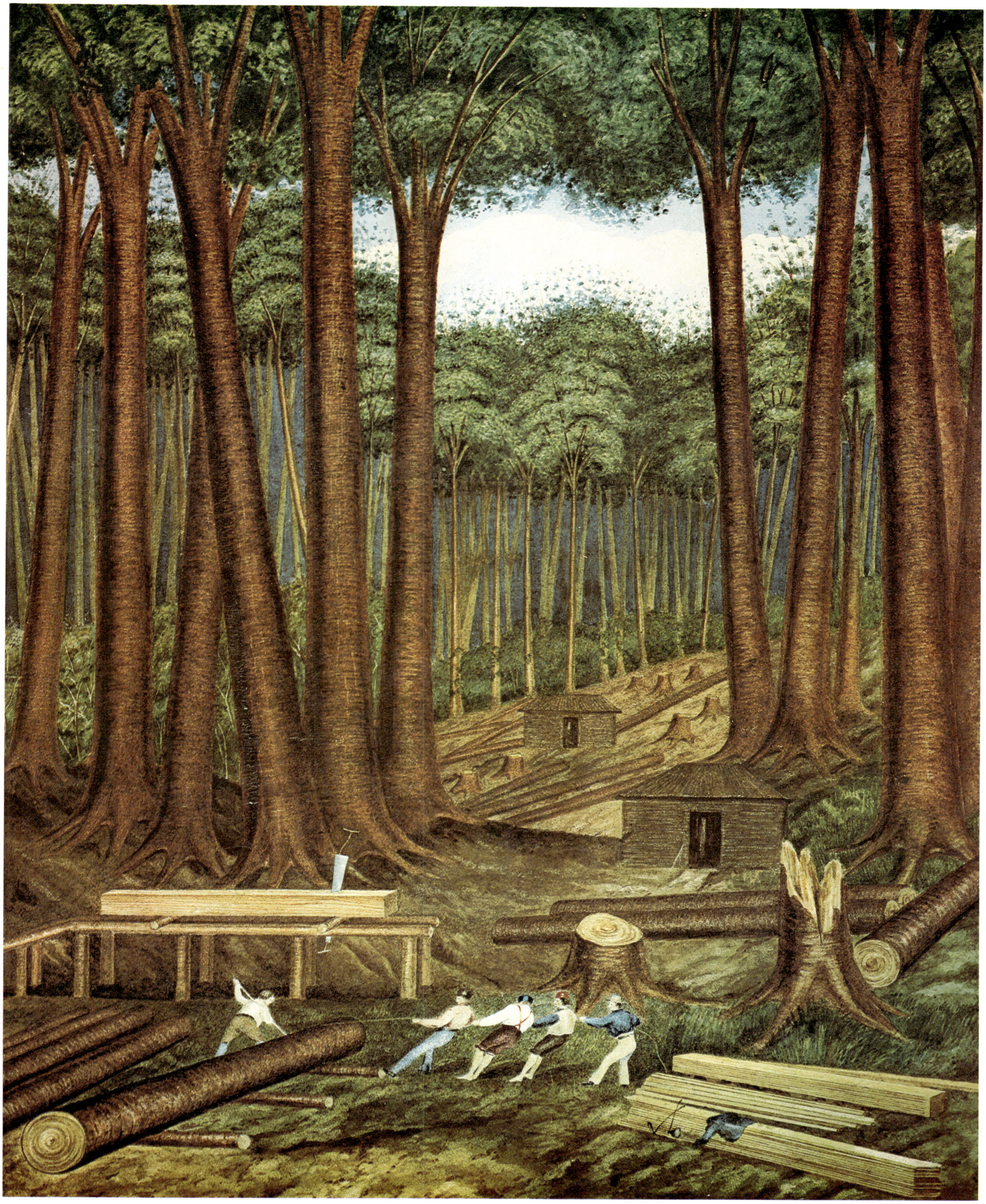

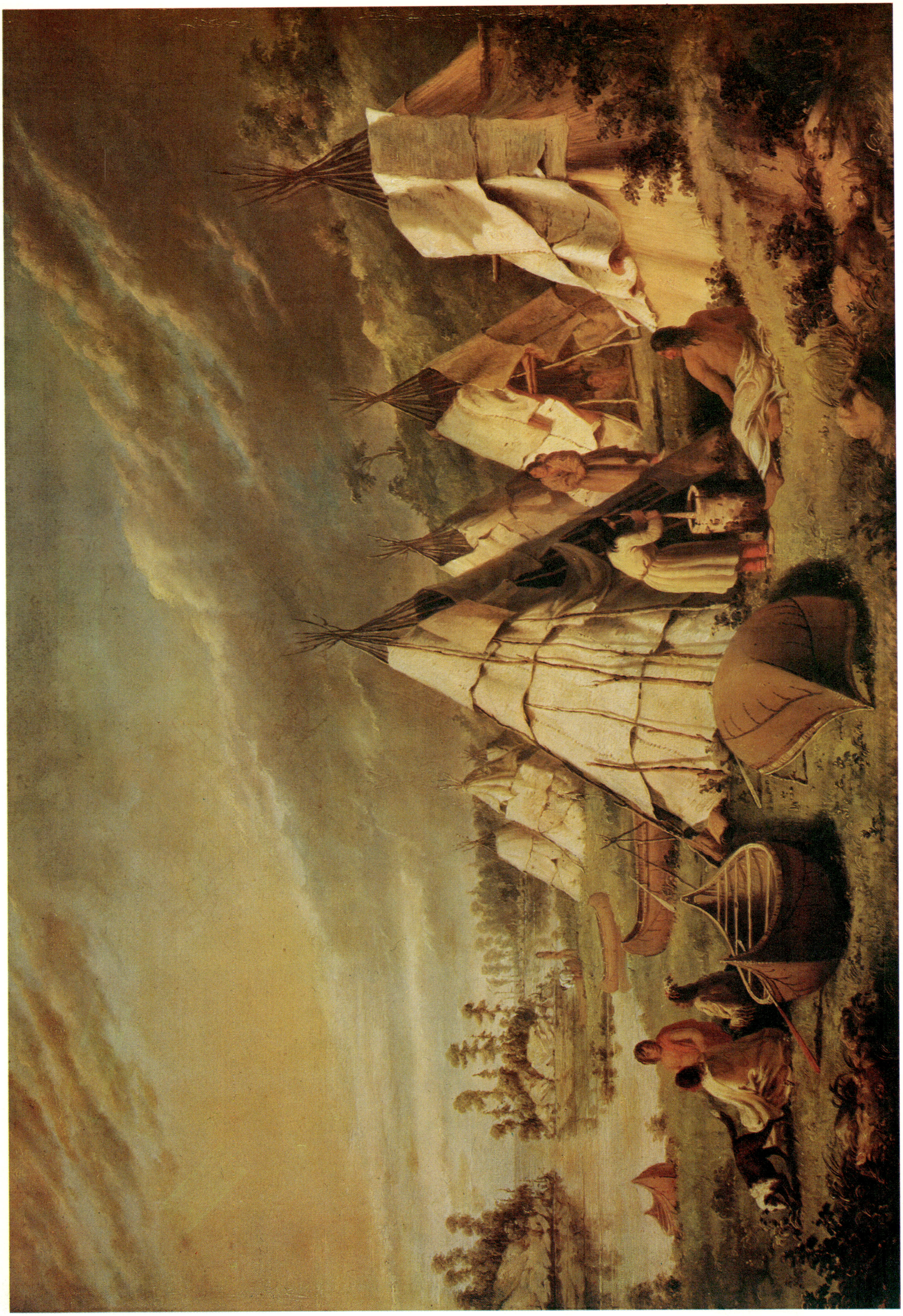

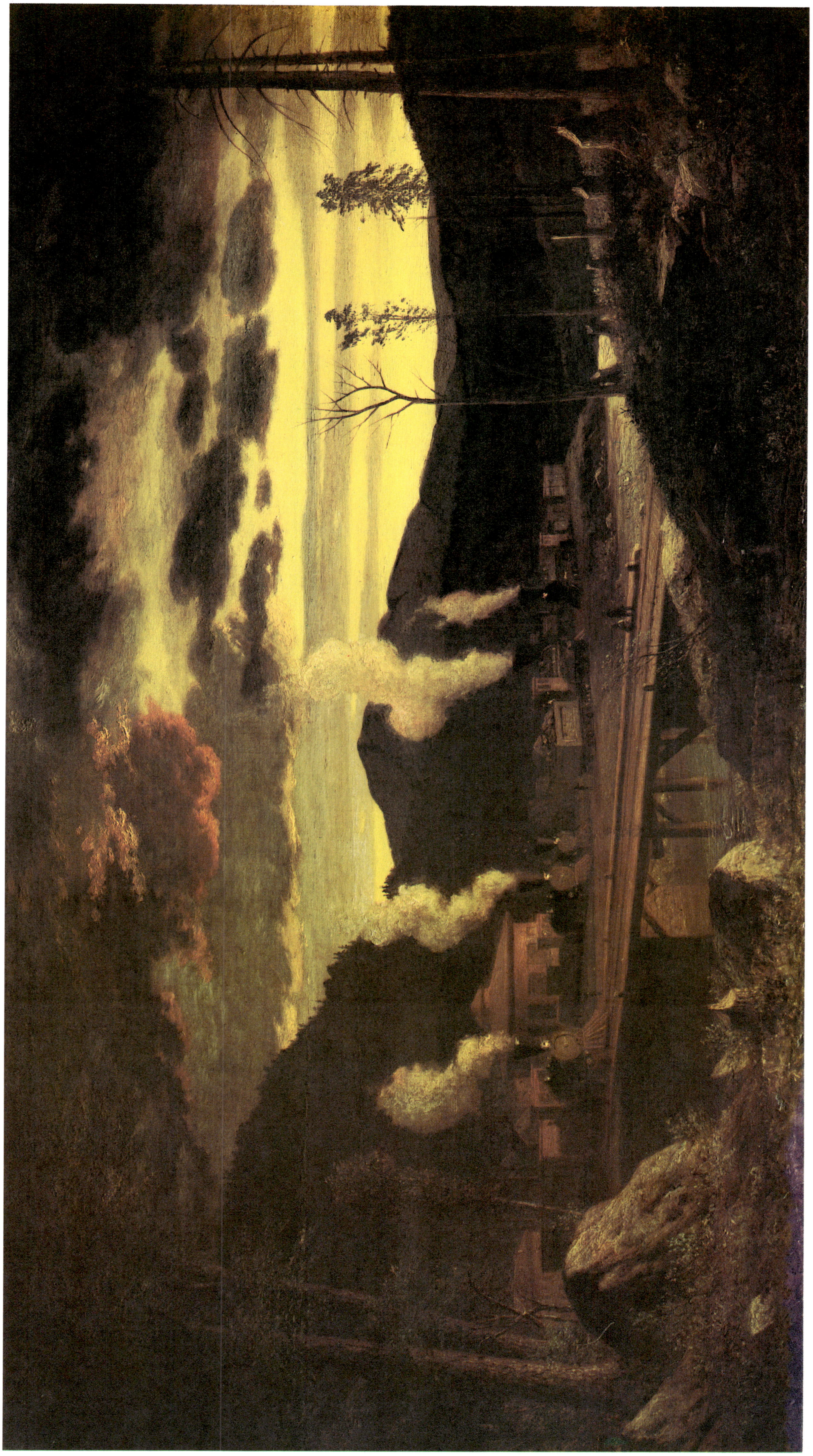

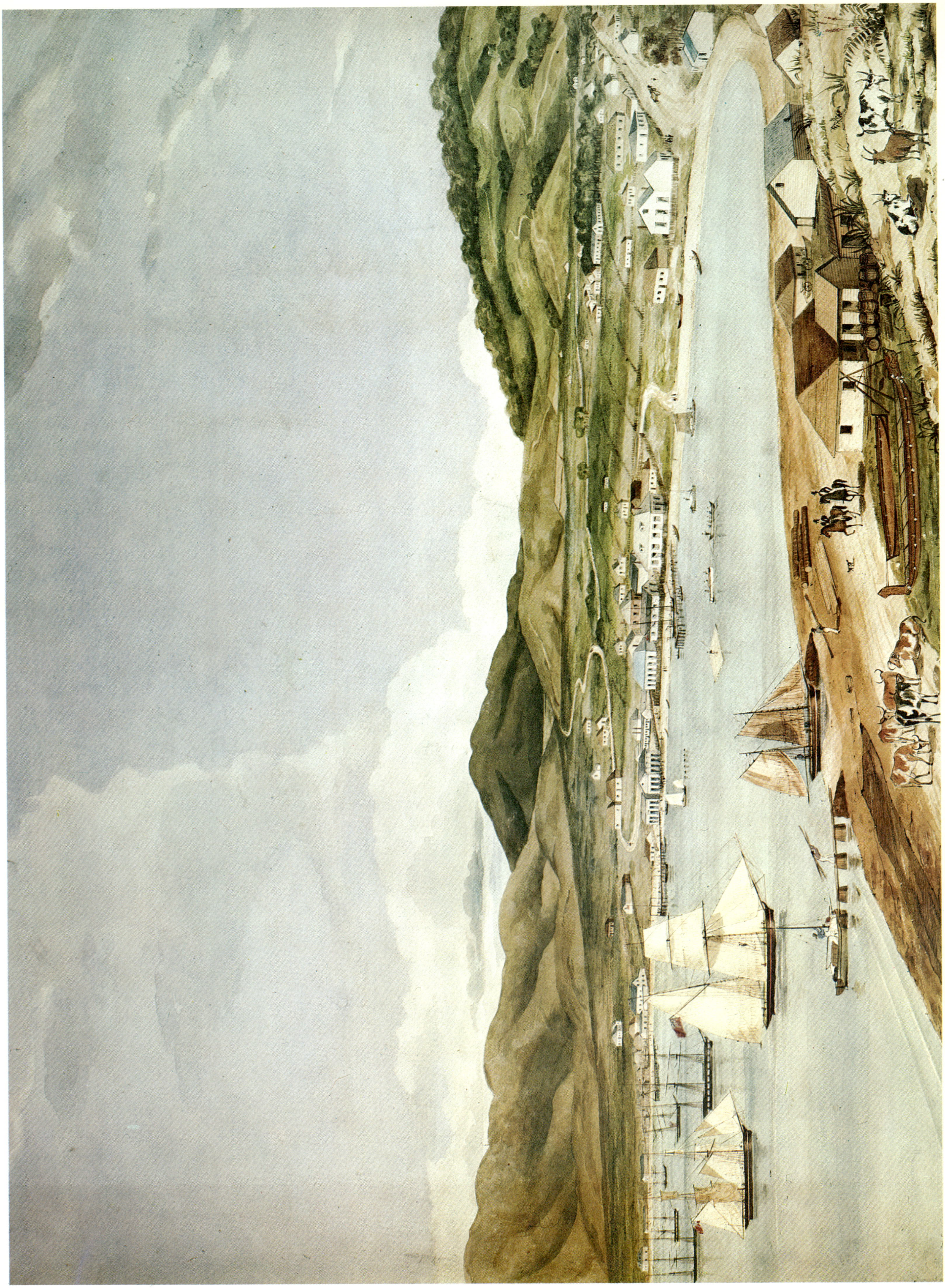

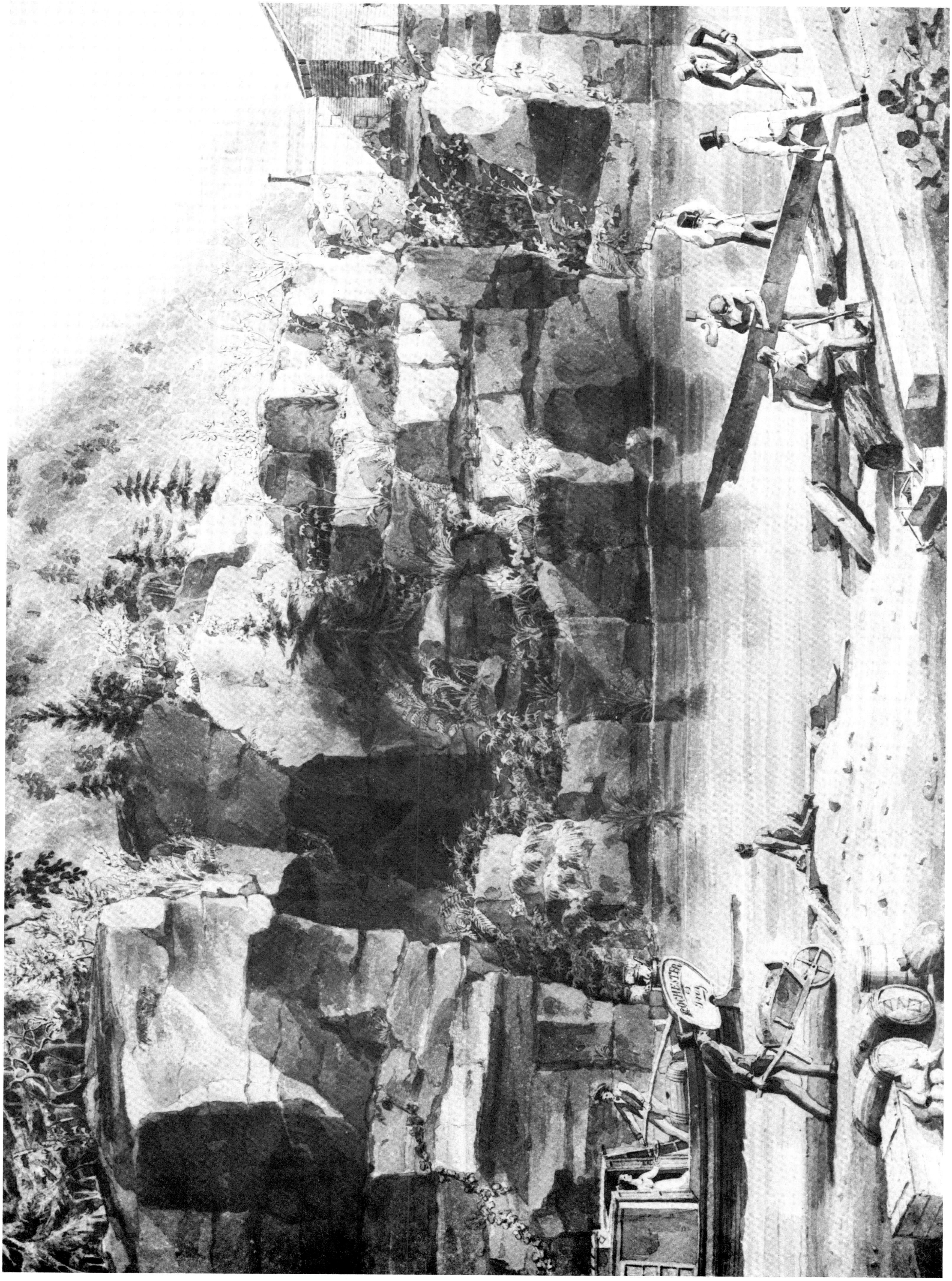
ROCHESTER

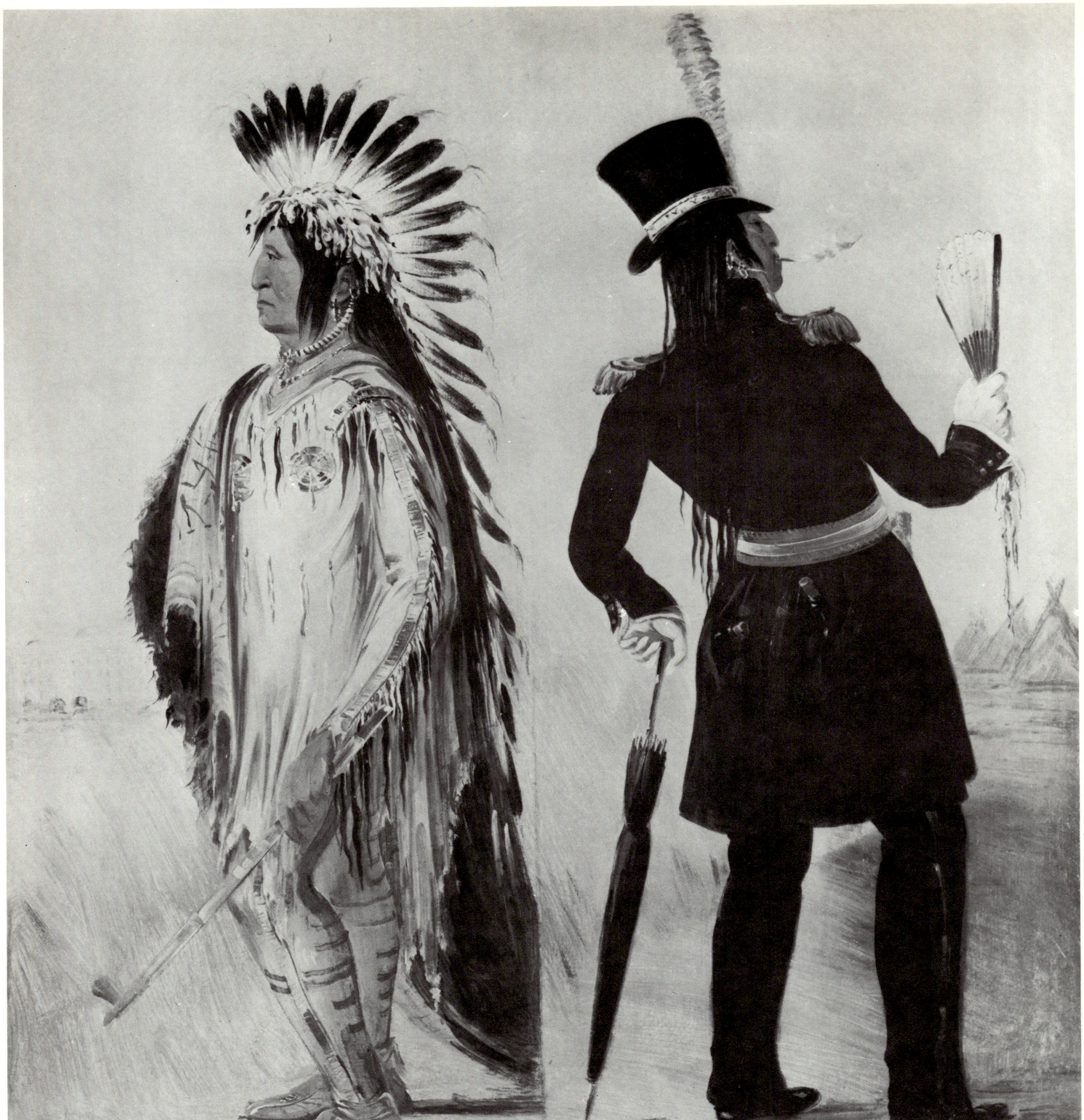

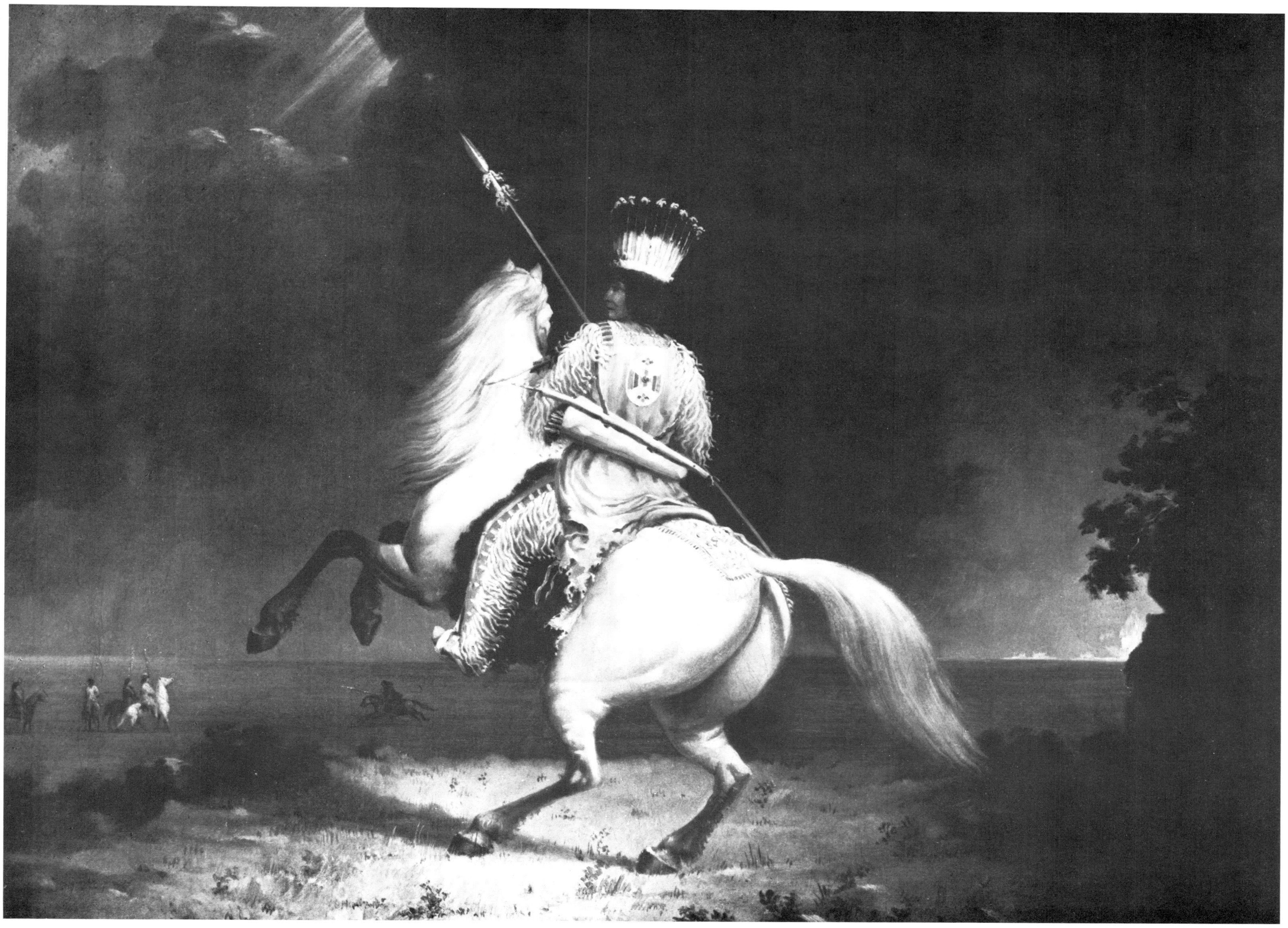

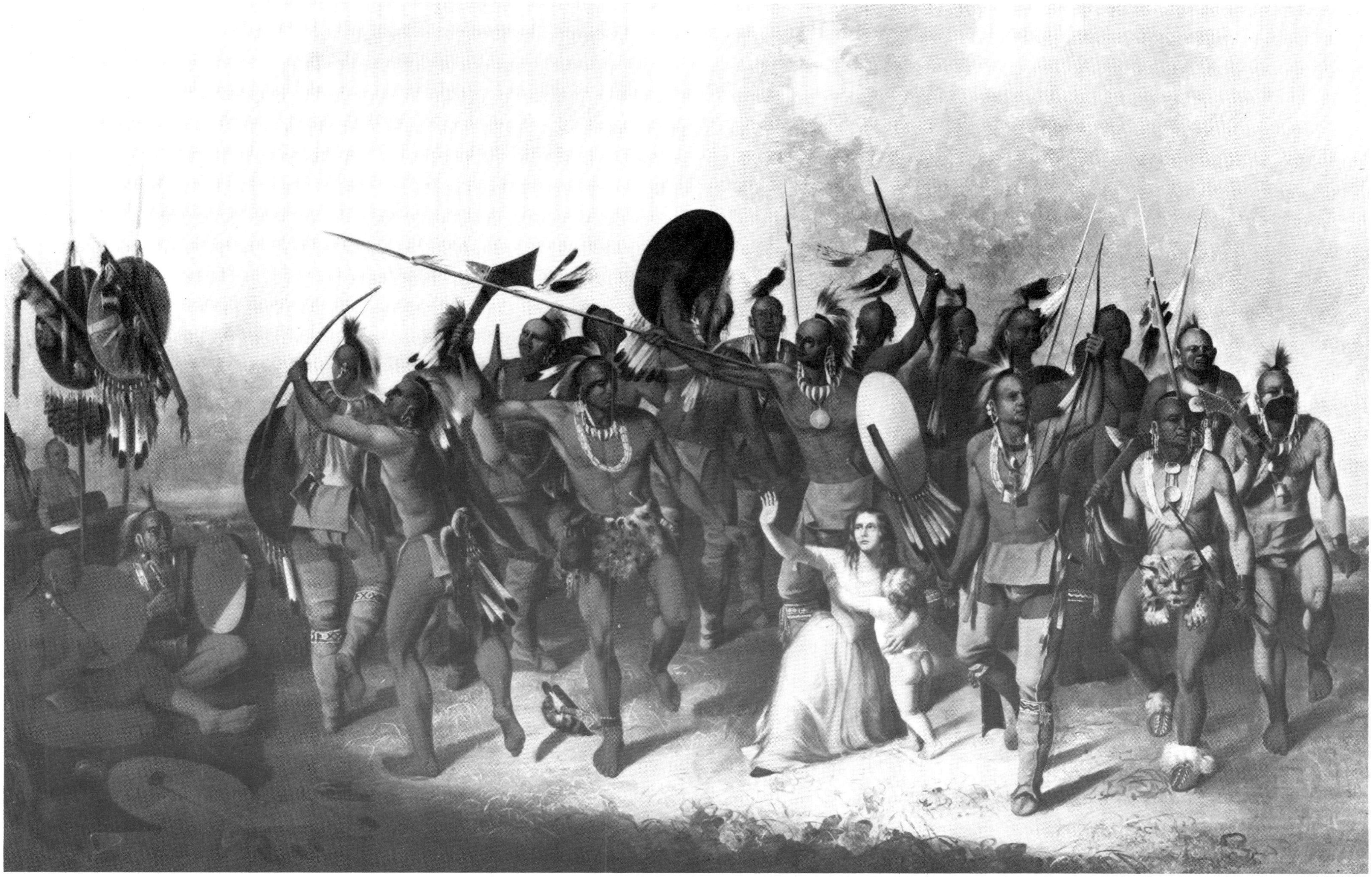

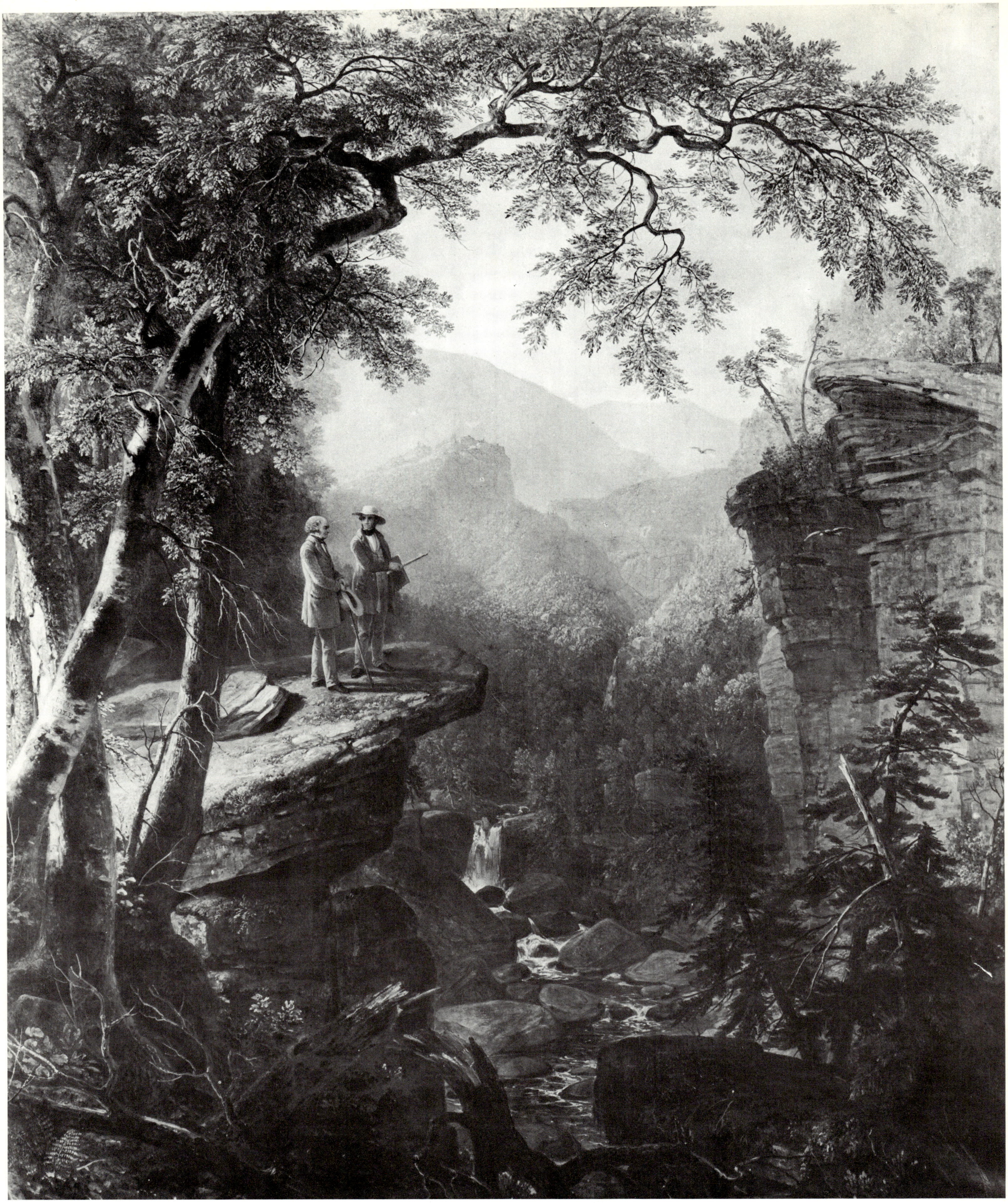

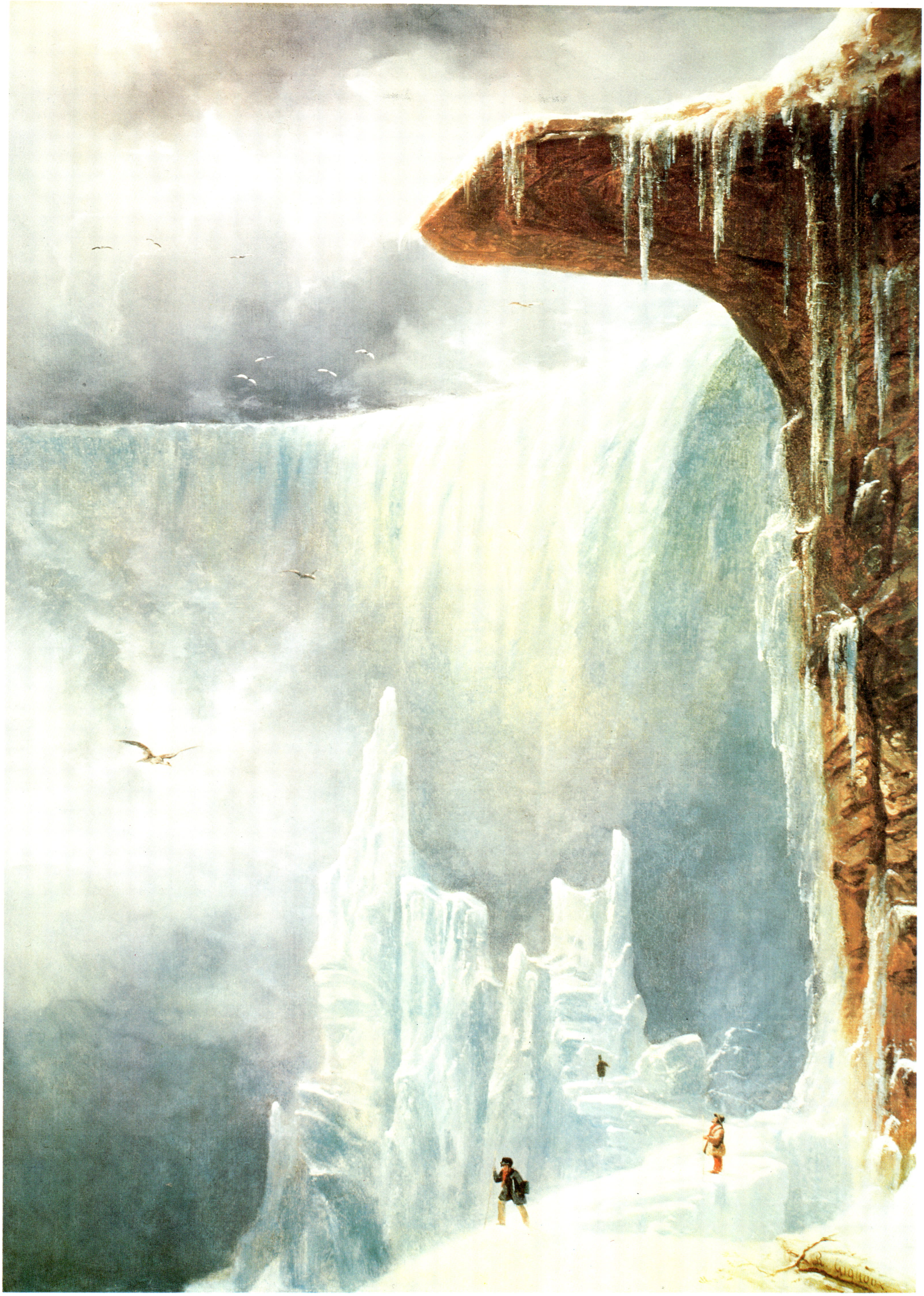

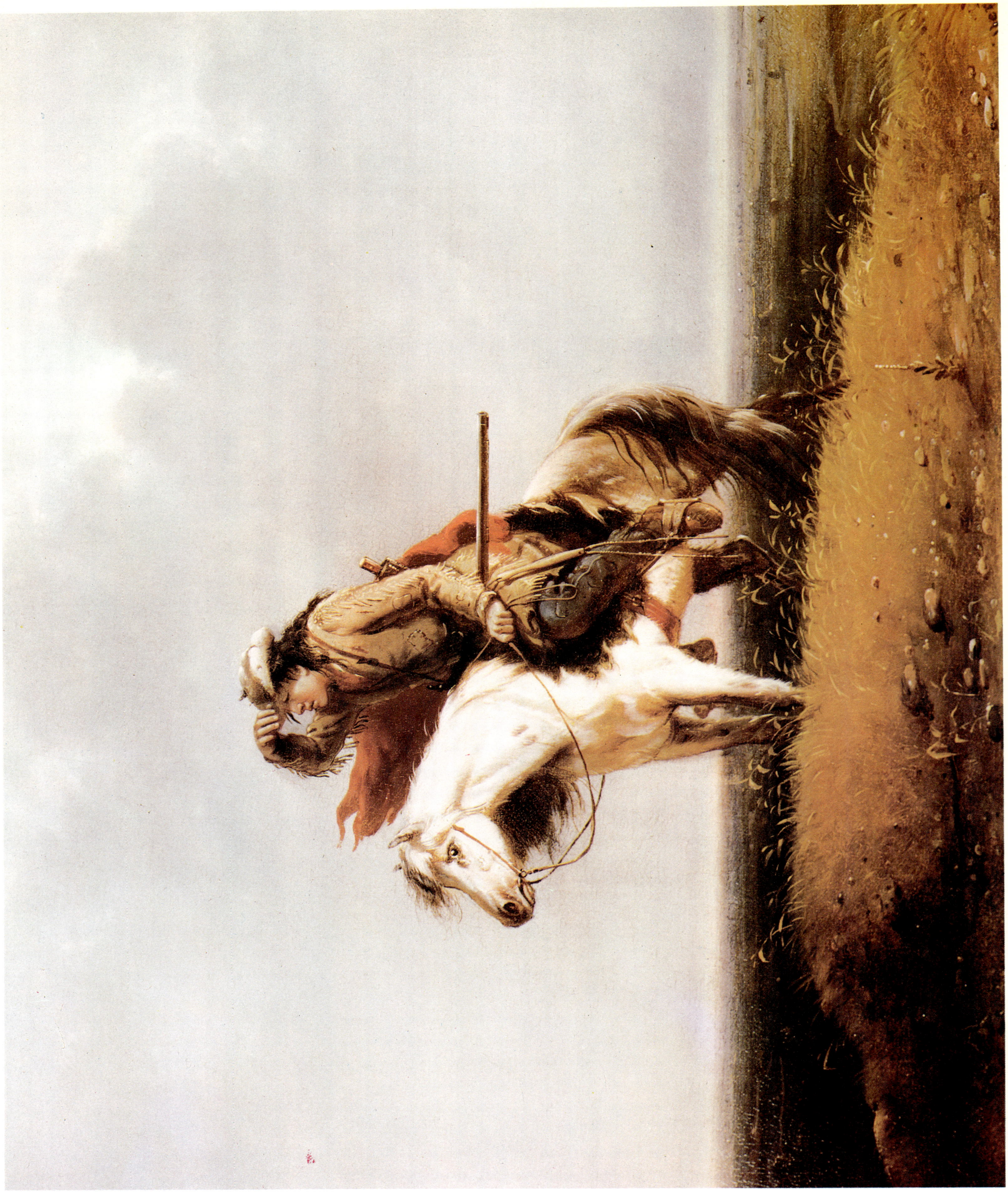

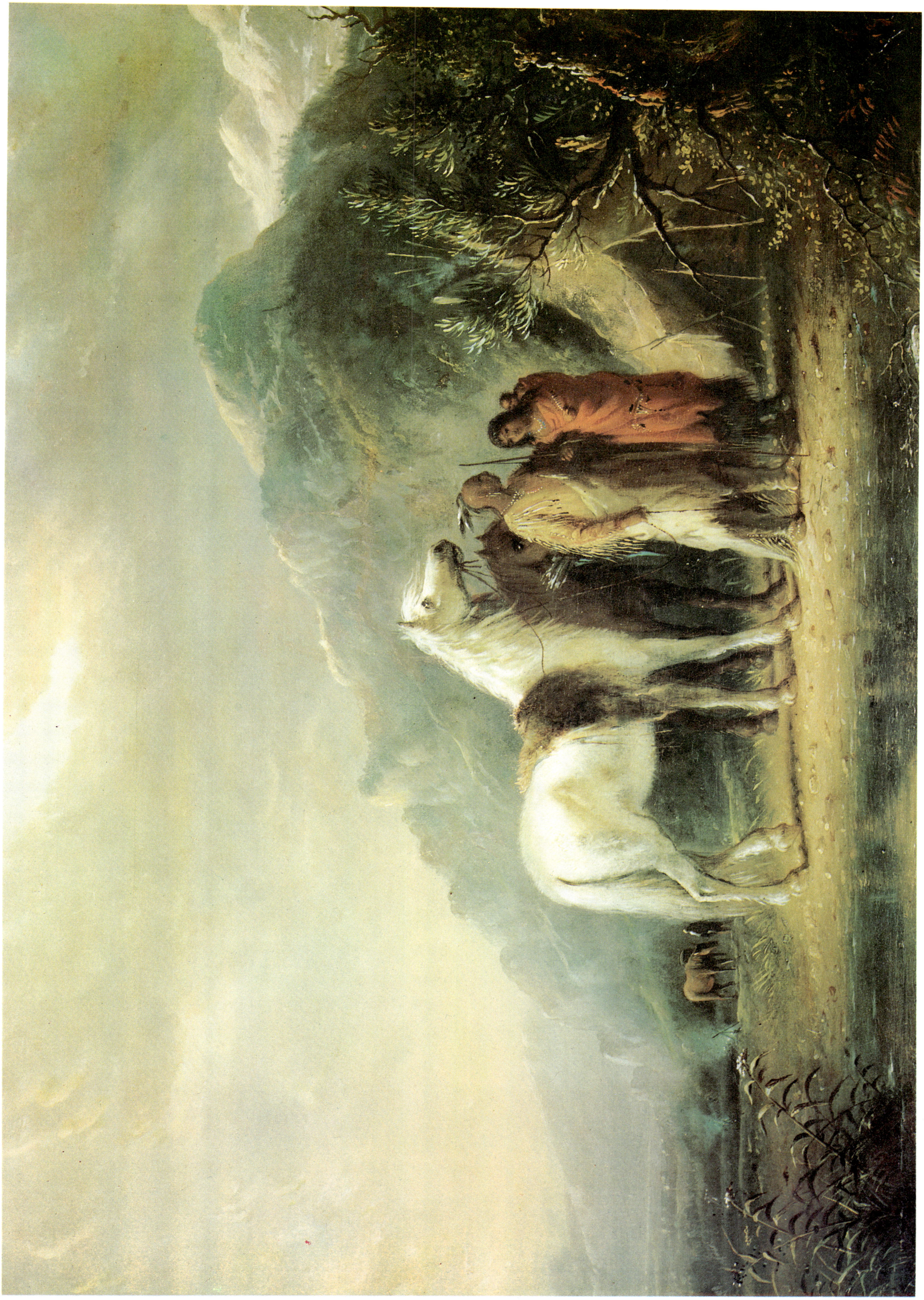

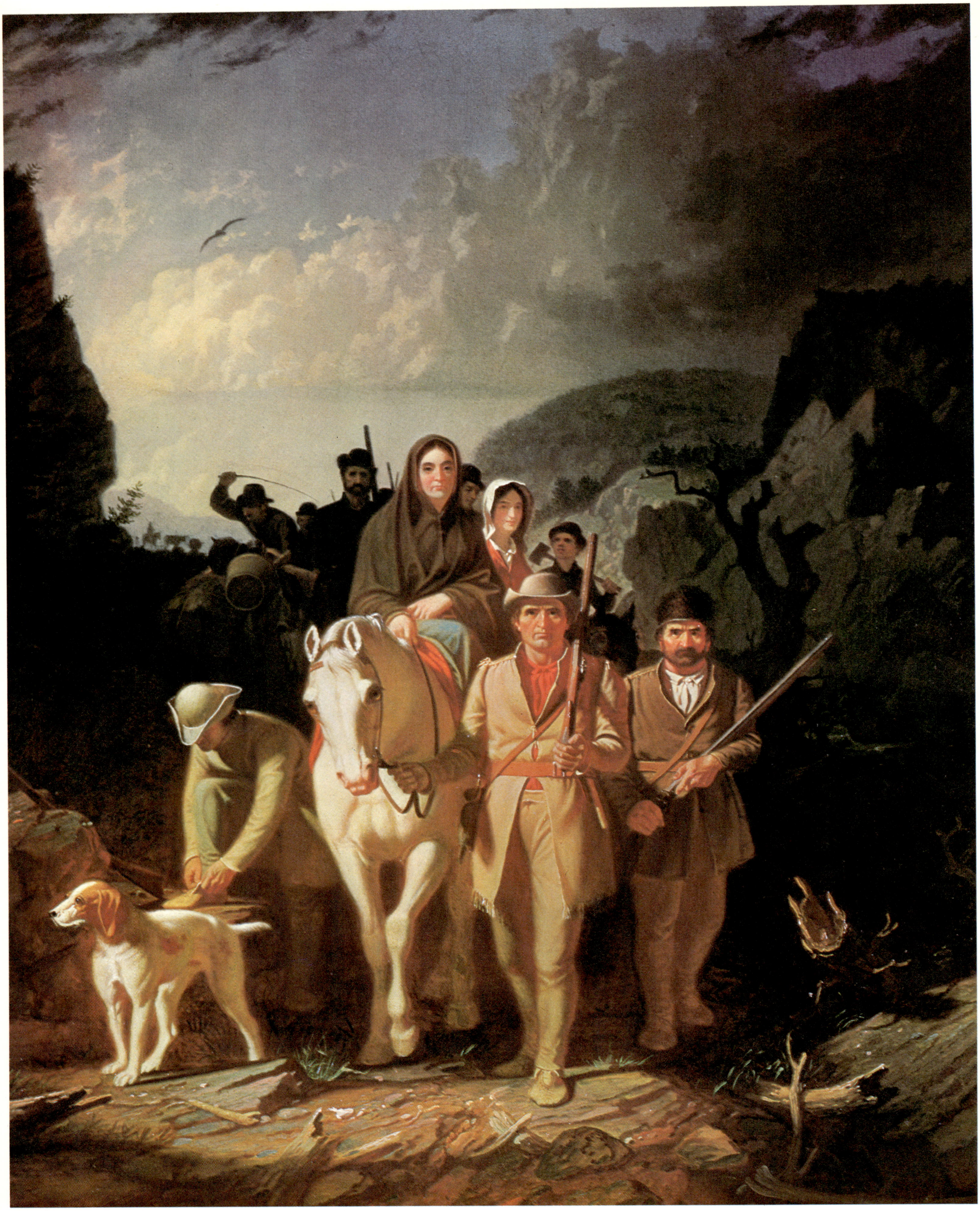

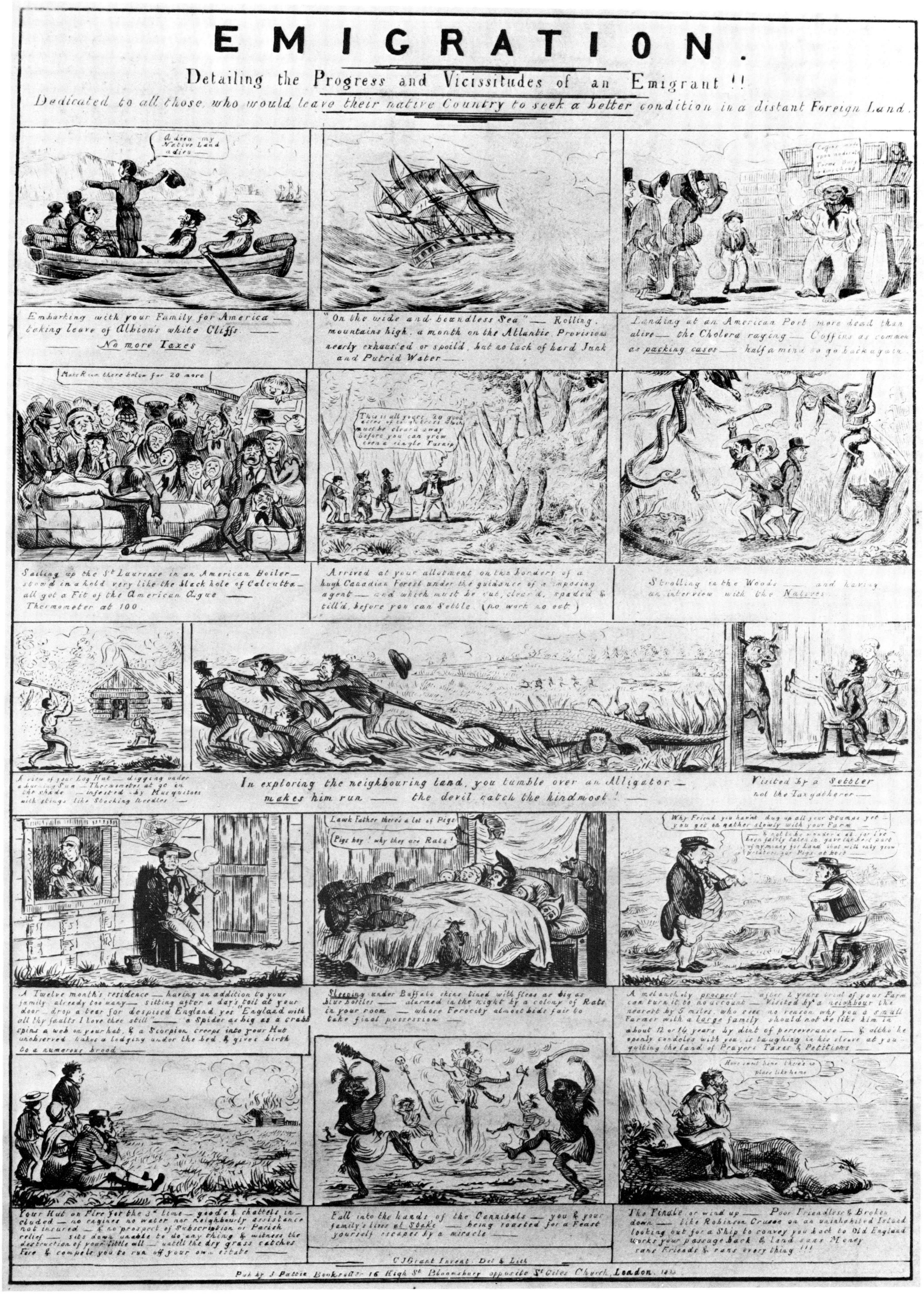
EMIGRATION.
Detailing the Progress and Vicissitudes of an Emigrant !!
Dedicated to all those, who would leave their native Country to seek a better condition in a distant Foreign Land.
Adieu my Native Land adieu
Embarking with your Family for America — taking leave of Albion's white Cliffs. — — No more Taxes —
"On the wide and boundless Sea" — Rolling, mountains high, a month on the Atlantic. Provisions nearly exhausted or spoil'd, but no lack of hard Junk and Putrid Water —.
Landing at an American Port more dead than alive — the Cholera raging — Coffins as common as packing cases — half a mind to go back again.
Make Room there below for 20 more
Sailing up the St Laurence in an American Boiler — stow'd in a hold very like the black hole of Calcutta — all got a Fit of the American Ague — Thermometer at 100.
Arrived at your allotment on the borders of a hugh Canadian Forest under the guidance of a imposing agent — and which must be cut, clear'd, spaded & till'd, before you can Settle. (no work no eat)
Strolling in the Woods — and having an interview with the Natives.
In exploring the neighbouring land, you tumble over an Alligator — makes him run — the devil catch the hindmost!
Visited by a Settler not the Tax gatherer —
Lawk Father there's a lot of Pigs
Pigs boy! why they are Rats!
A Twelve month's residence — having an addition to your family already too many — sitting after a day's toil at your door — drop a tear for despised England, yes "England with all thy faults I love thee still" — a Spider as big as a crabb spins a web on your hat, & a Scorpion creeps into your Hut unobserved takes a lodging under the bed & gives birth to a numerous brood —
Sleeping under Buffalo skins lined with fleas as big as blue bottles — alarmed in the night by a colony of Rats in your room — whose Ferocity almost bids fair to take final possession —
A melancholy prospect — after 2 years trial of your Farm can turn it to no account — Visited by a neighbour the nearest by 5 miles, who sees no reason why you a small Farmer with a large family should not be like him in about 12 or 14 years by dint of perseverance — & altho' he openly condoles with you, is laughing in his sleeve at you quiting the land of Prayers Taxes & Petitions —
Home sweet home there's no place like home
Your Hut on Fire for the 3d time — goods & chattels included — no engines no water nor neighbourly assistance not insured — & no prospect of Subscription or Parish relief — sits down unable to do any thing & witness the destruction of your little all — until the dry grass catches Fire & compels you to run off your own estate —
Fall into the hands of the Cannibals — you & your family's lives at Stake — being roasted for a Feast yourself escapes by a miracle —
The Finale or wind up — Poor Friendless & Broken down — like Robinson Crusoe on an uninhabited Island looking out for a Ship to convey you back to Old England works your passage back & land sans Money sans Friends & sans every thing !!!
C J Grant Invent. Del & Lith
Pub by J Pattie Bookseller 16 High St Bloomsbury opposite St Giles Church, London. 1830

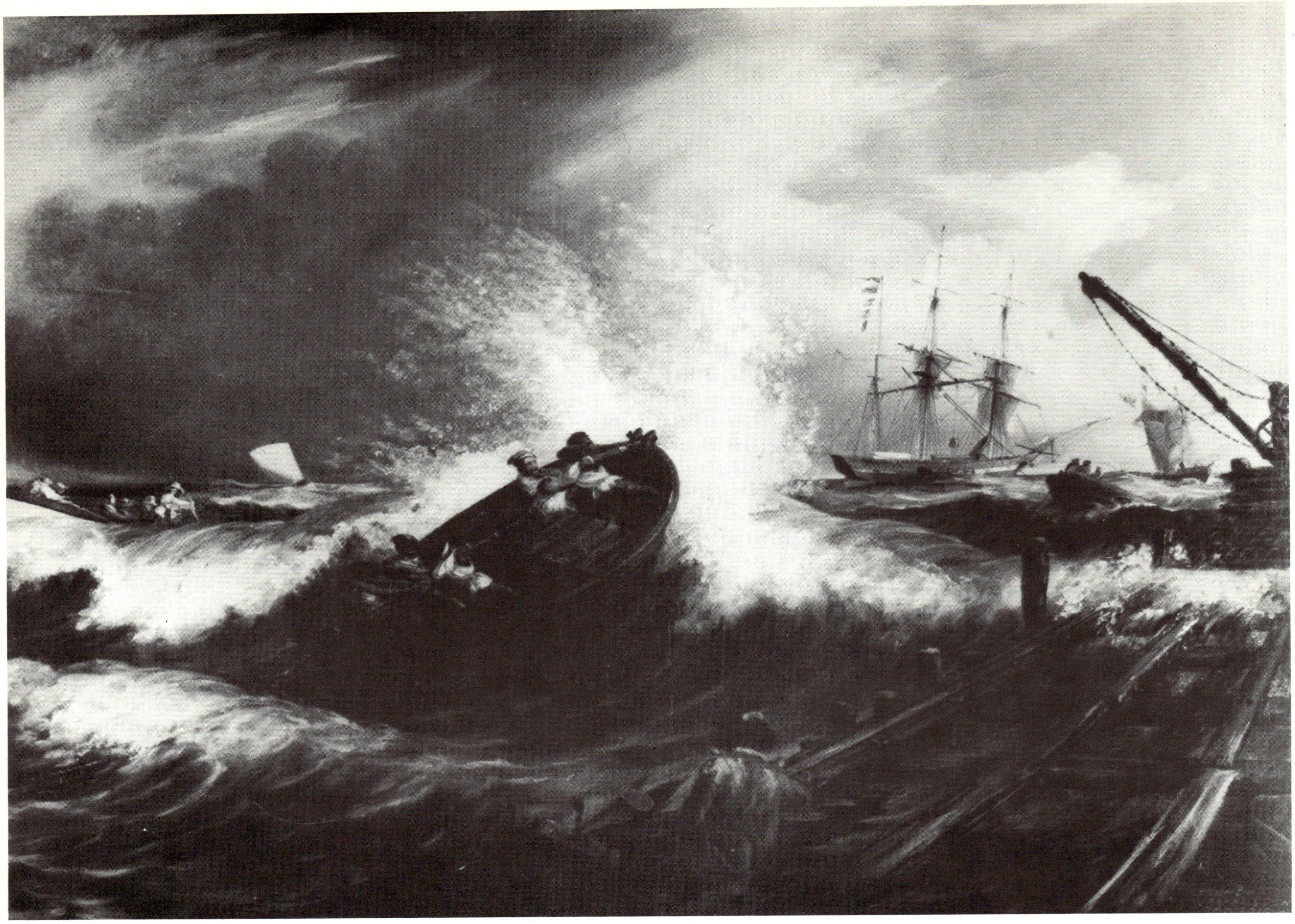

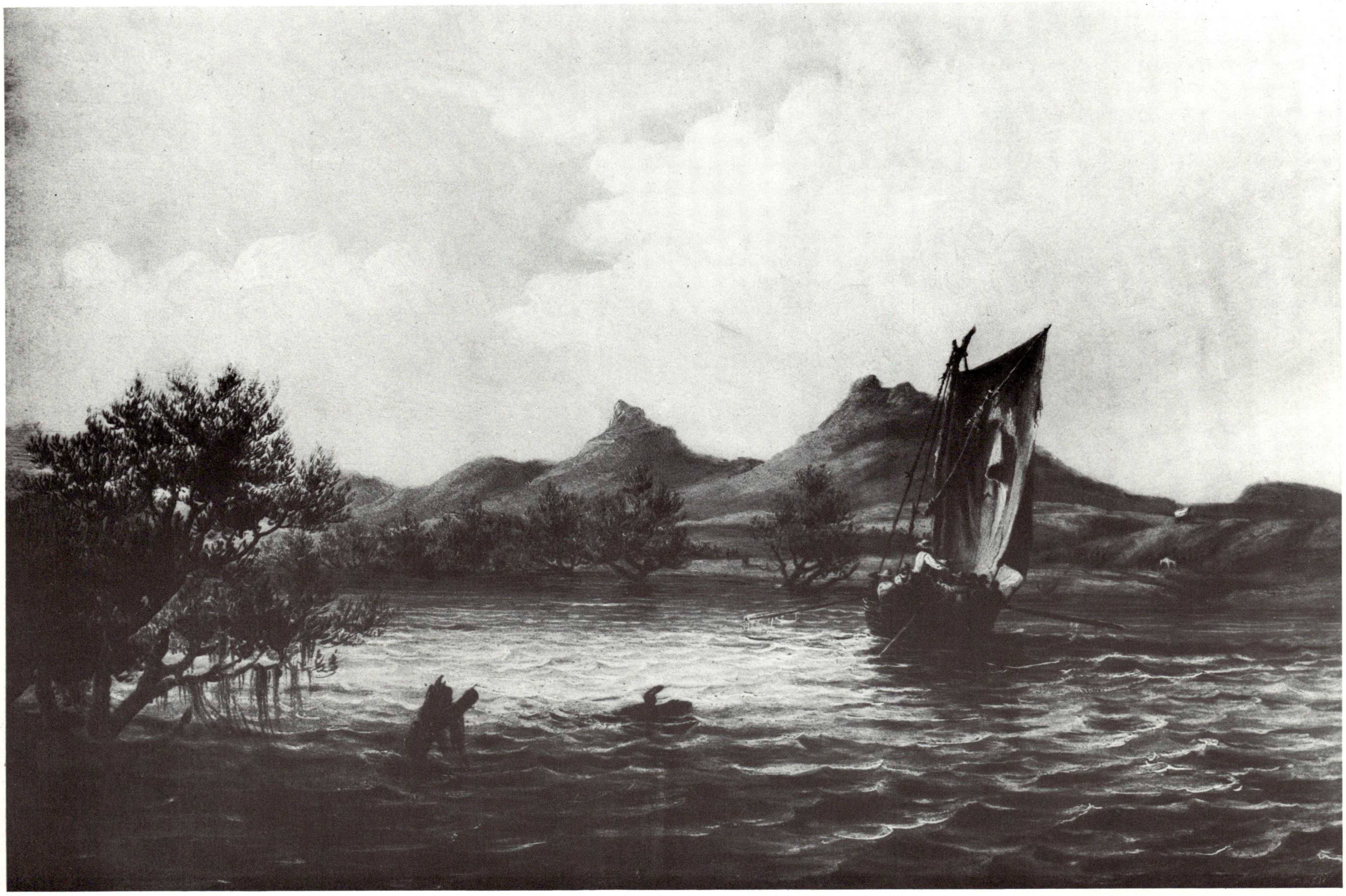

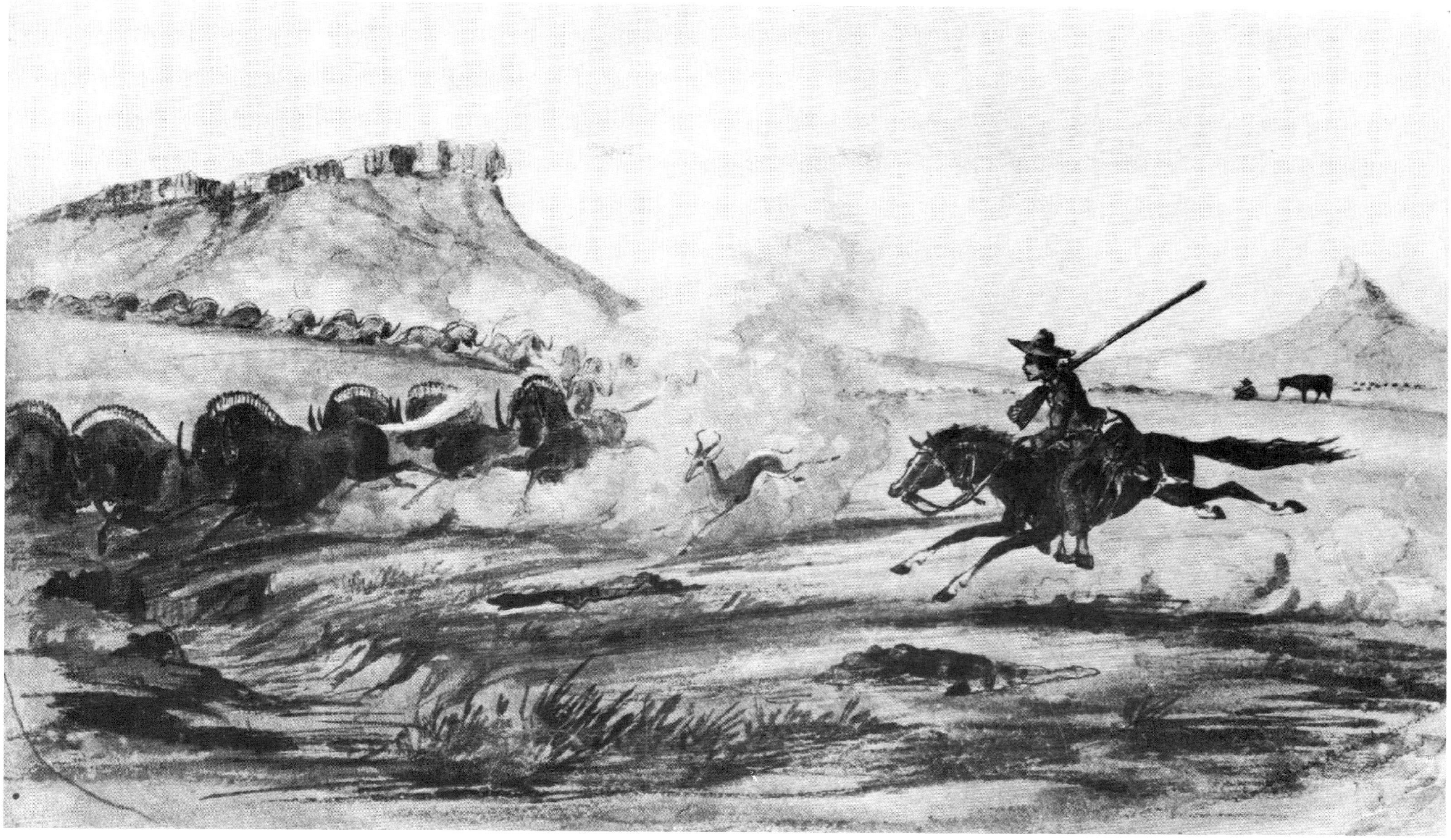

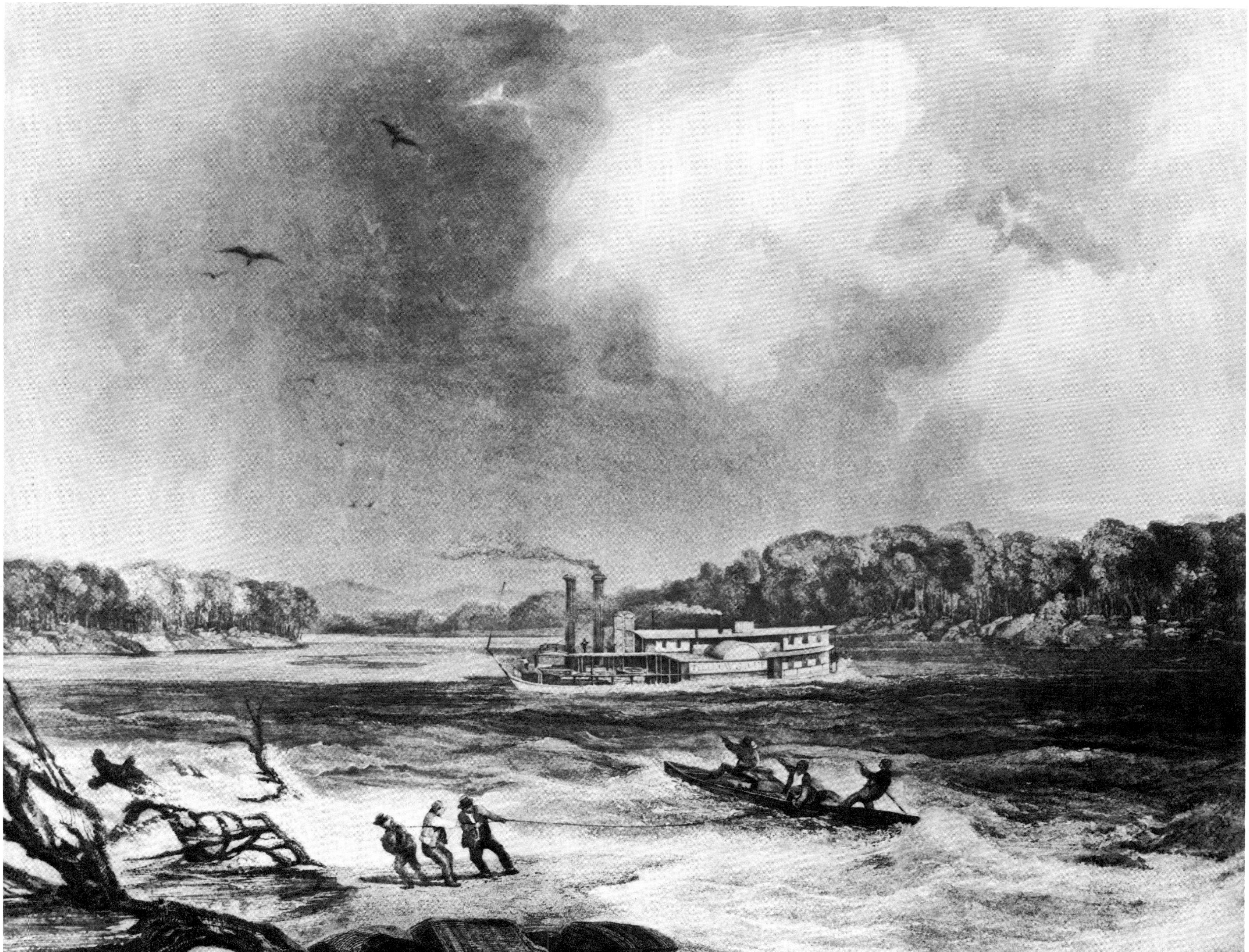

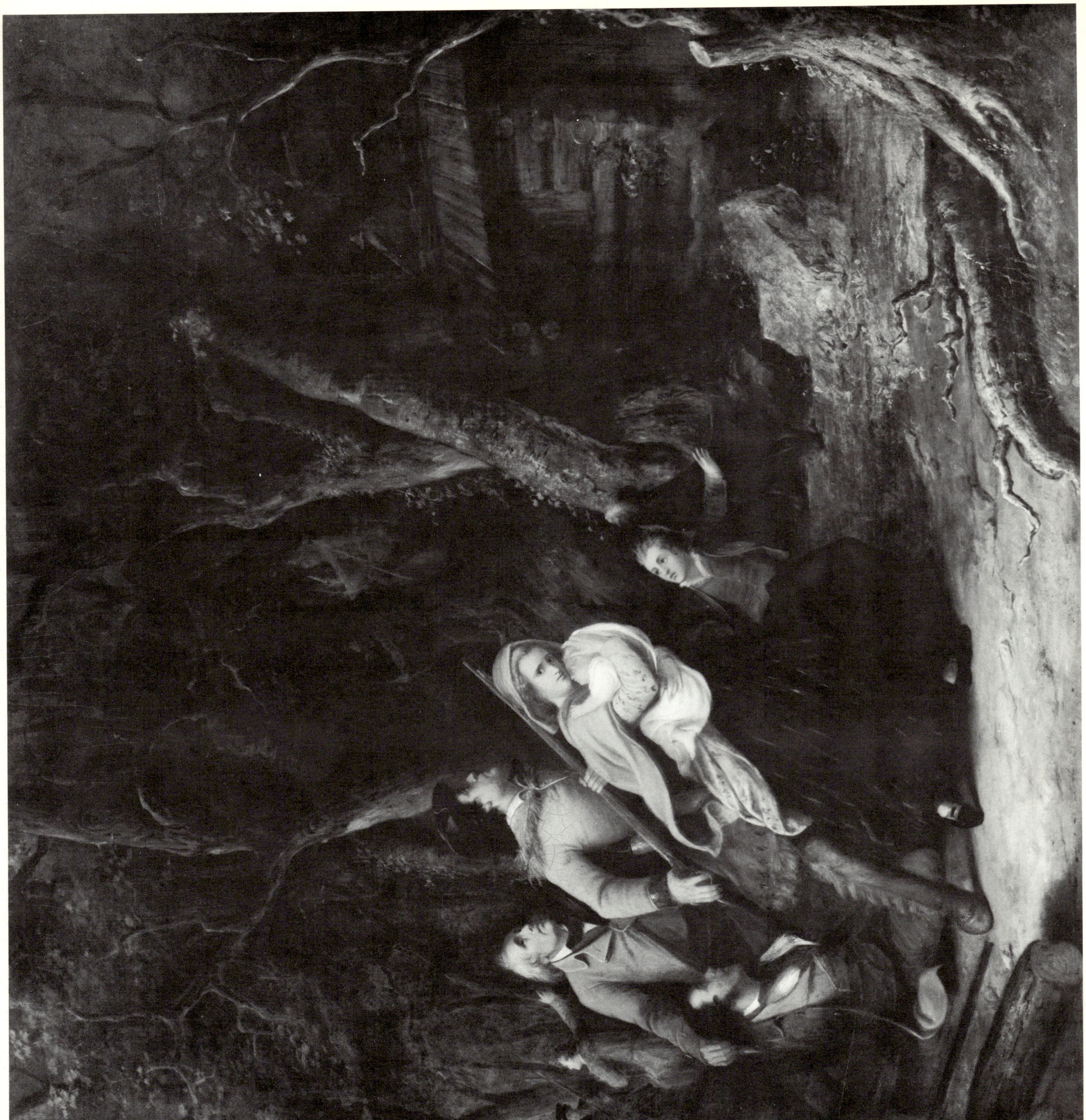

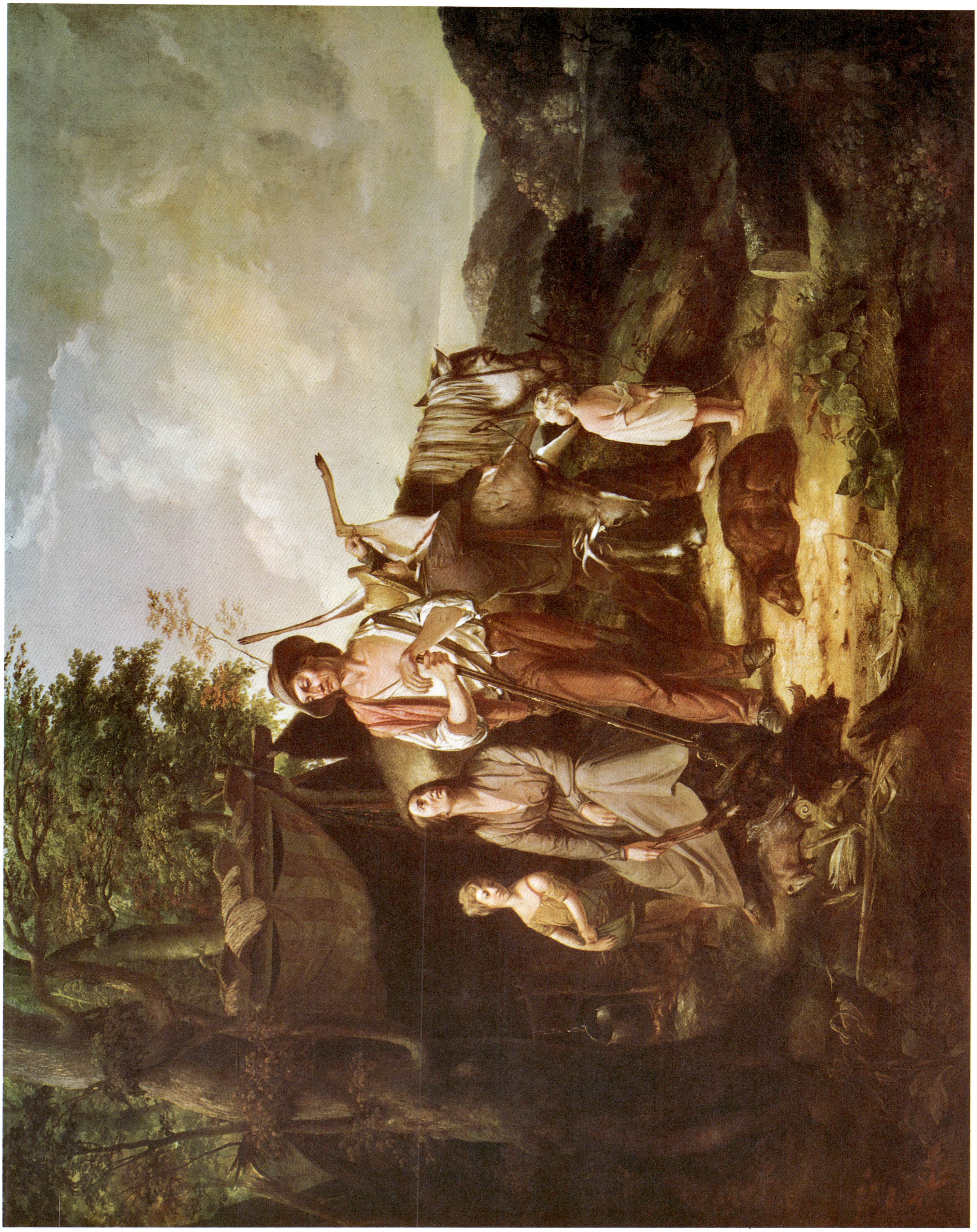

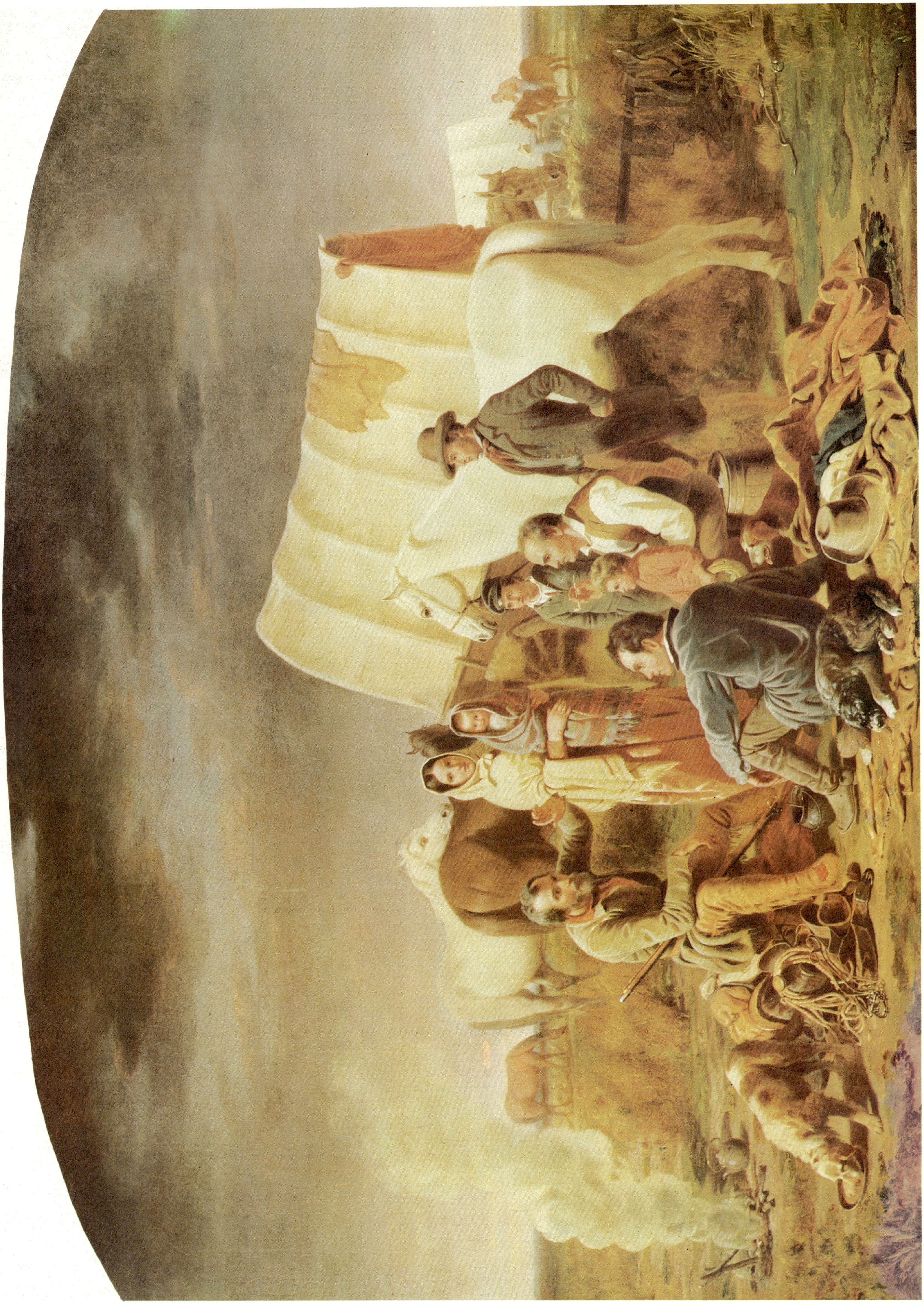

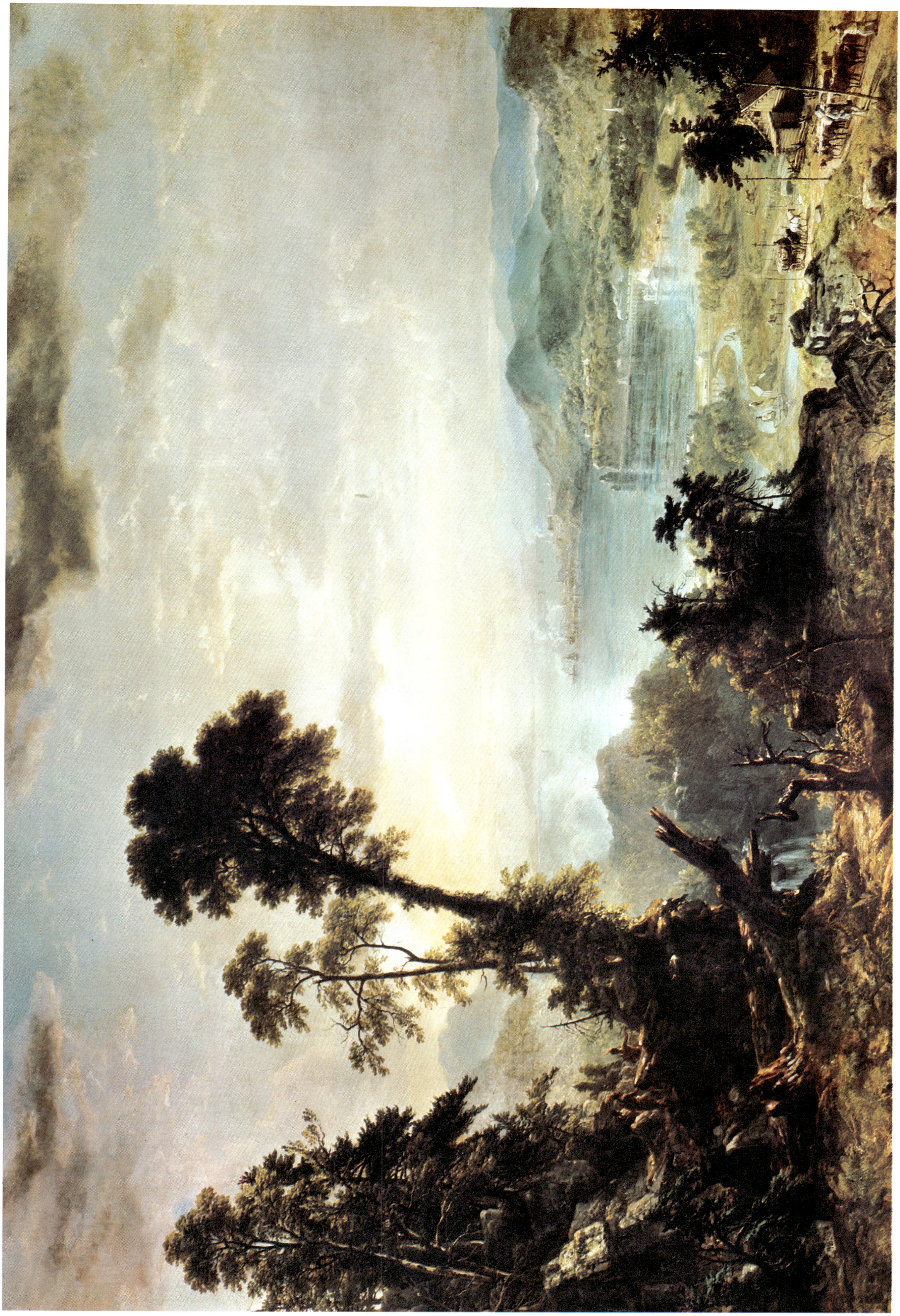

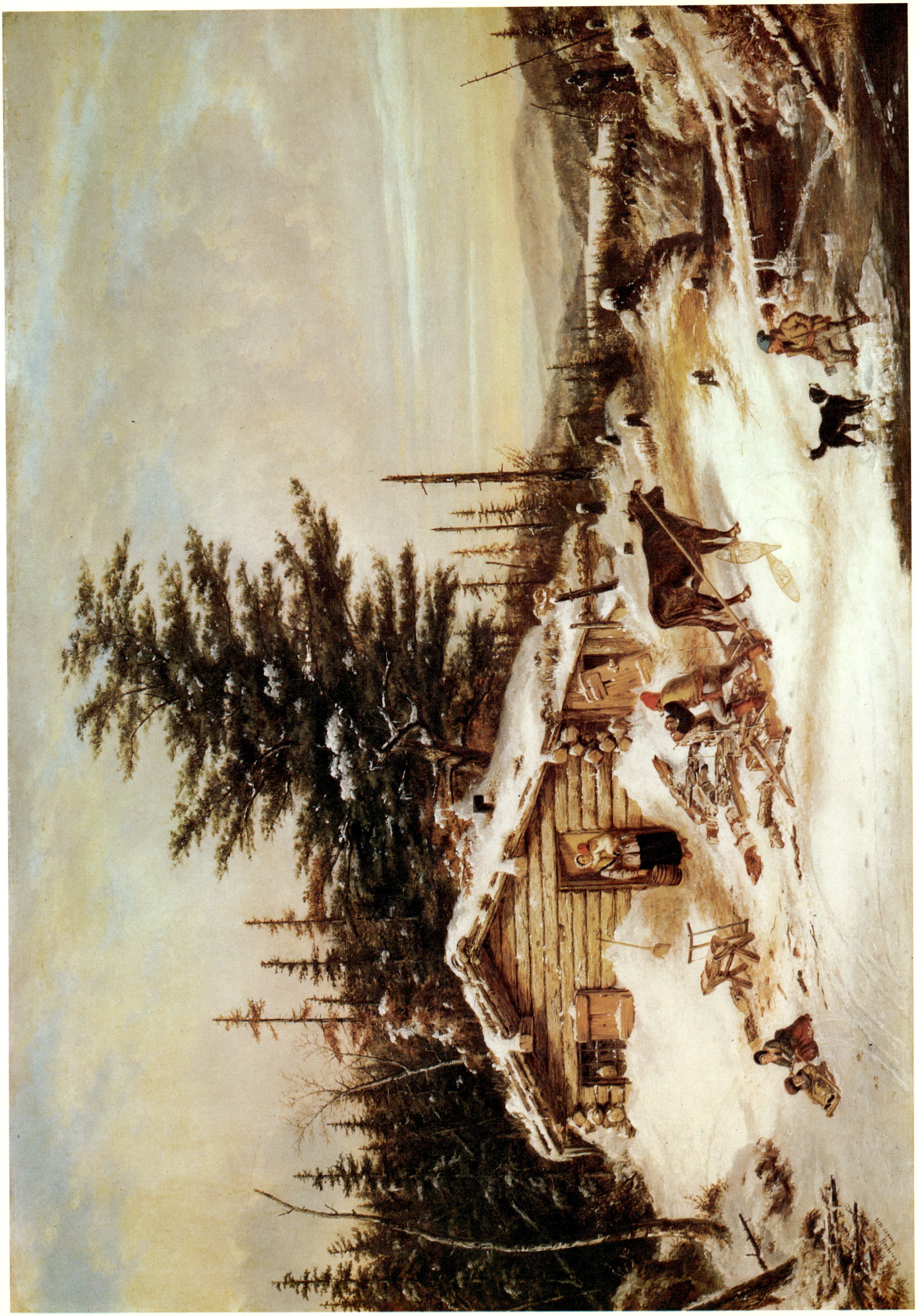

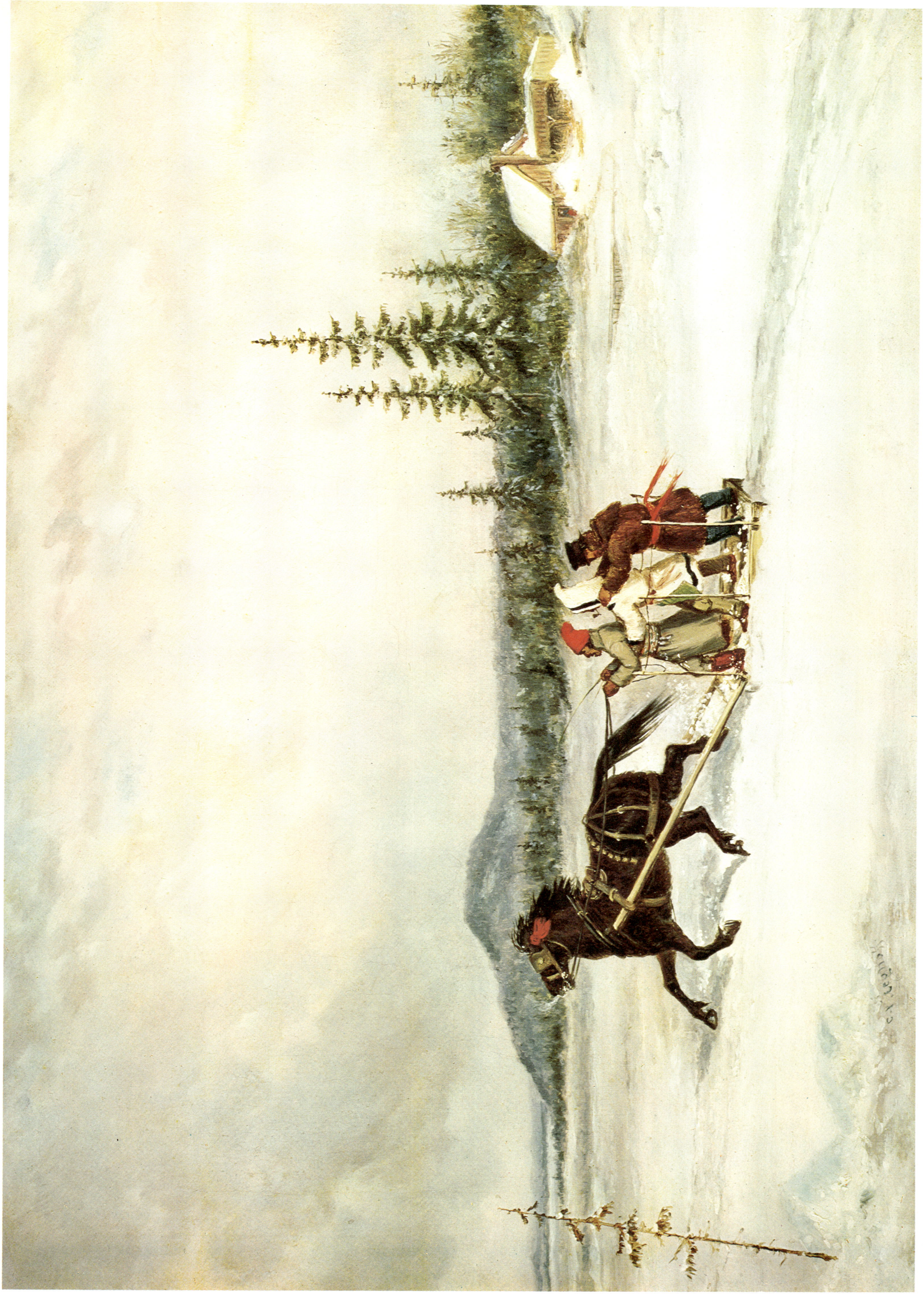

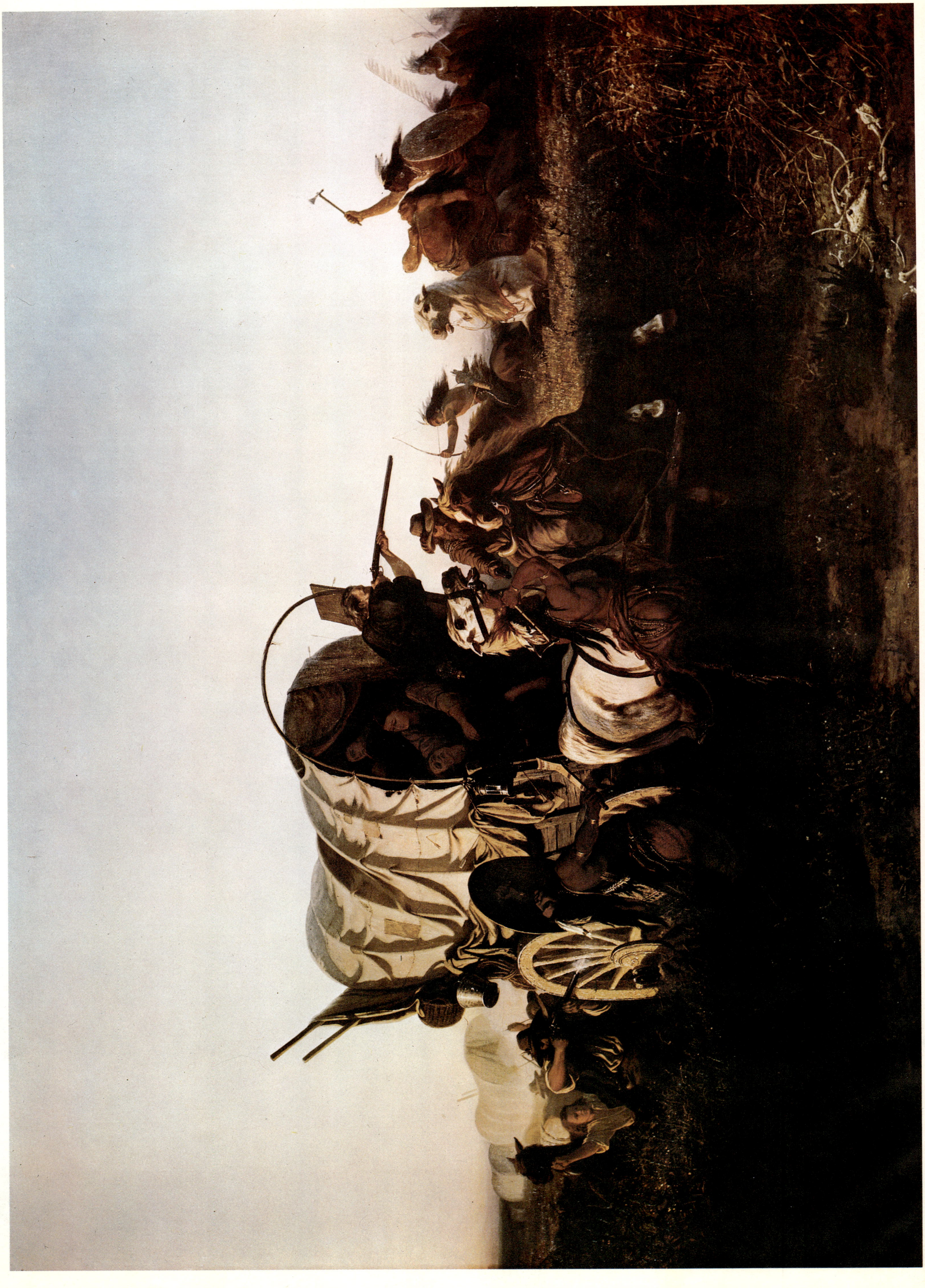

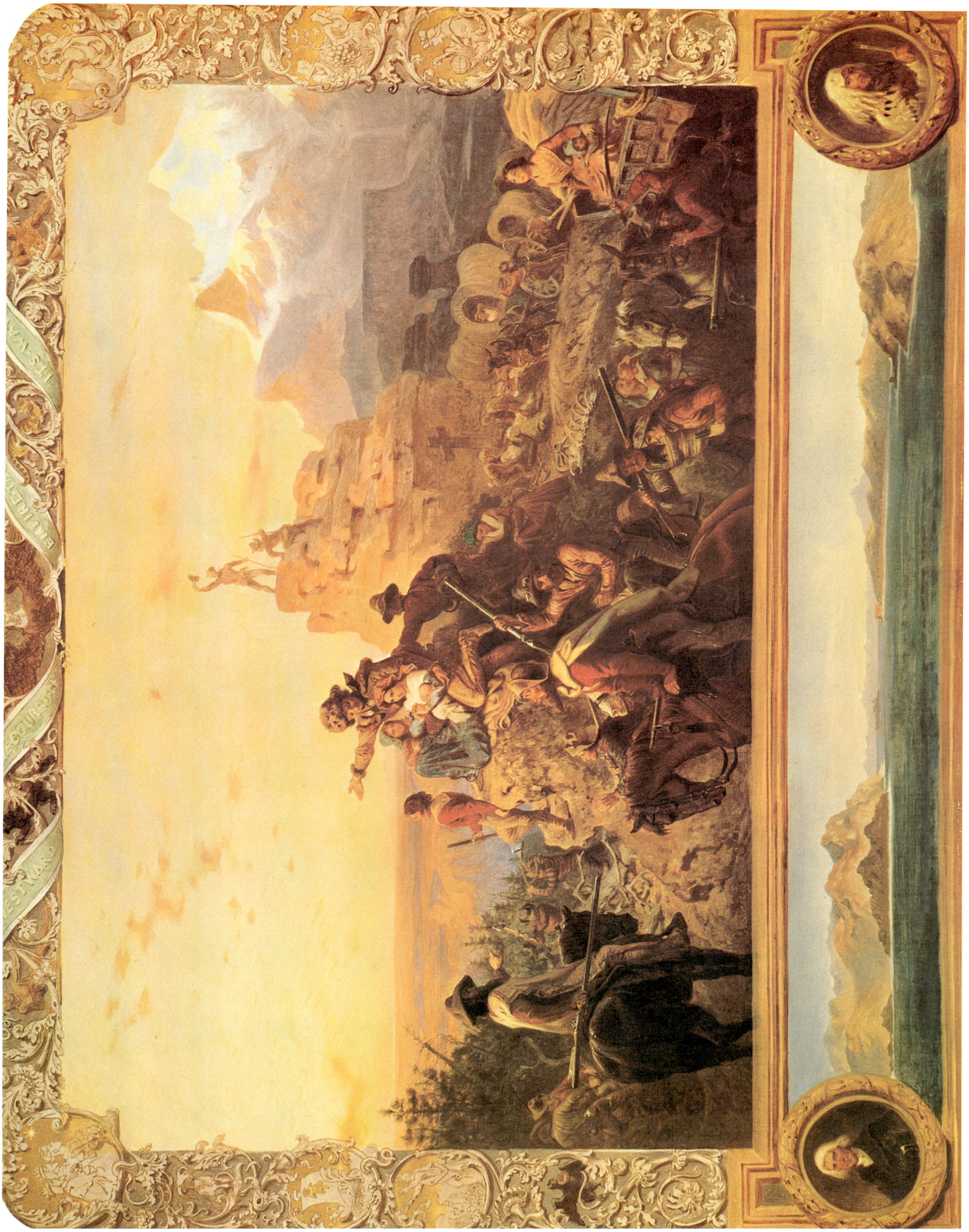

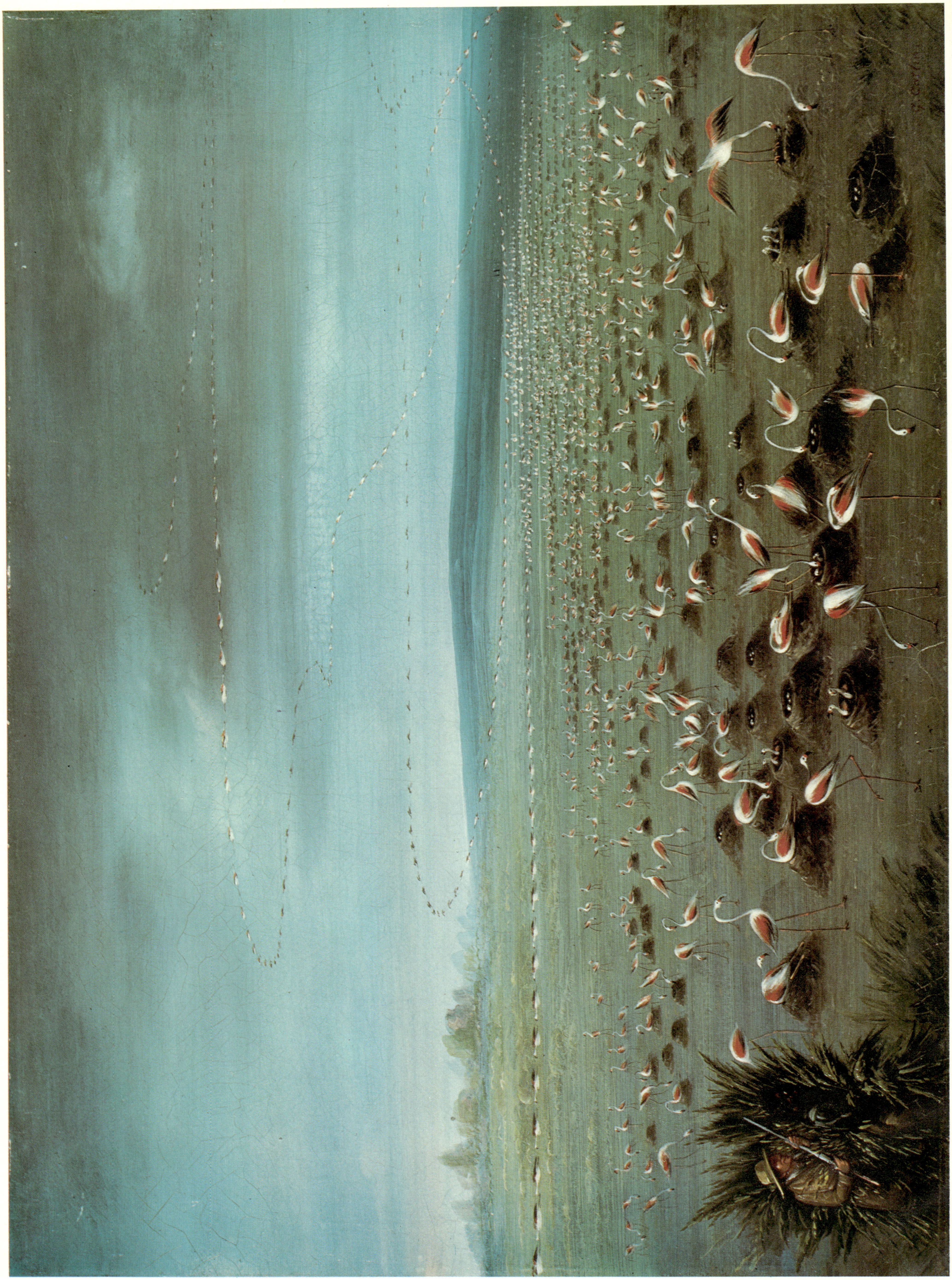

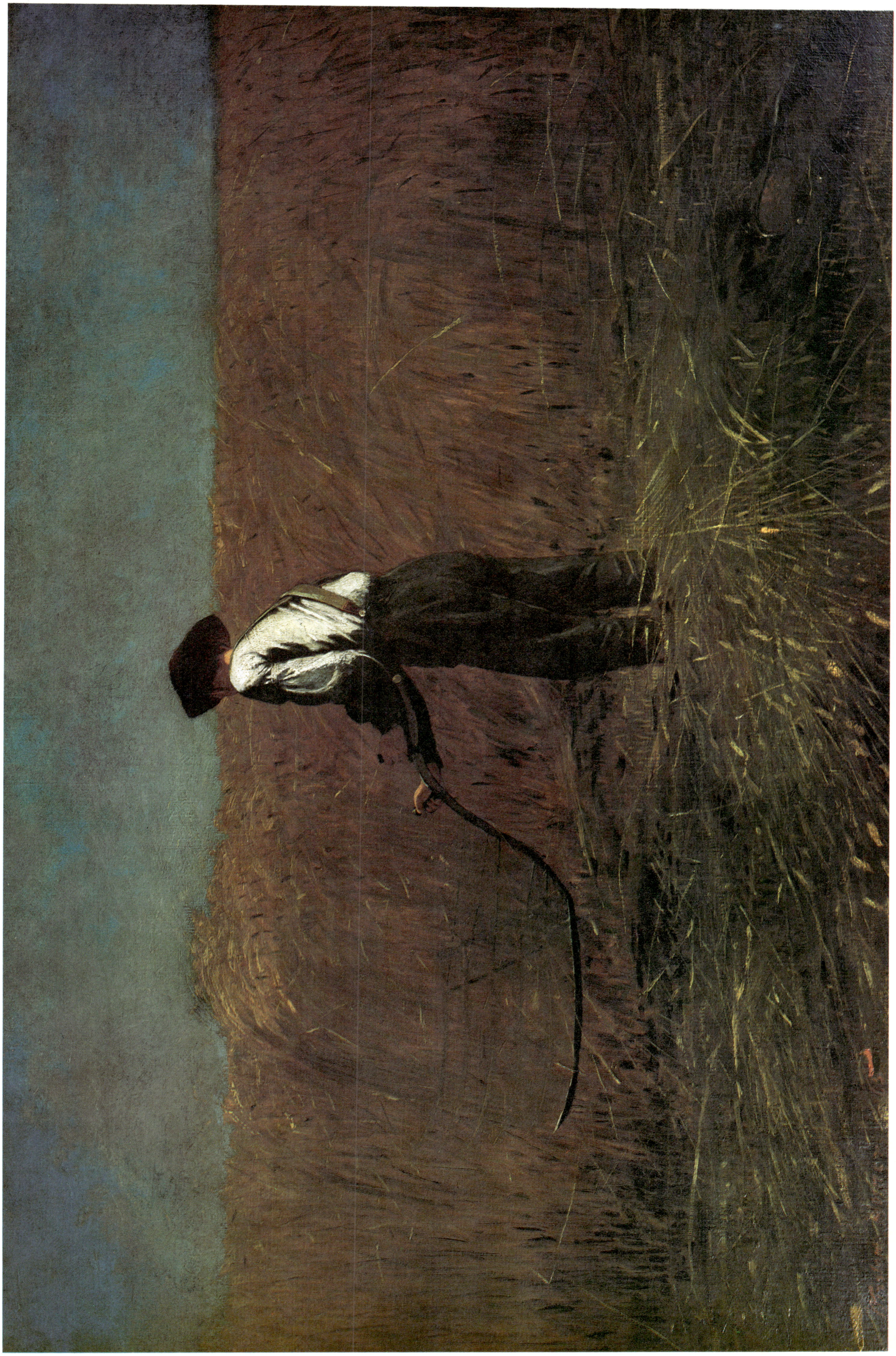

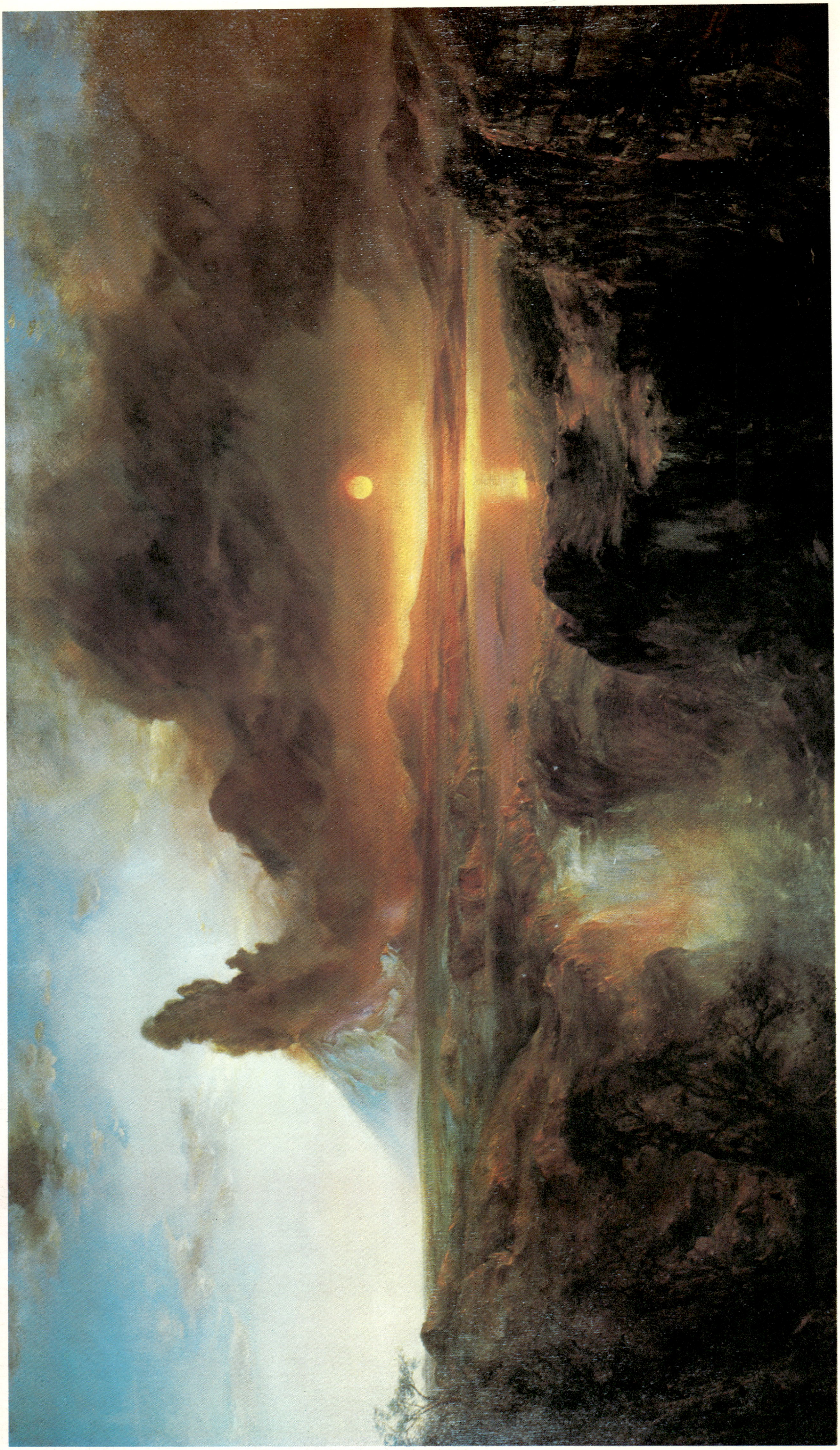

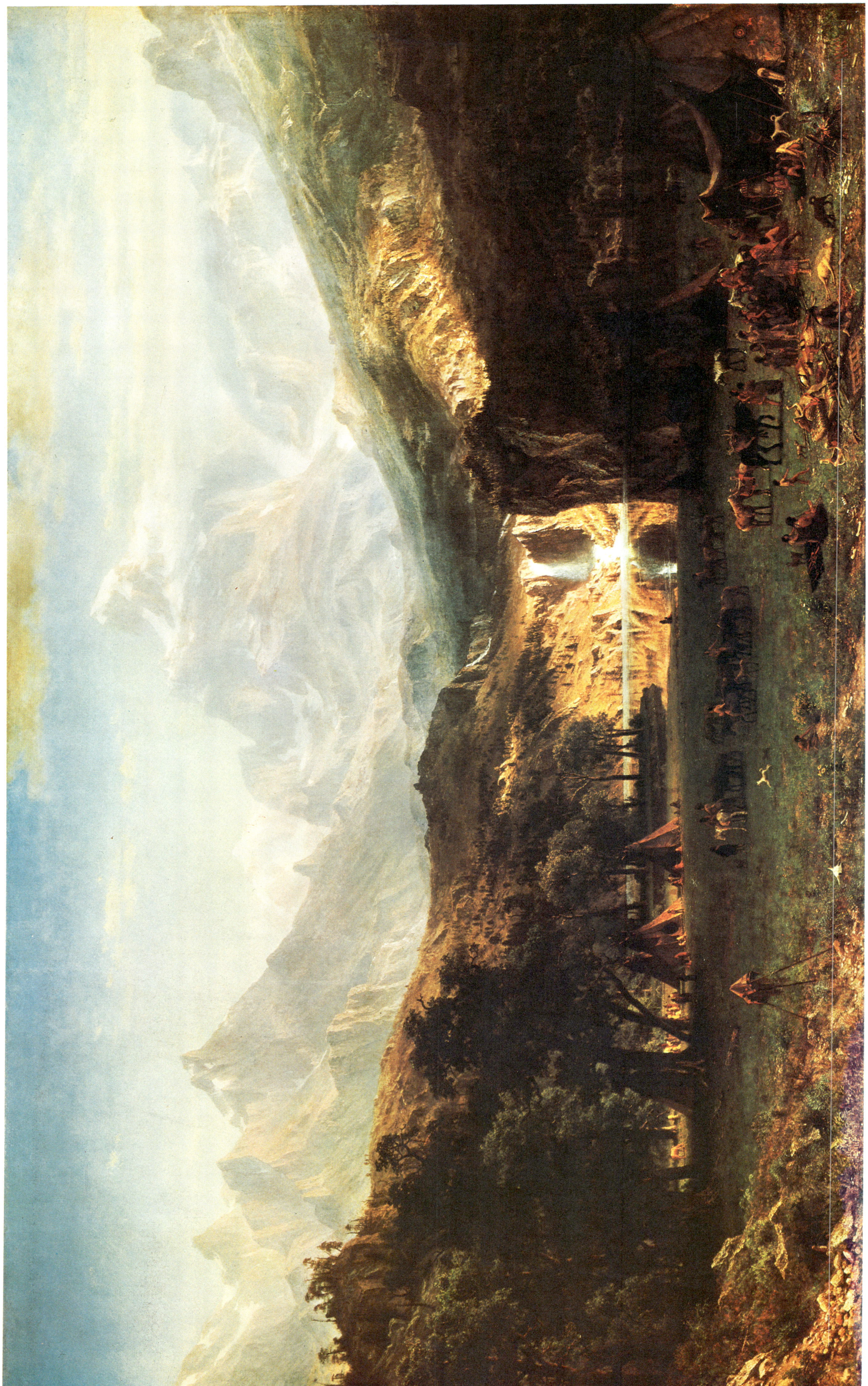

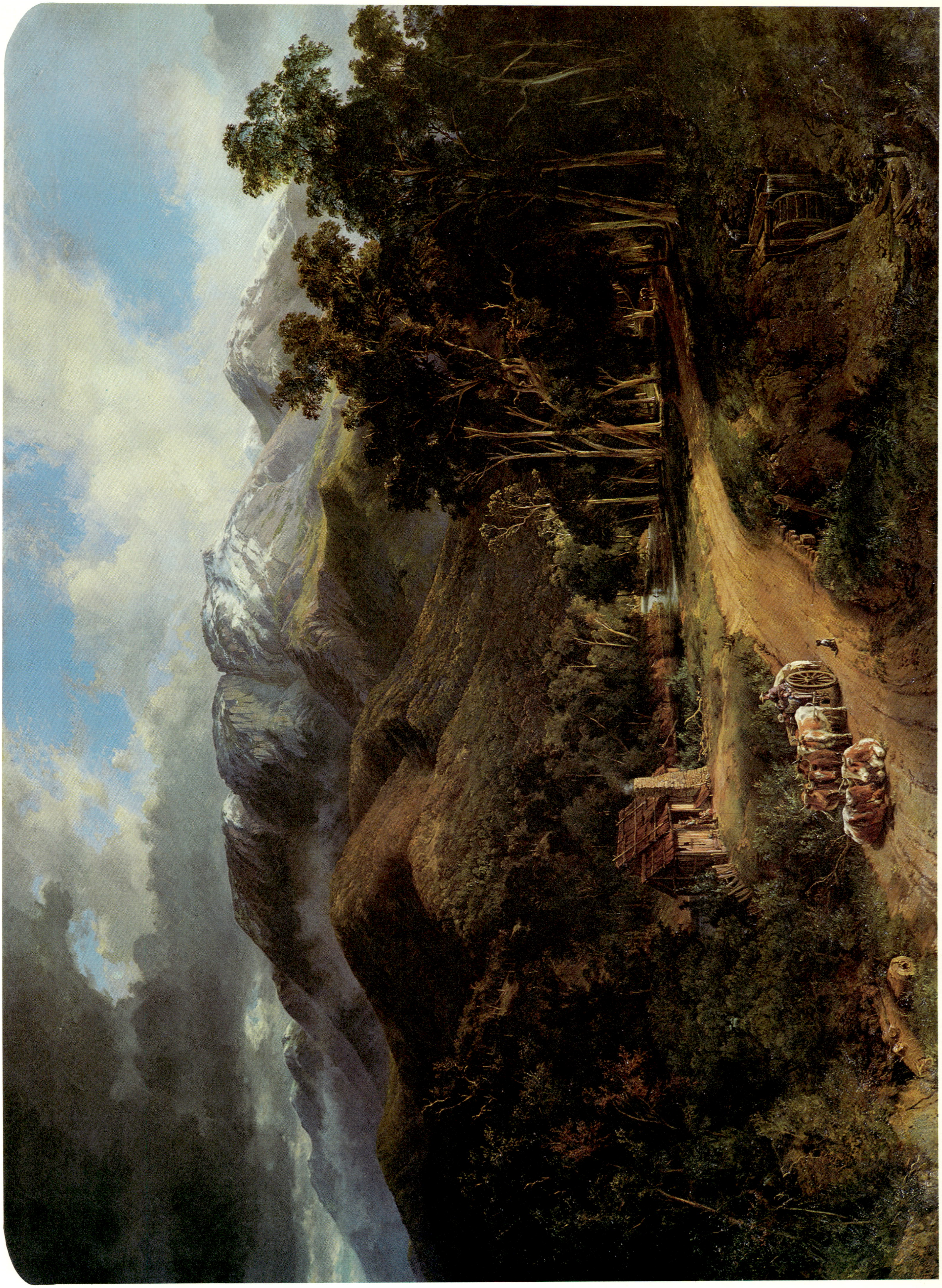

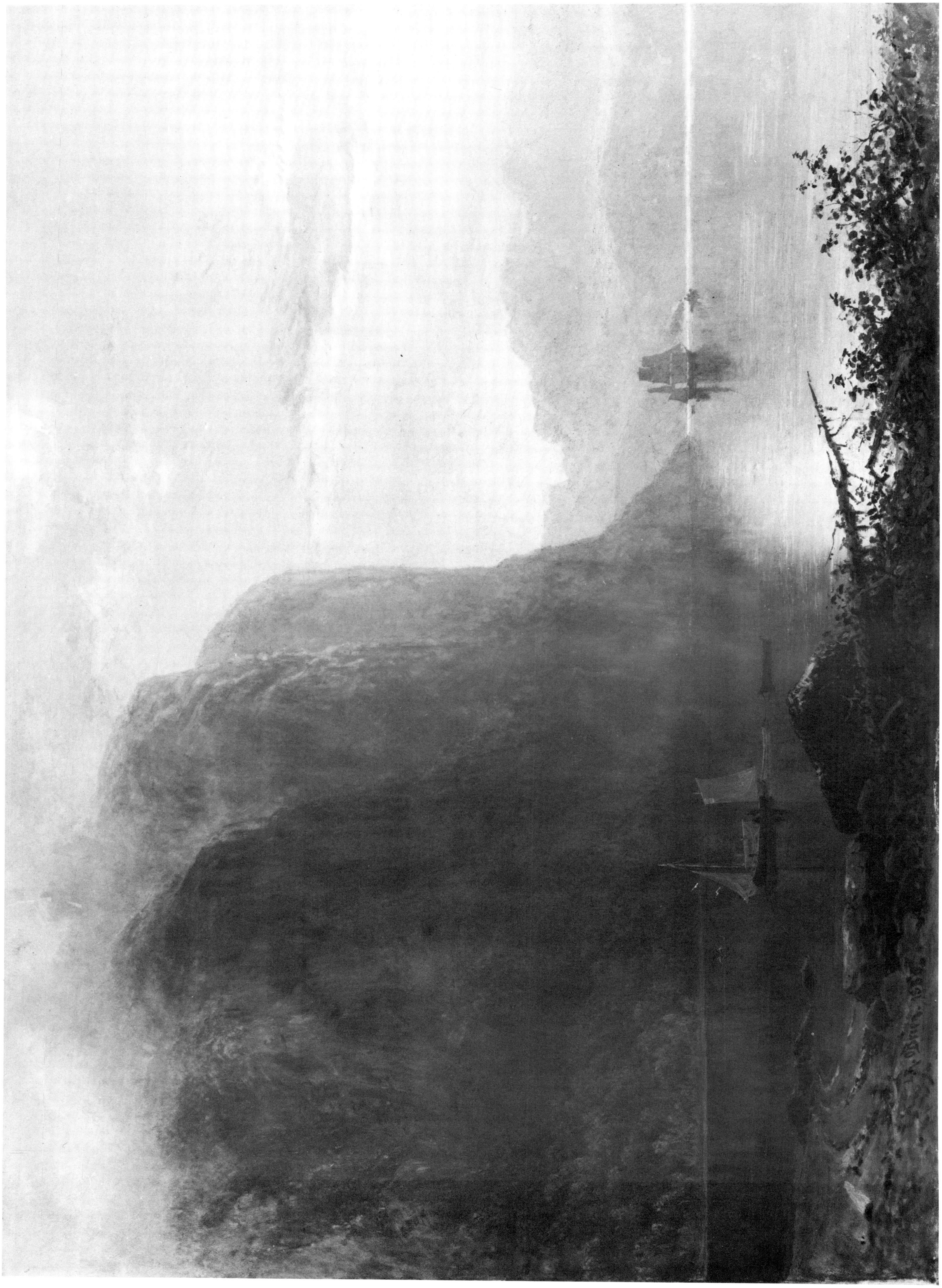

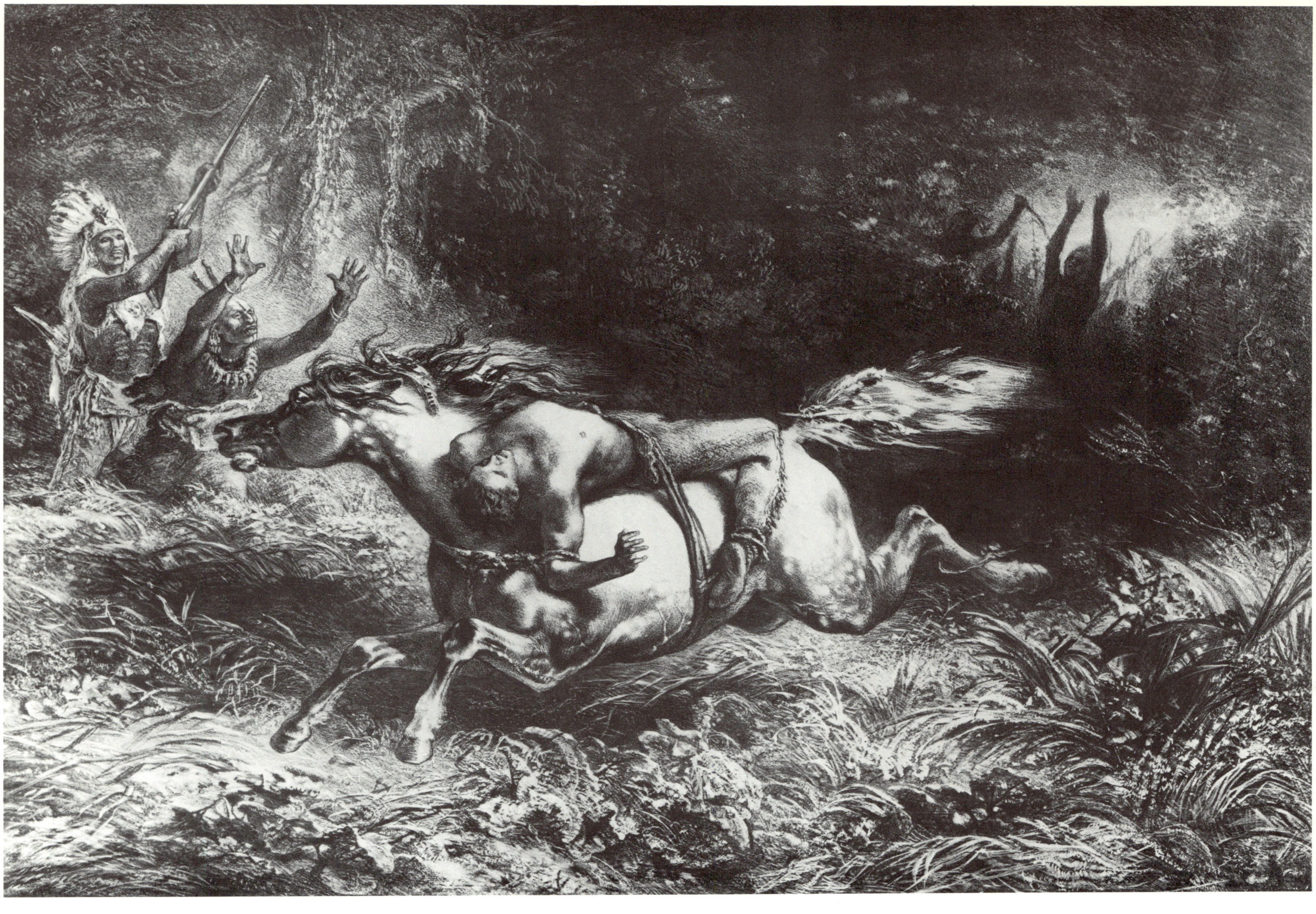

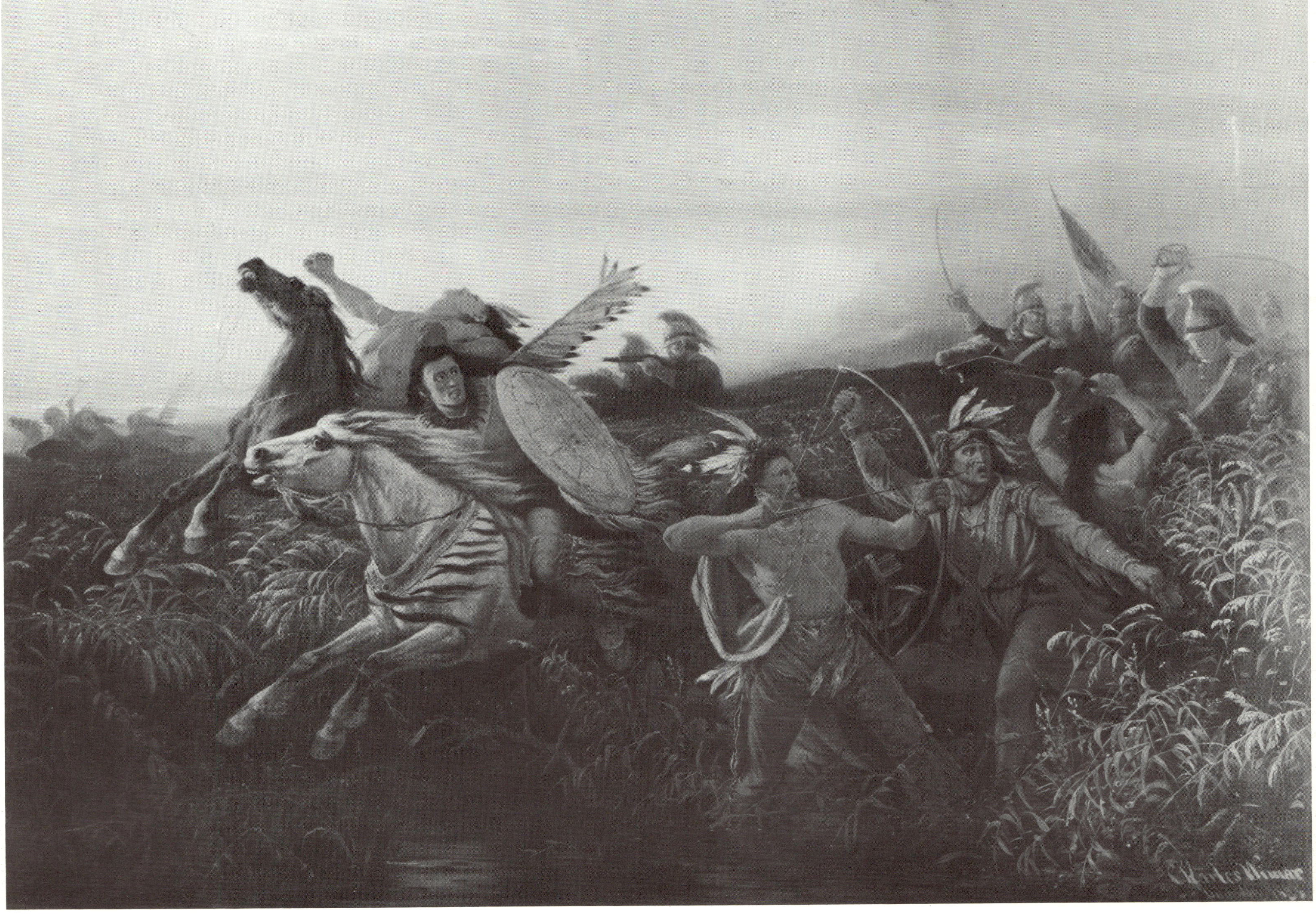
Charles Wimar

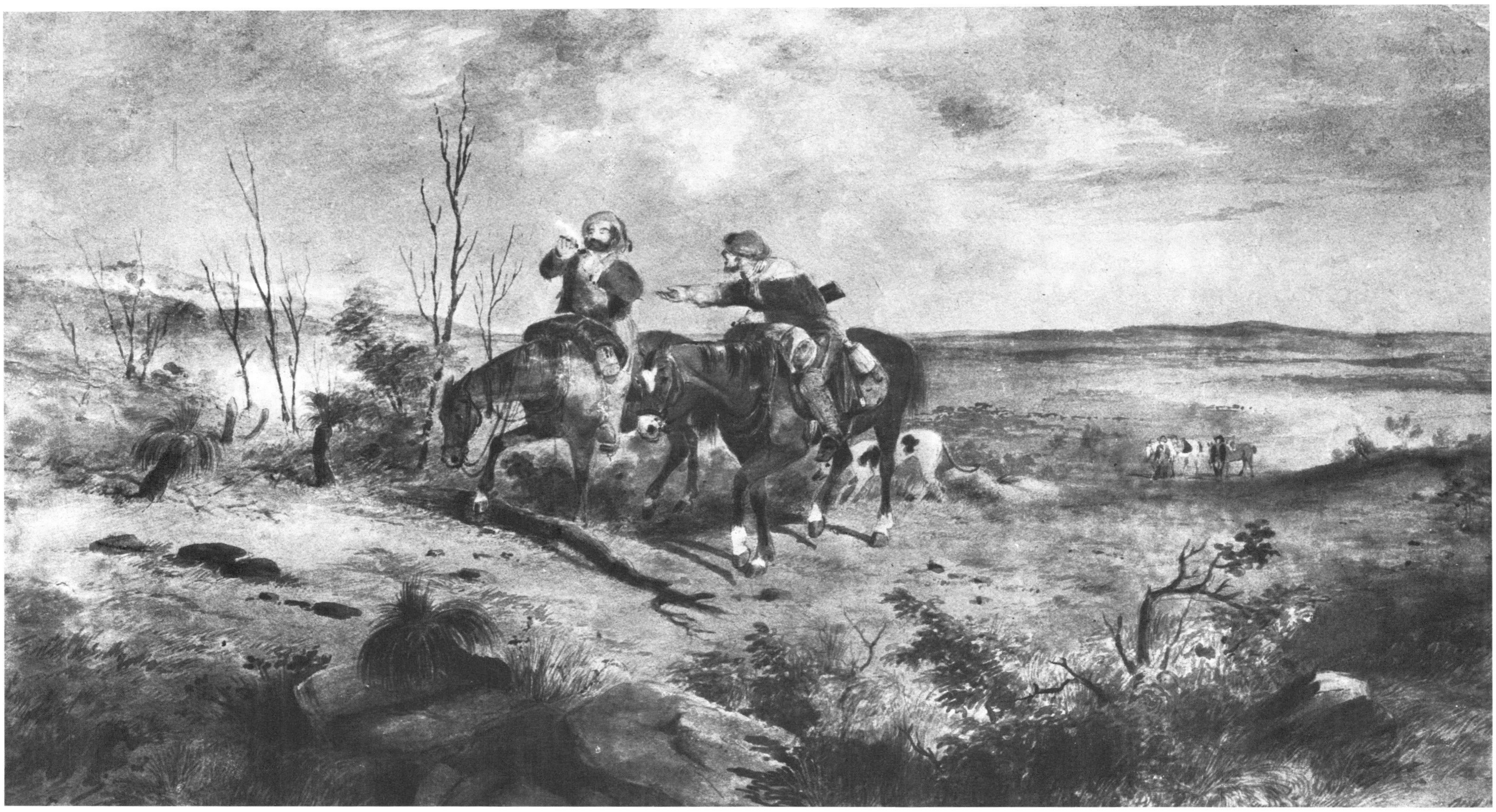

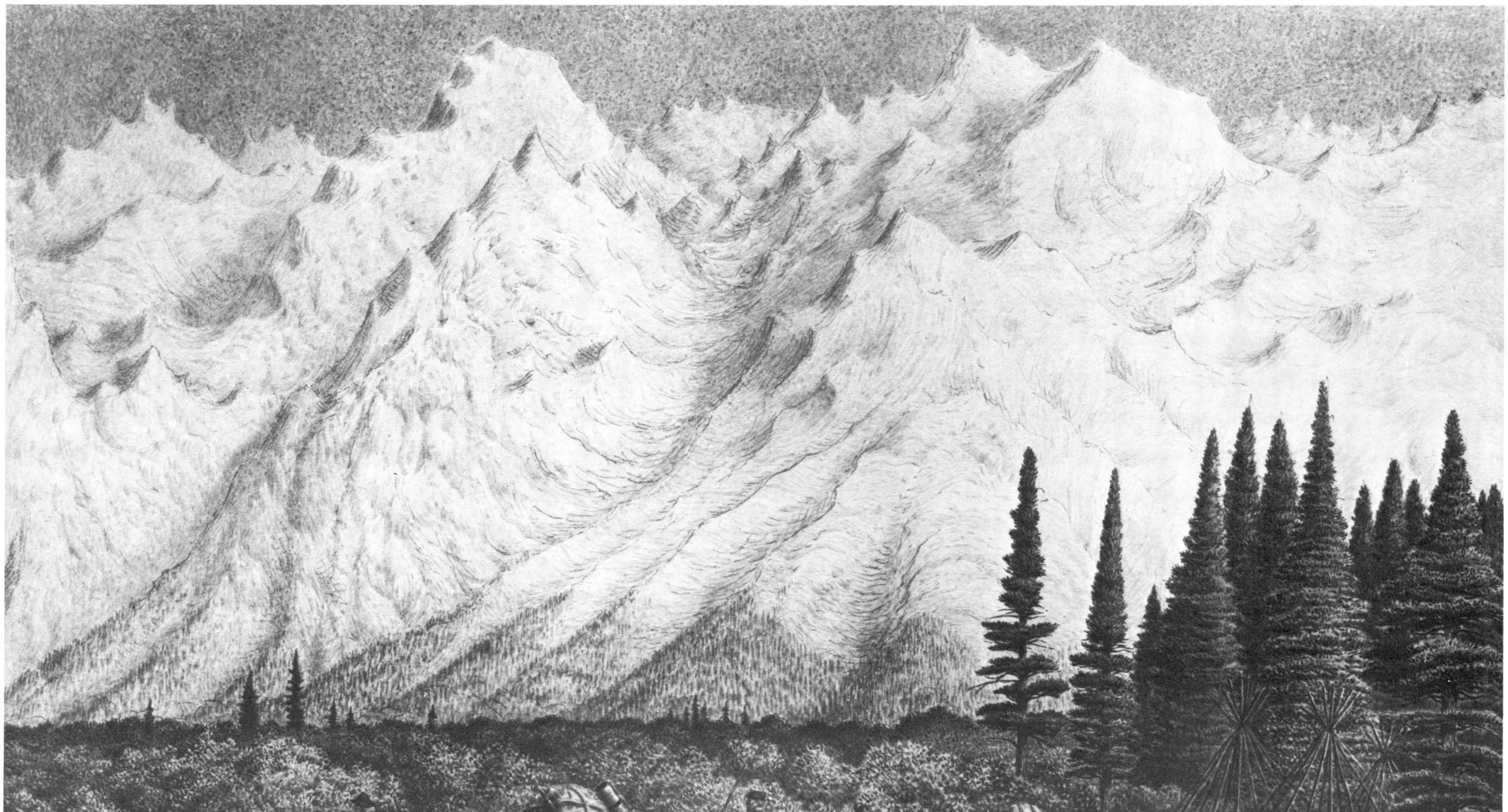

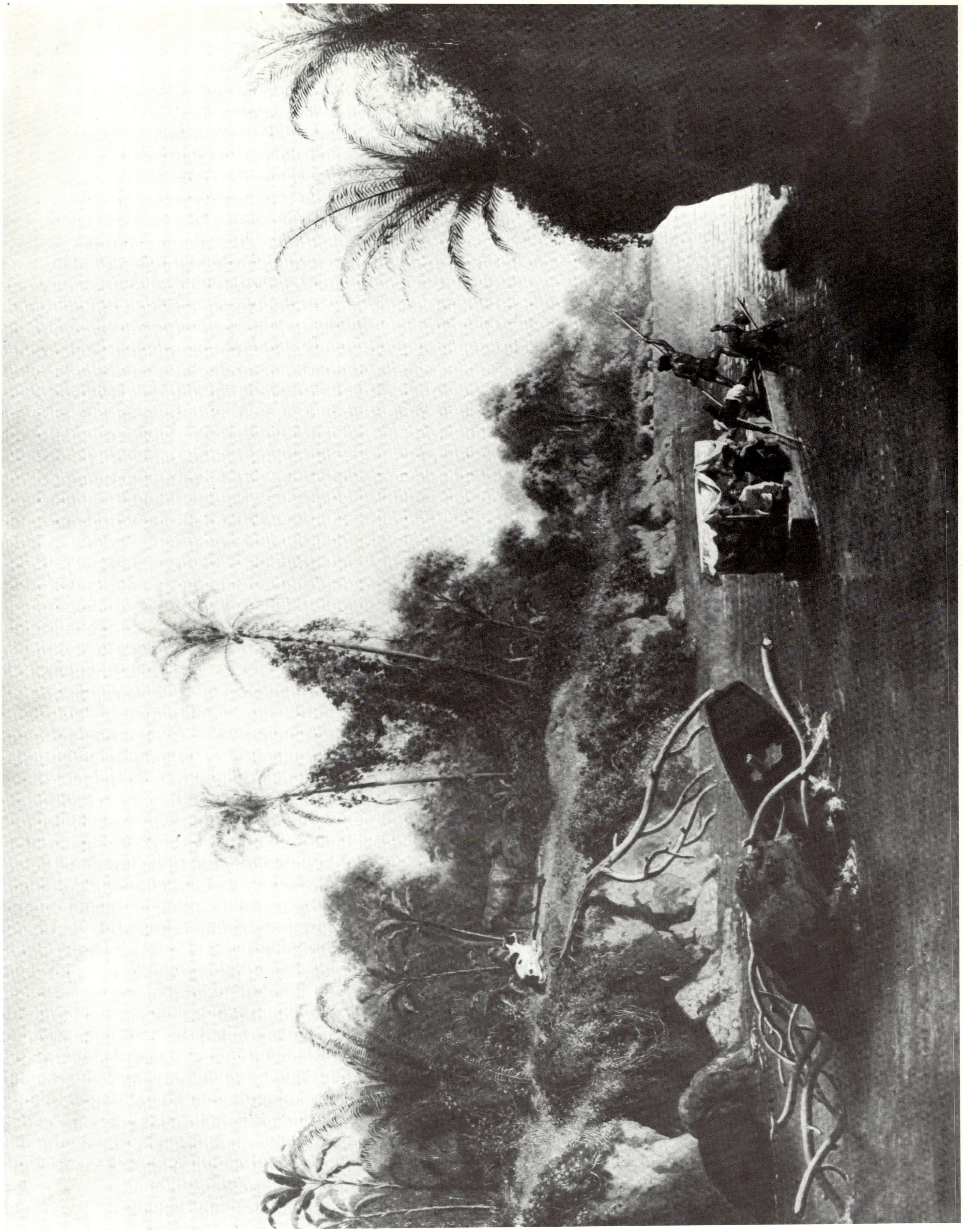

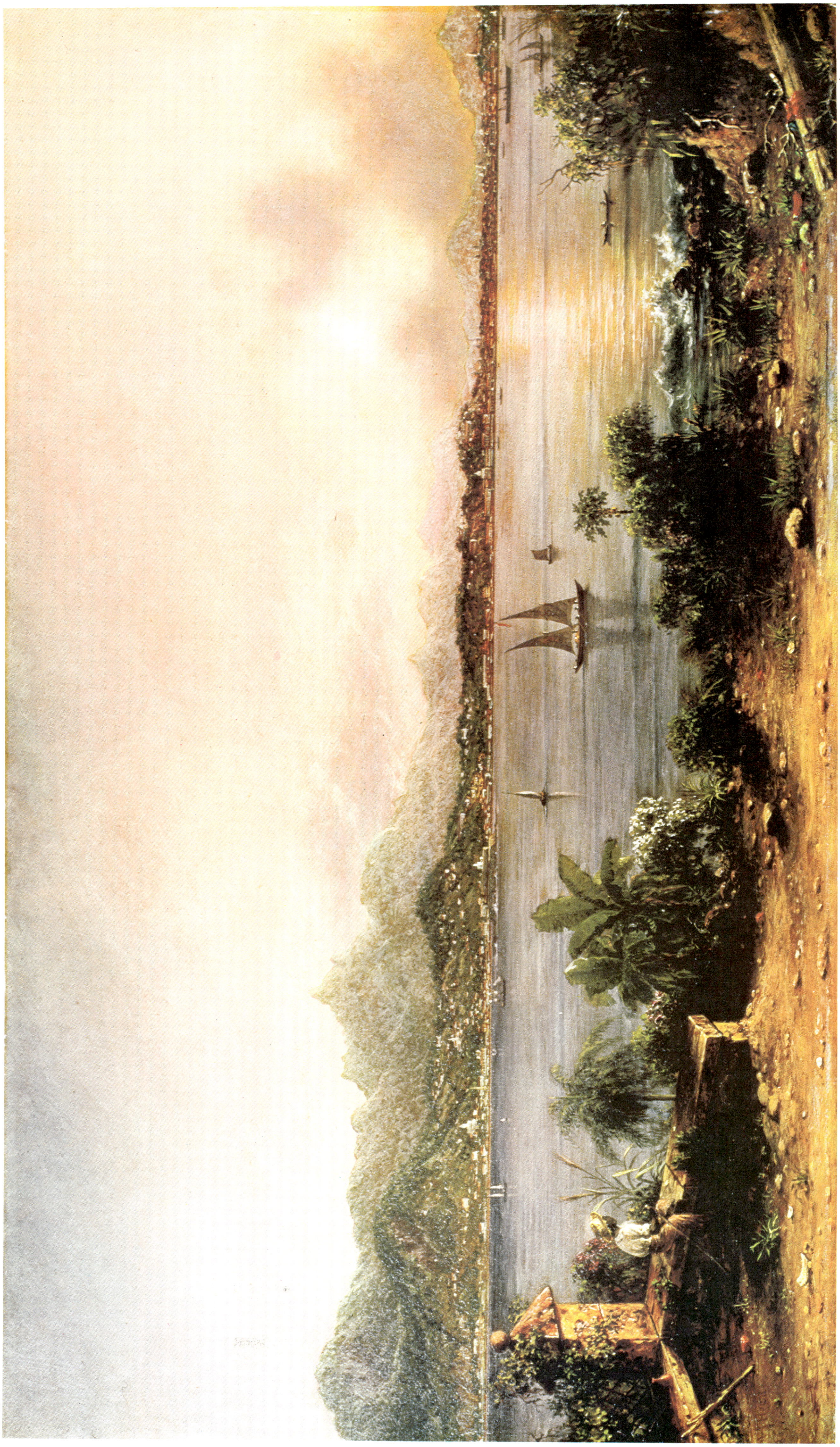

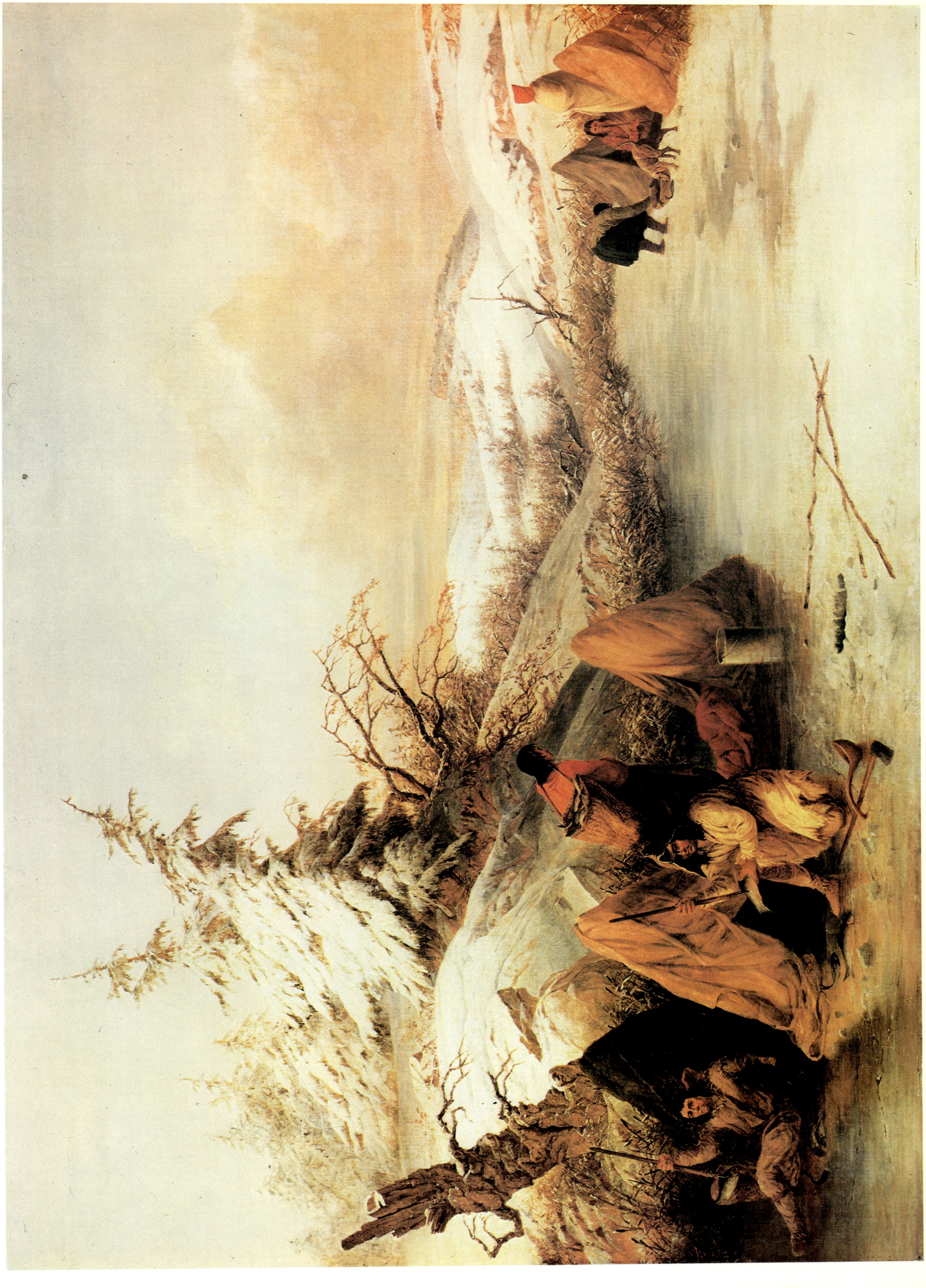

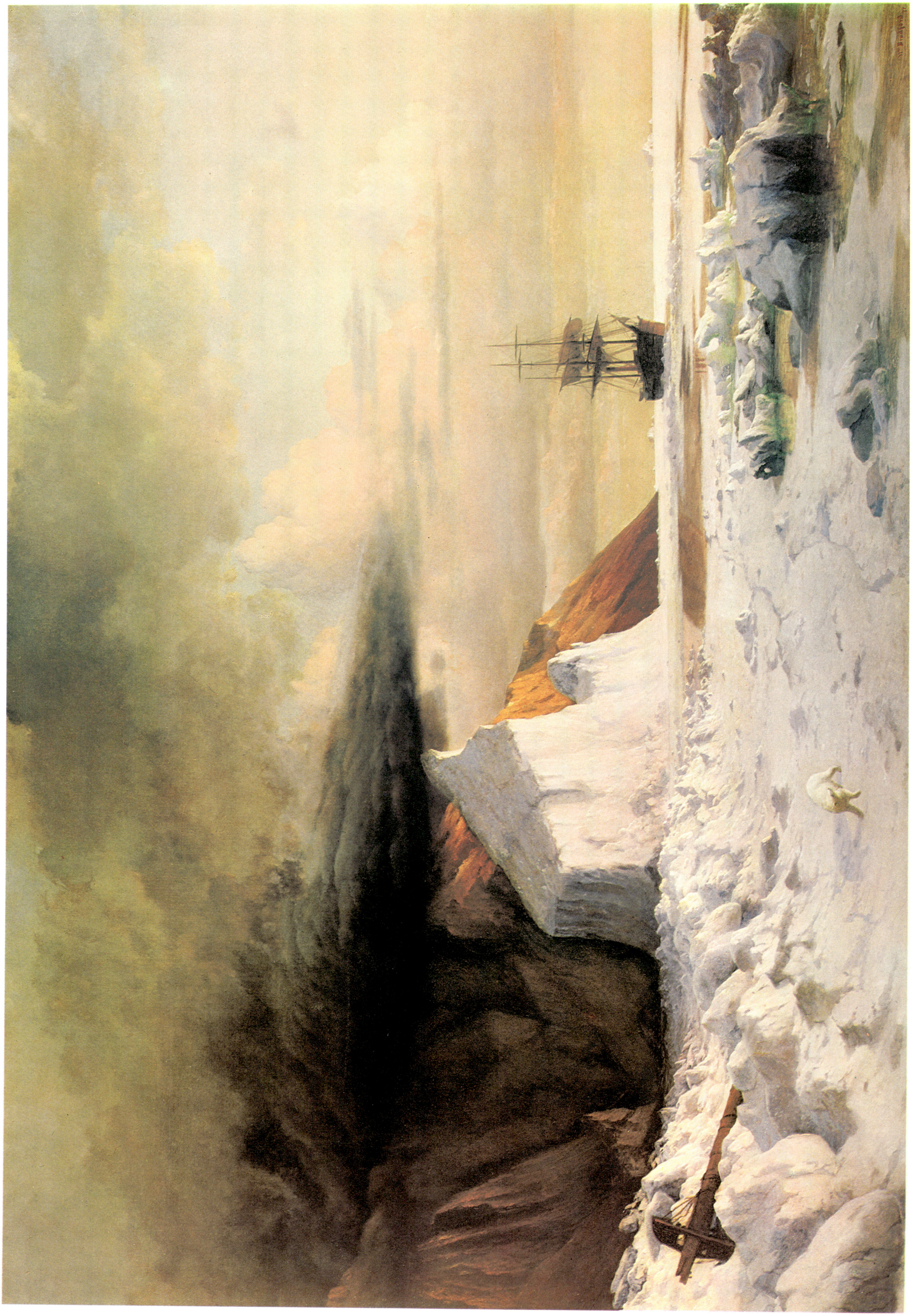

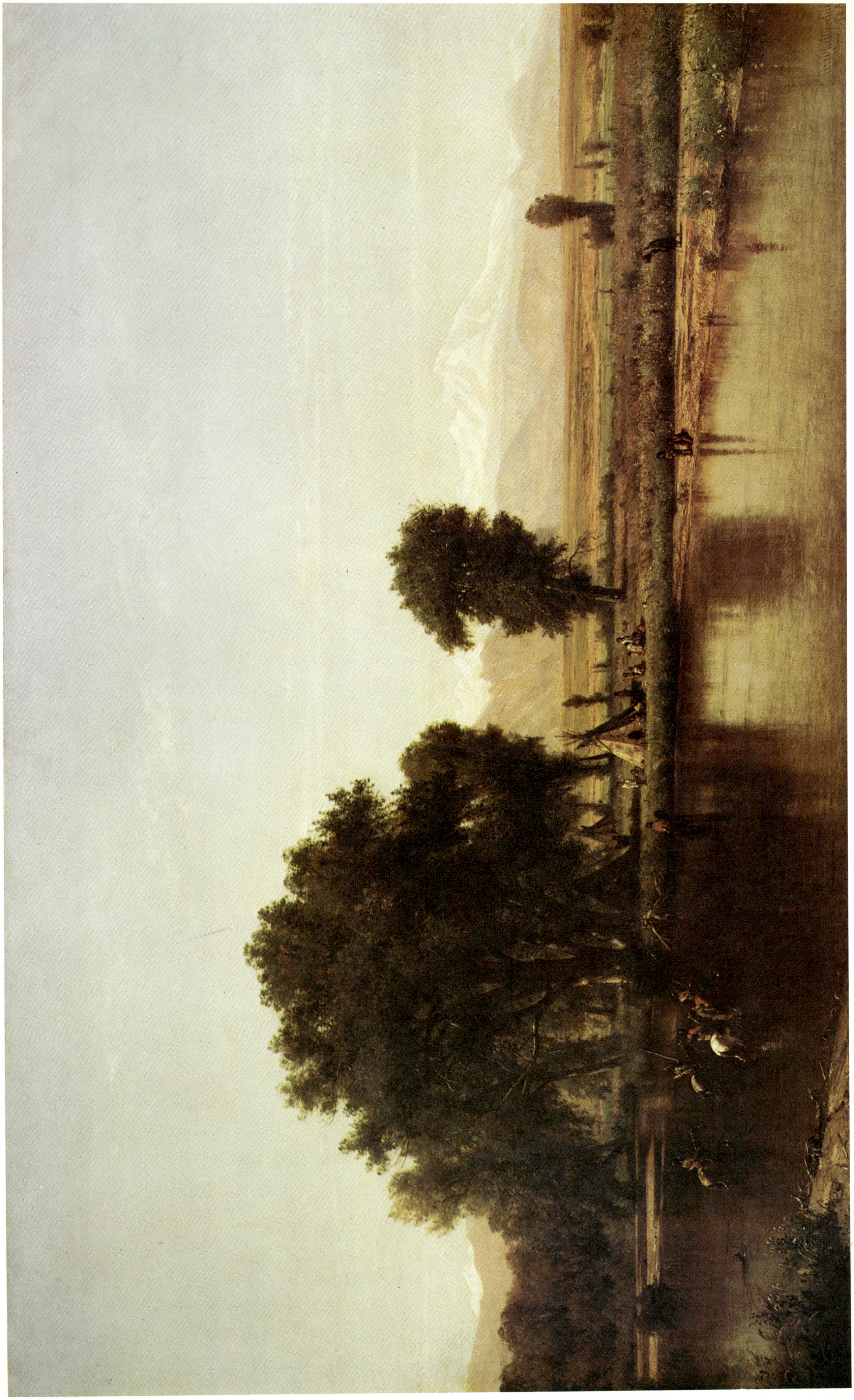

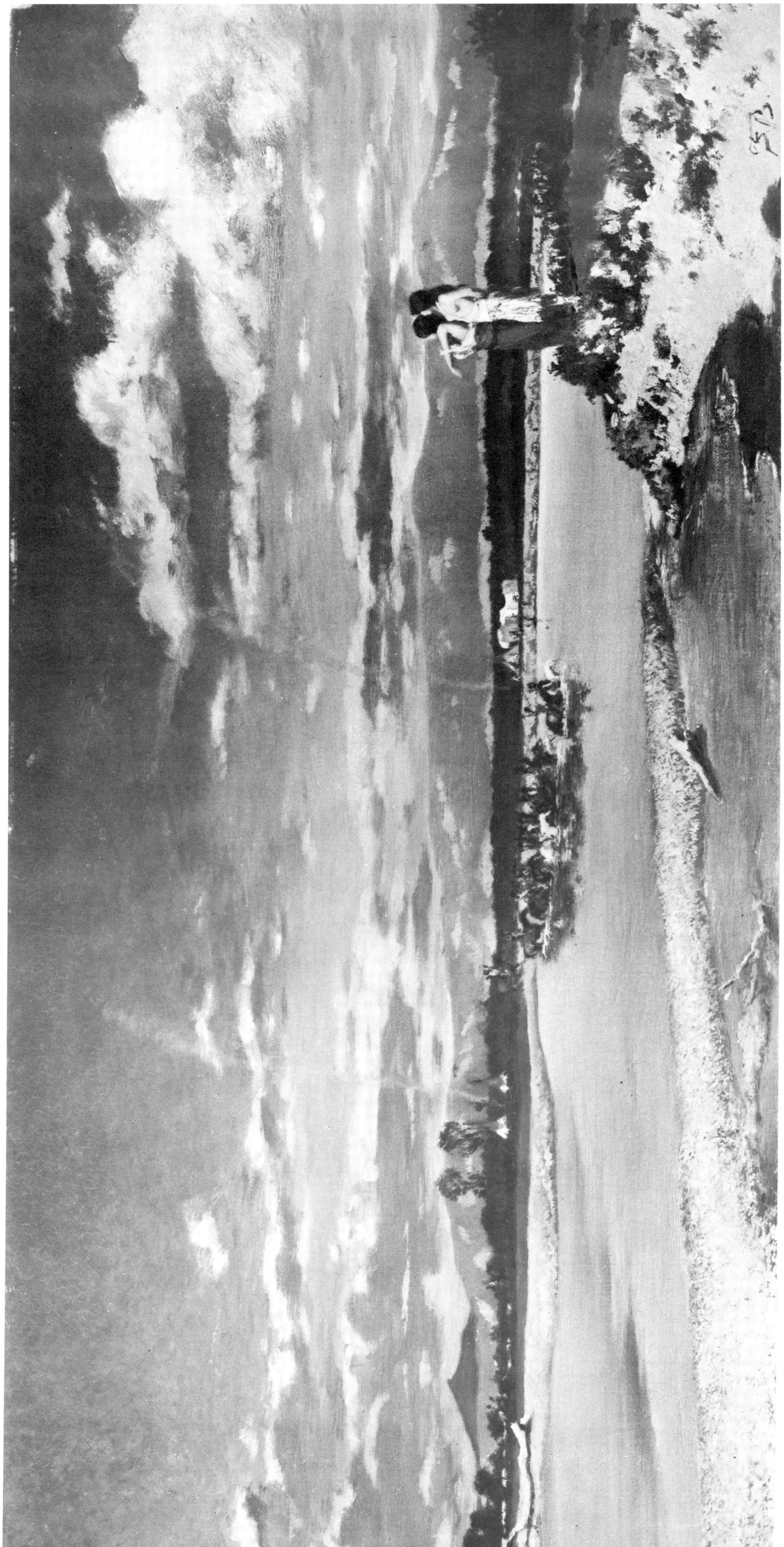

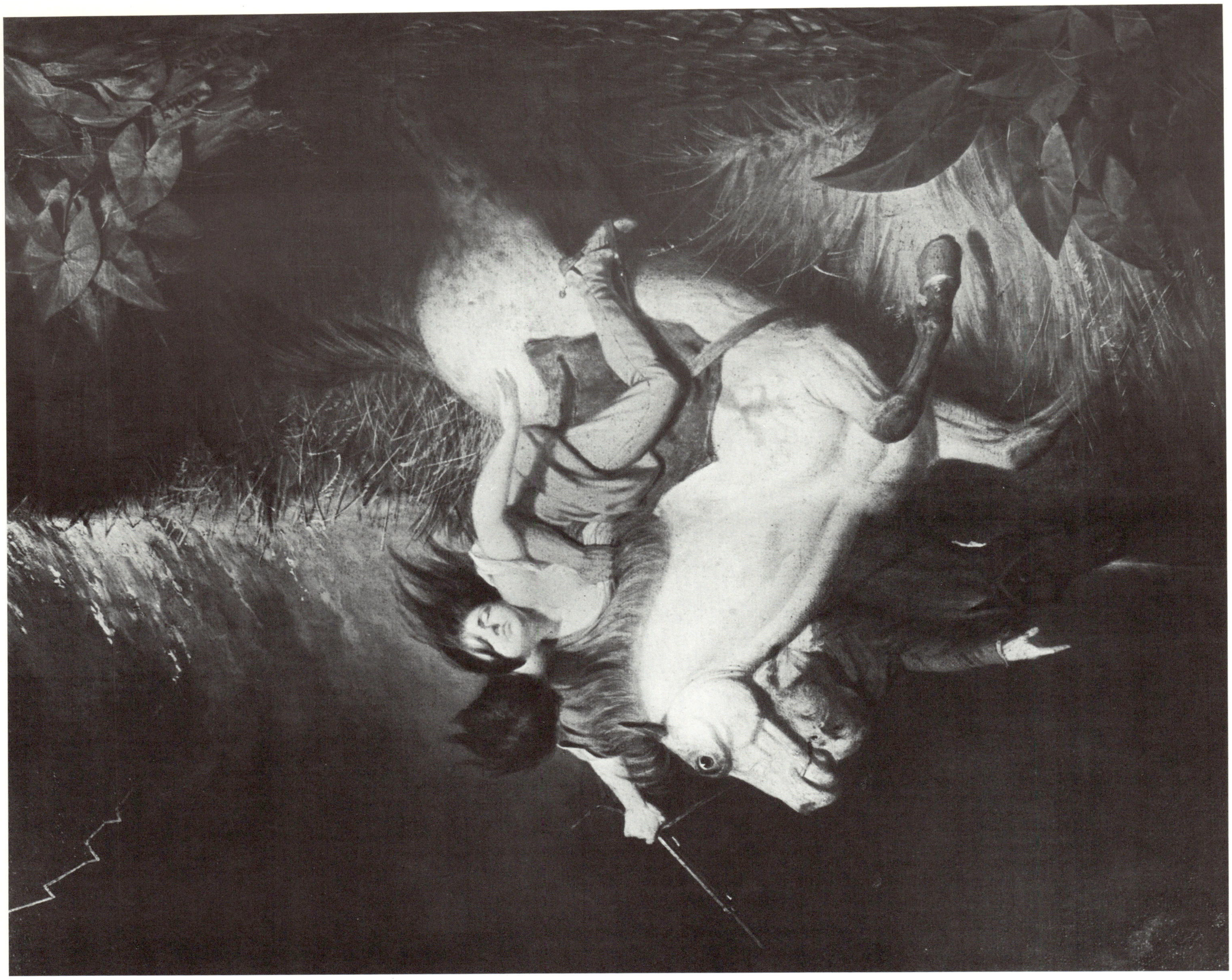

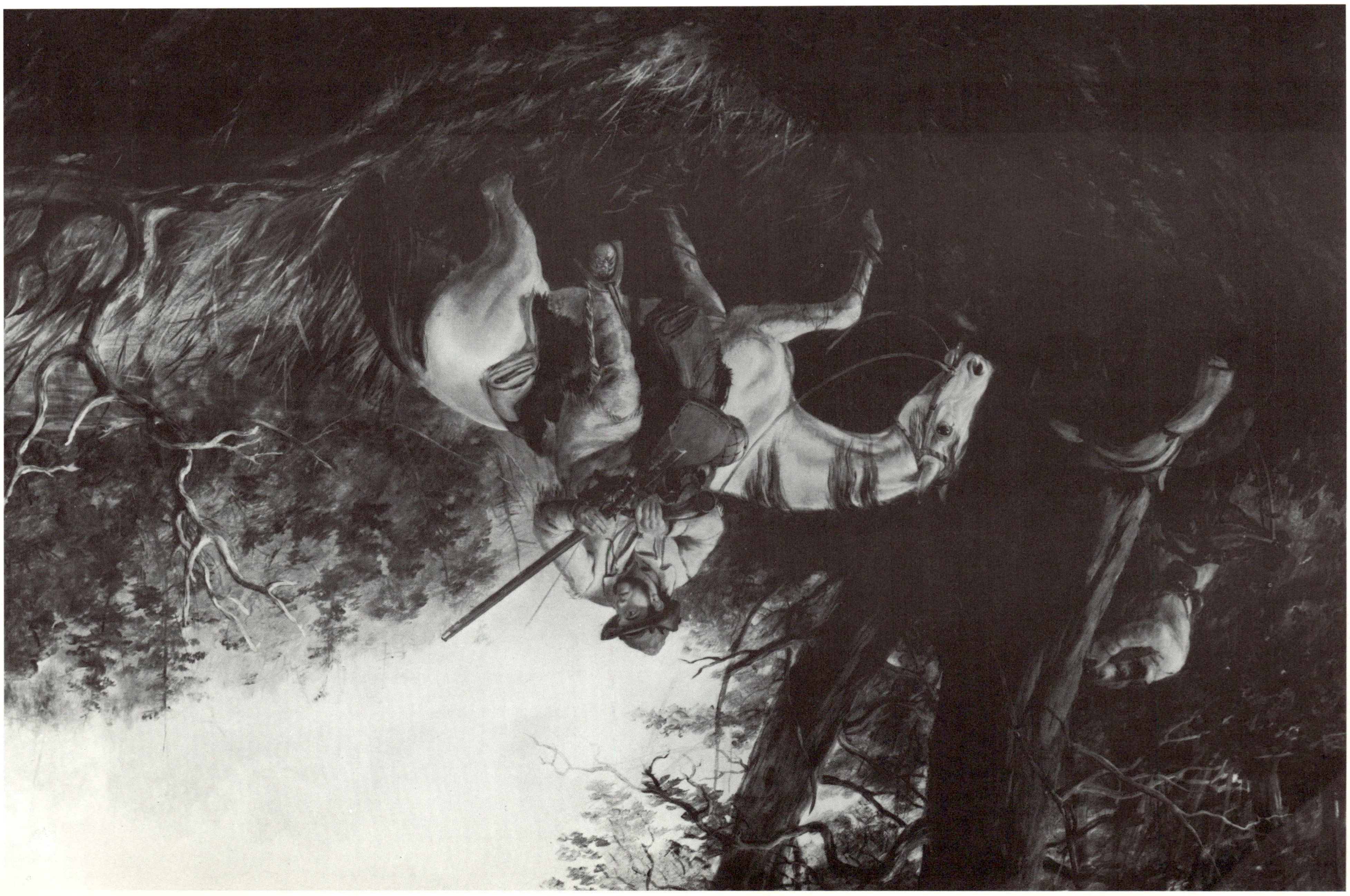

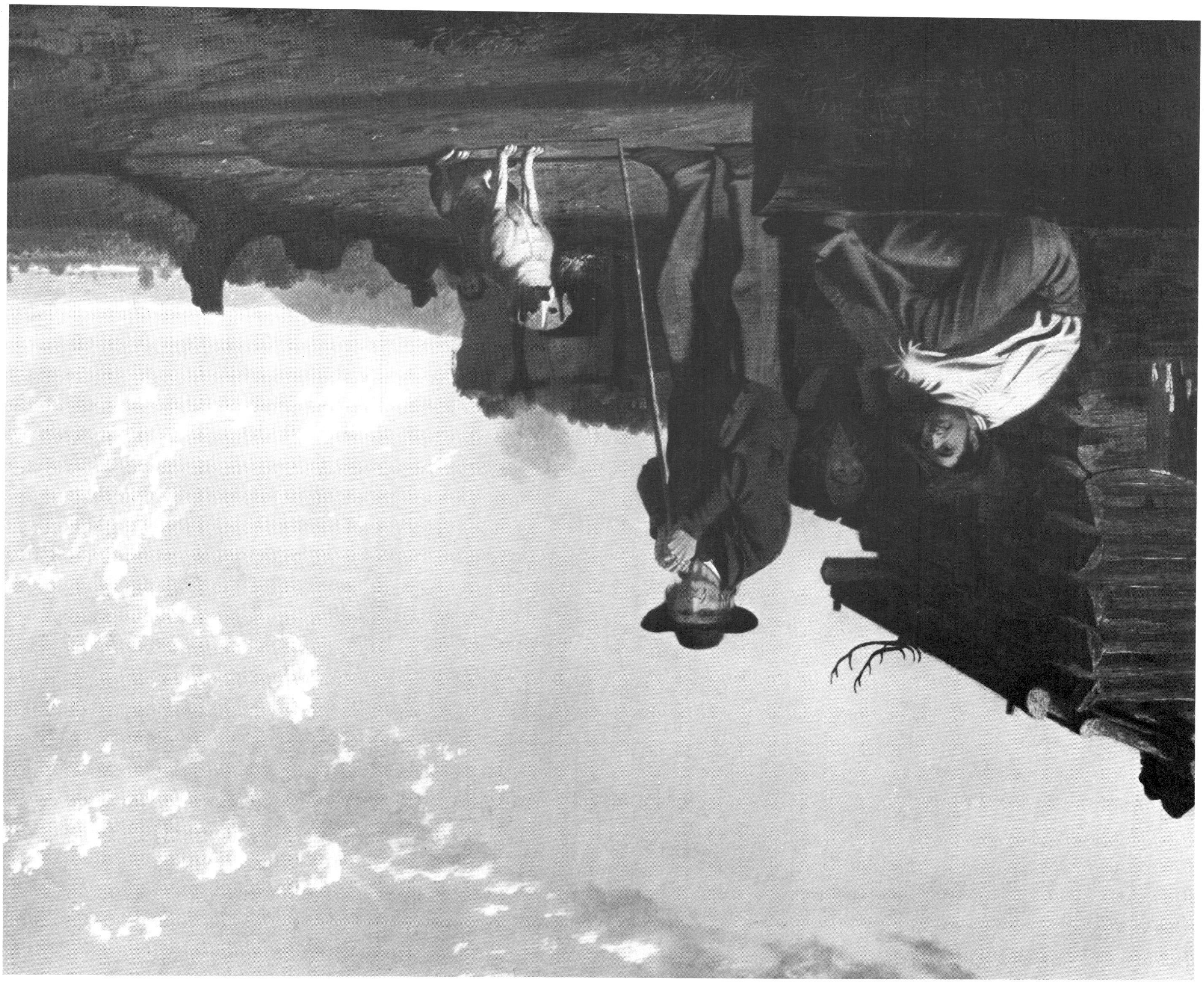

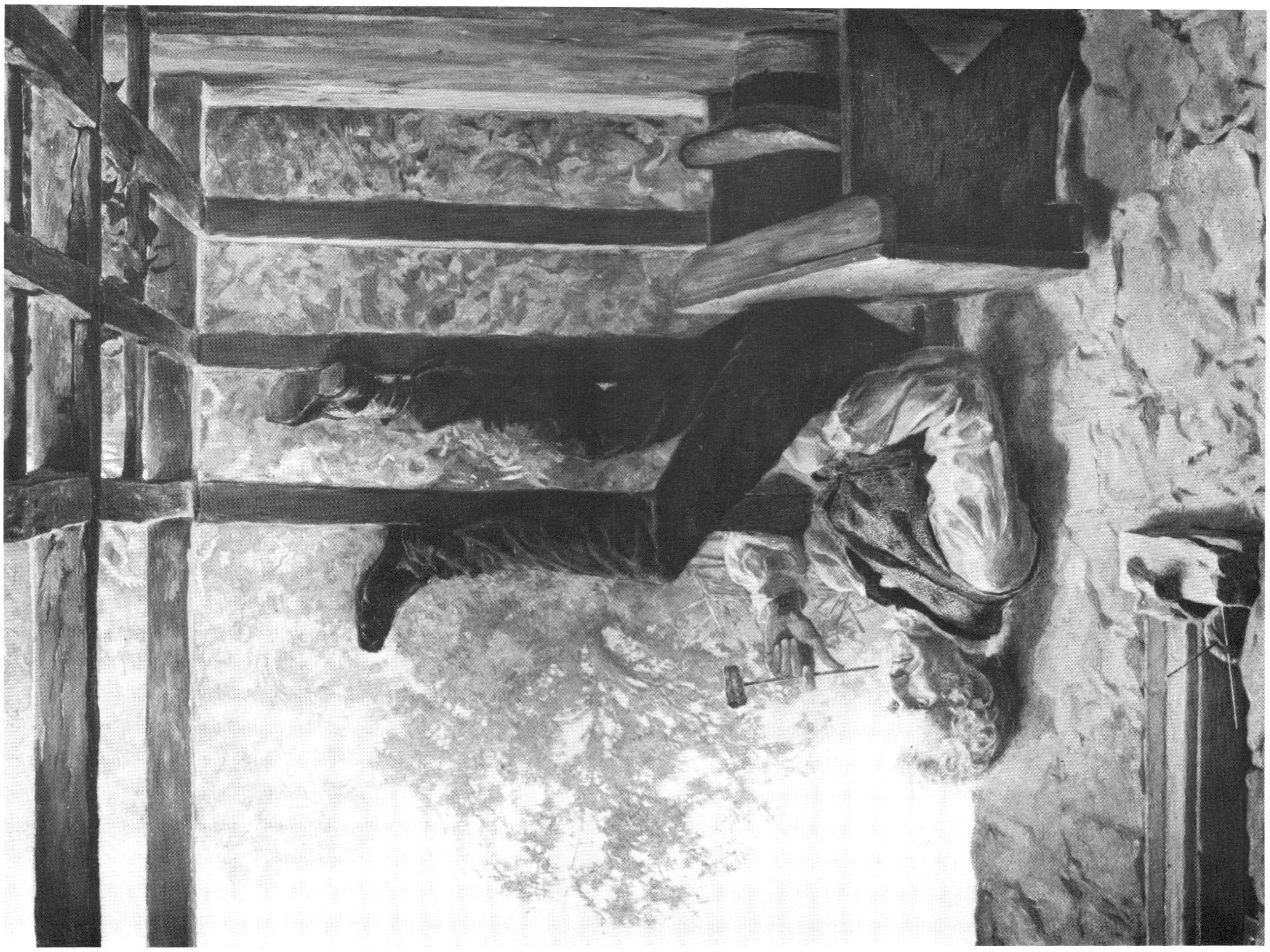

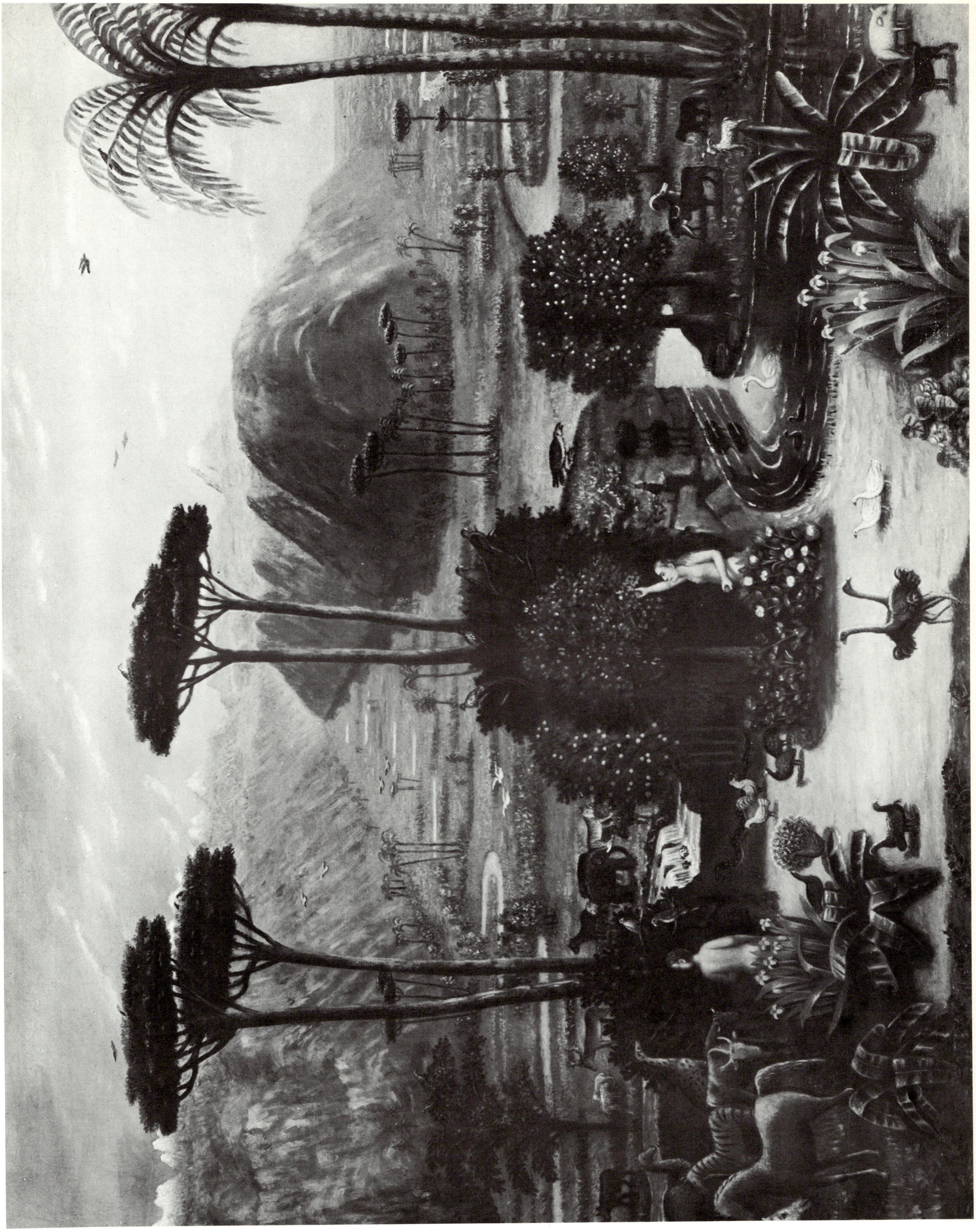

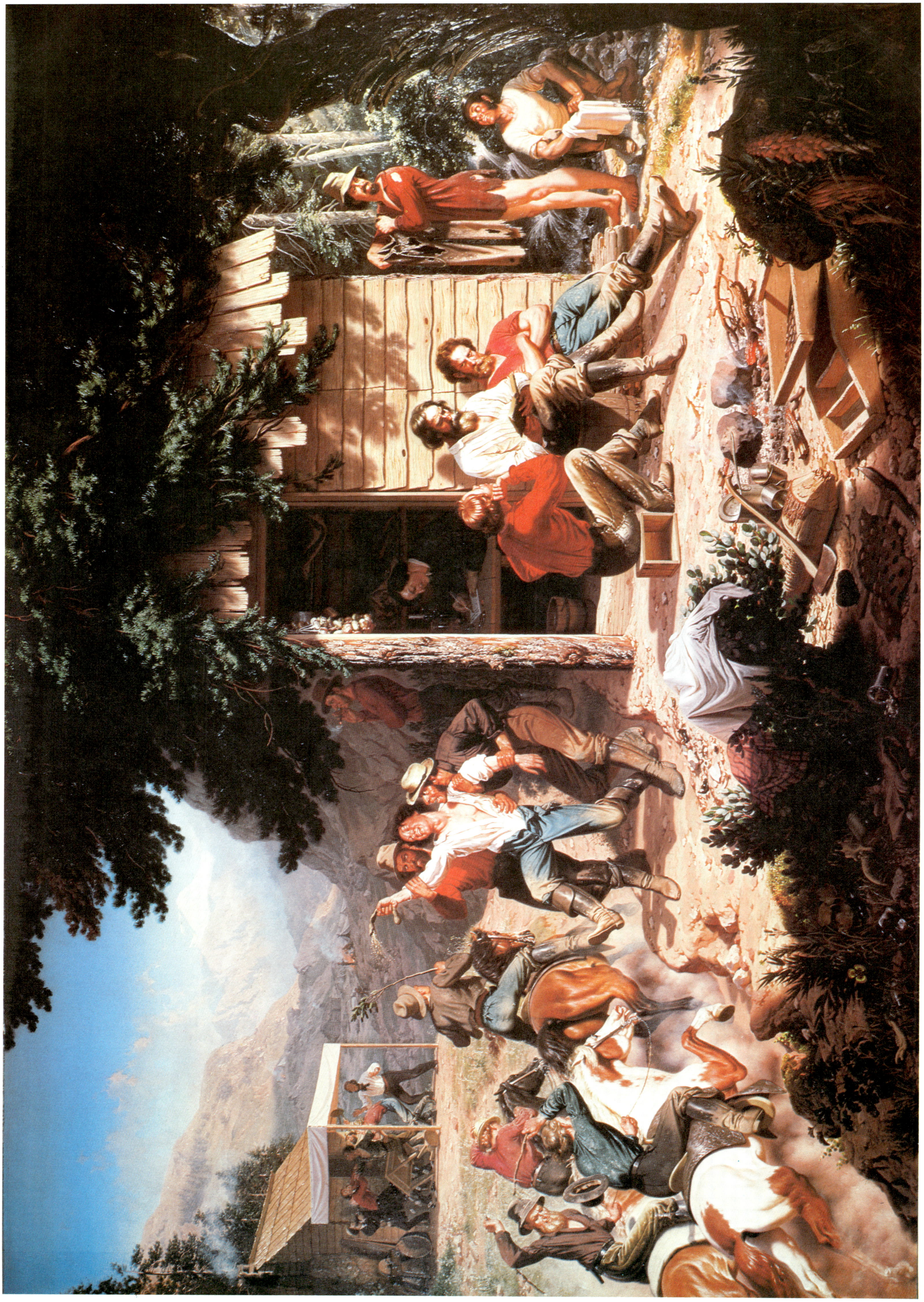

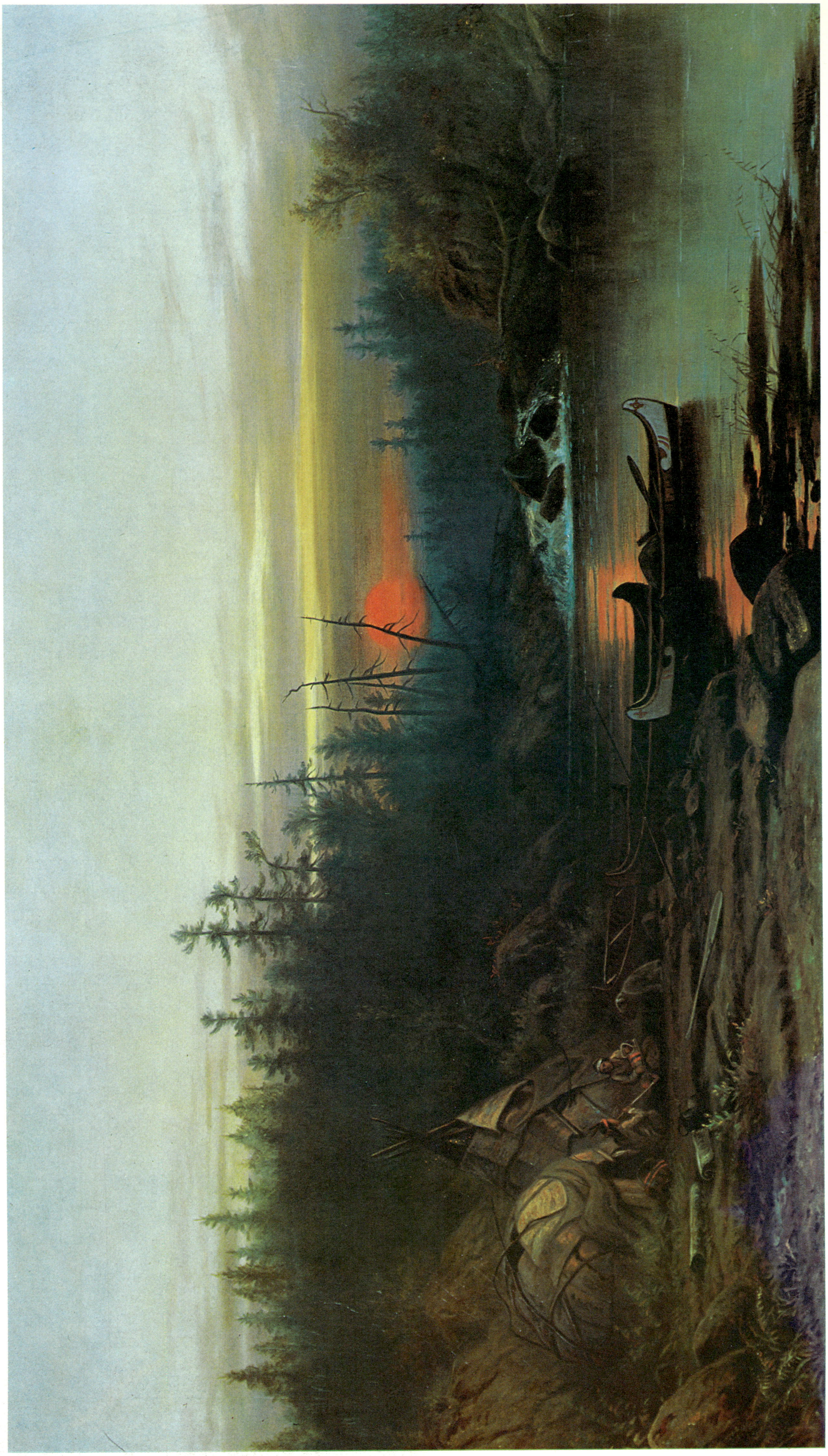

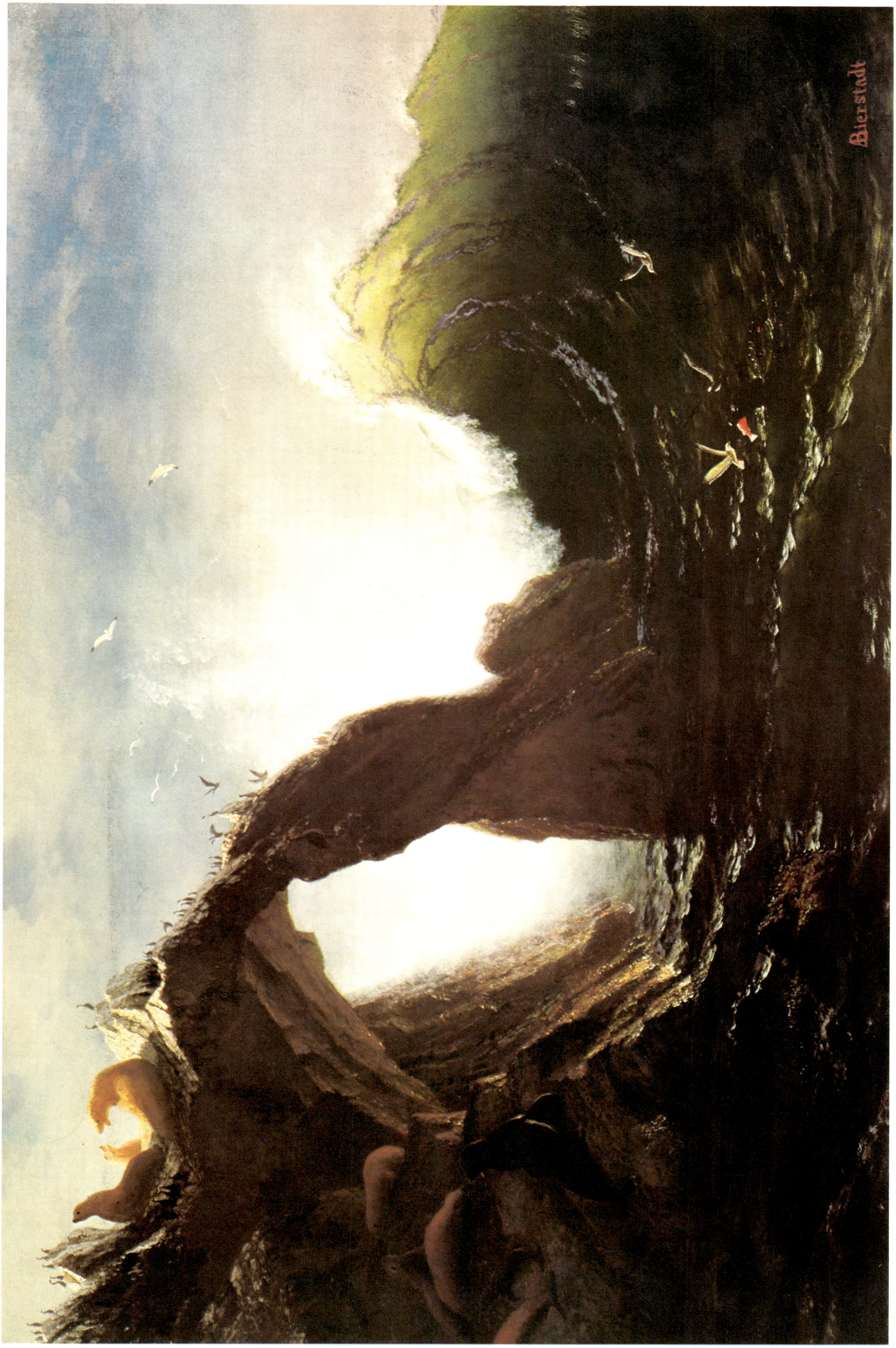
Bierstadt

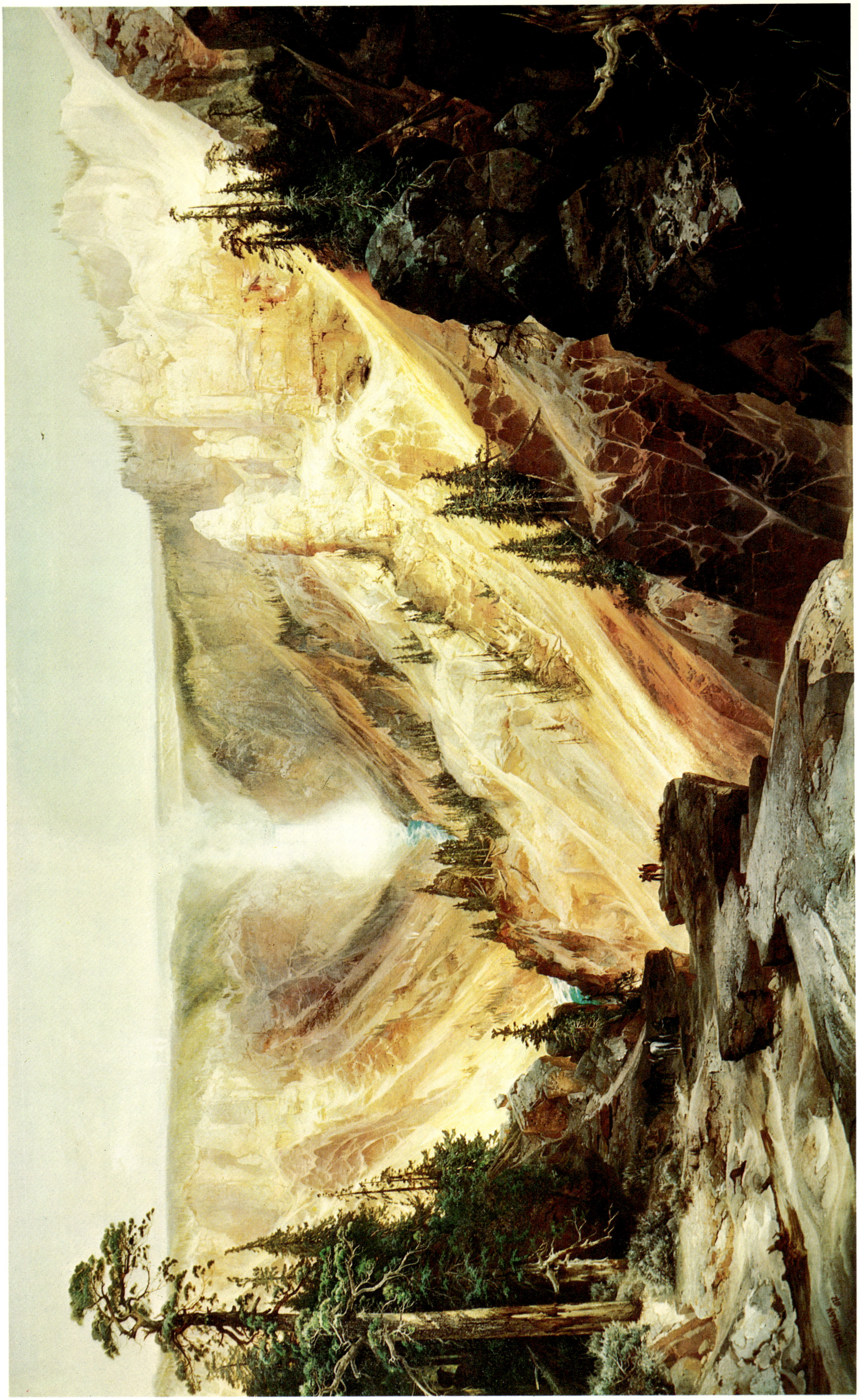

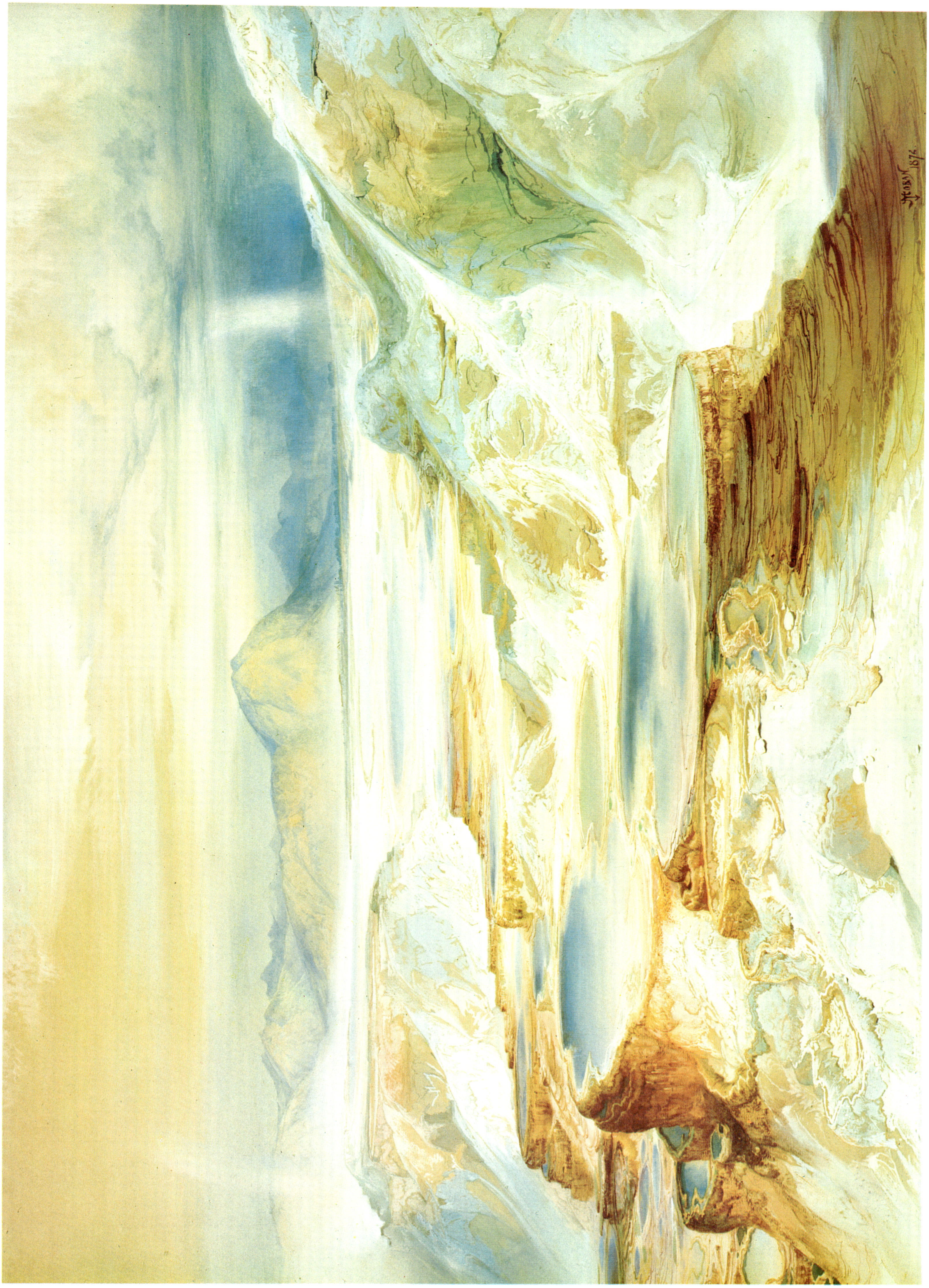

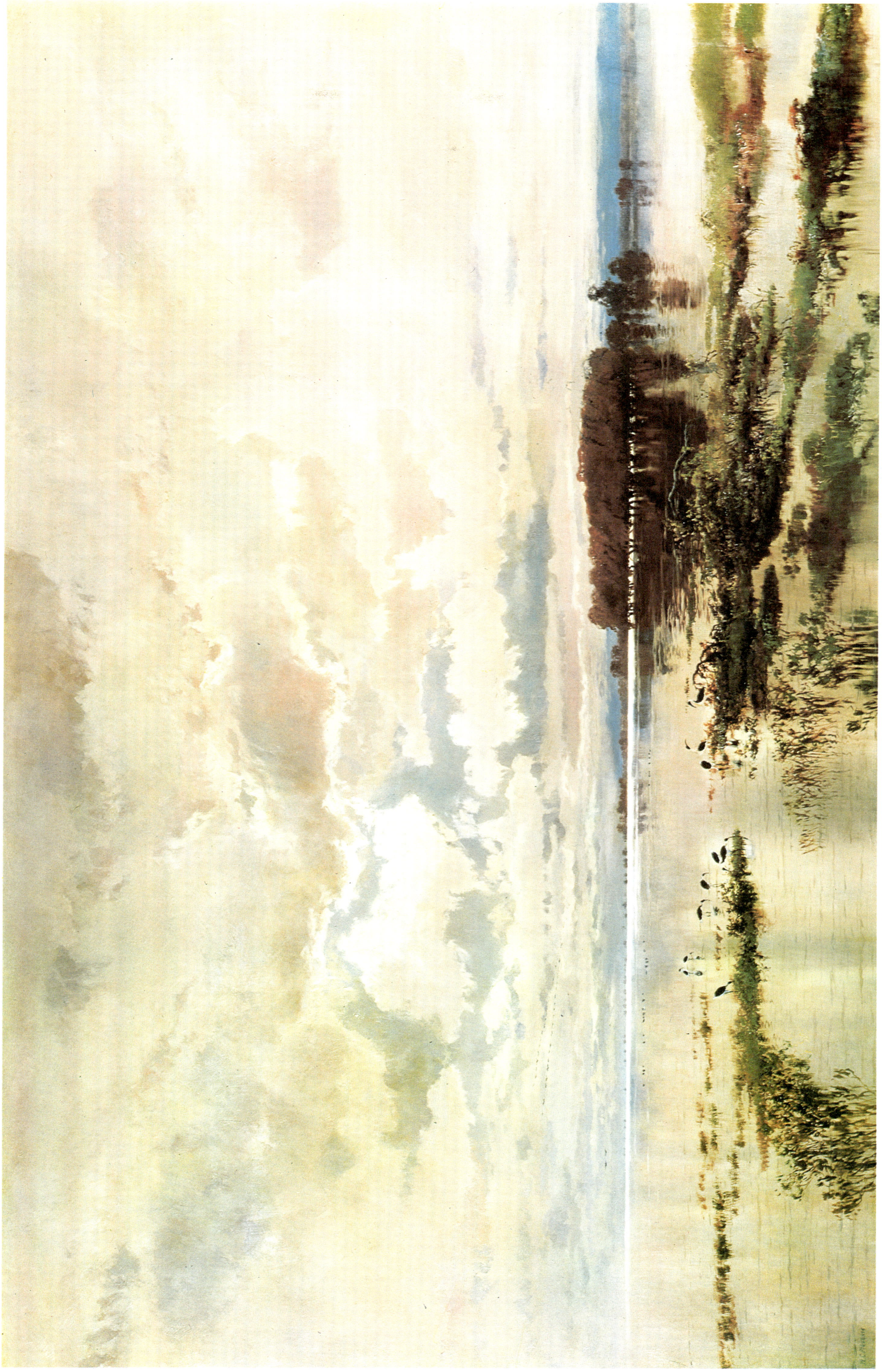

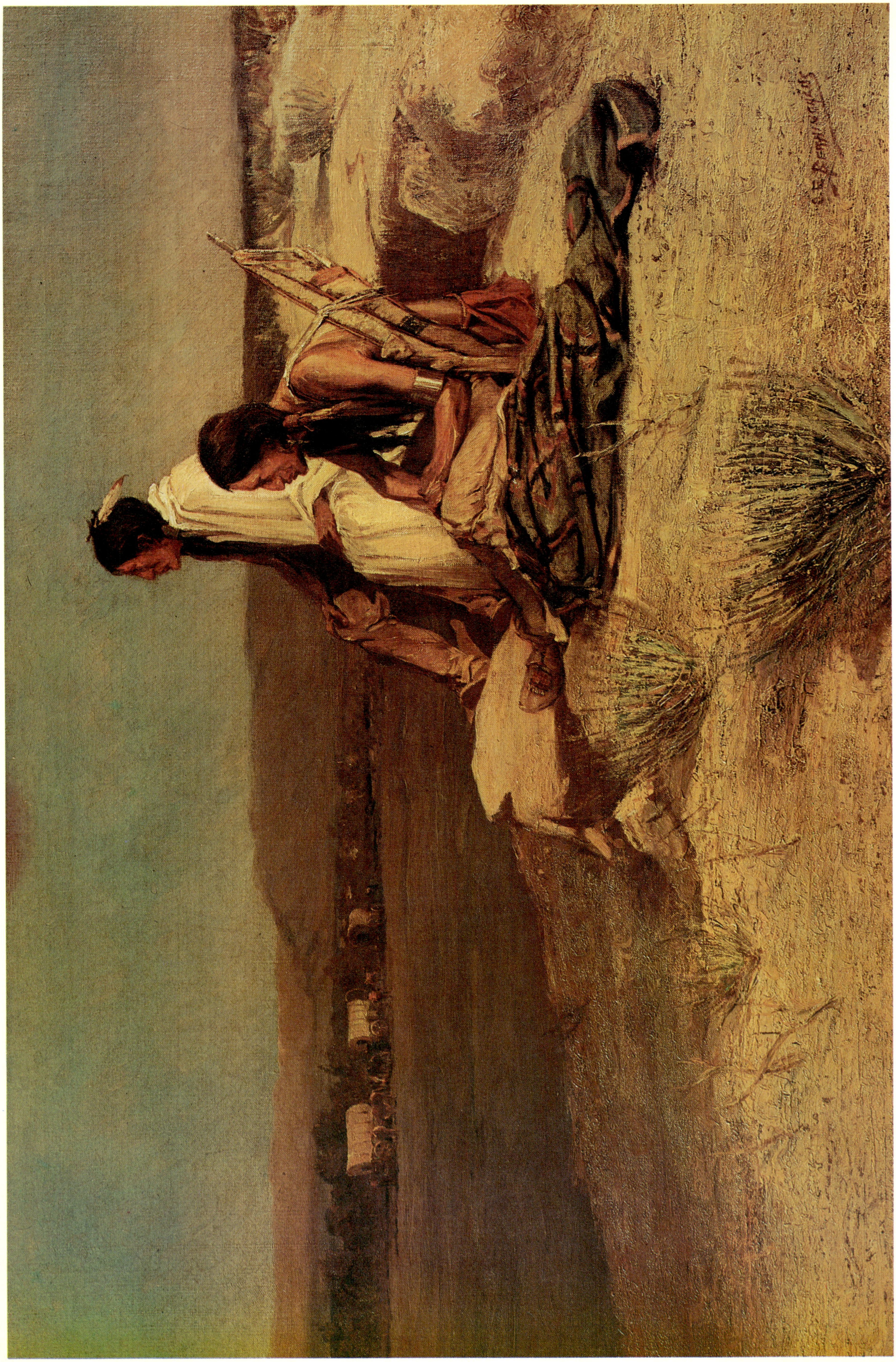

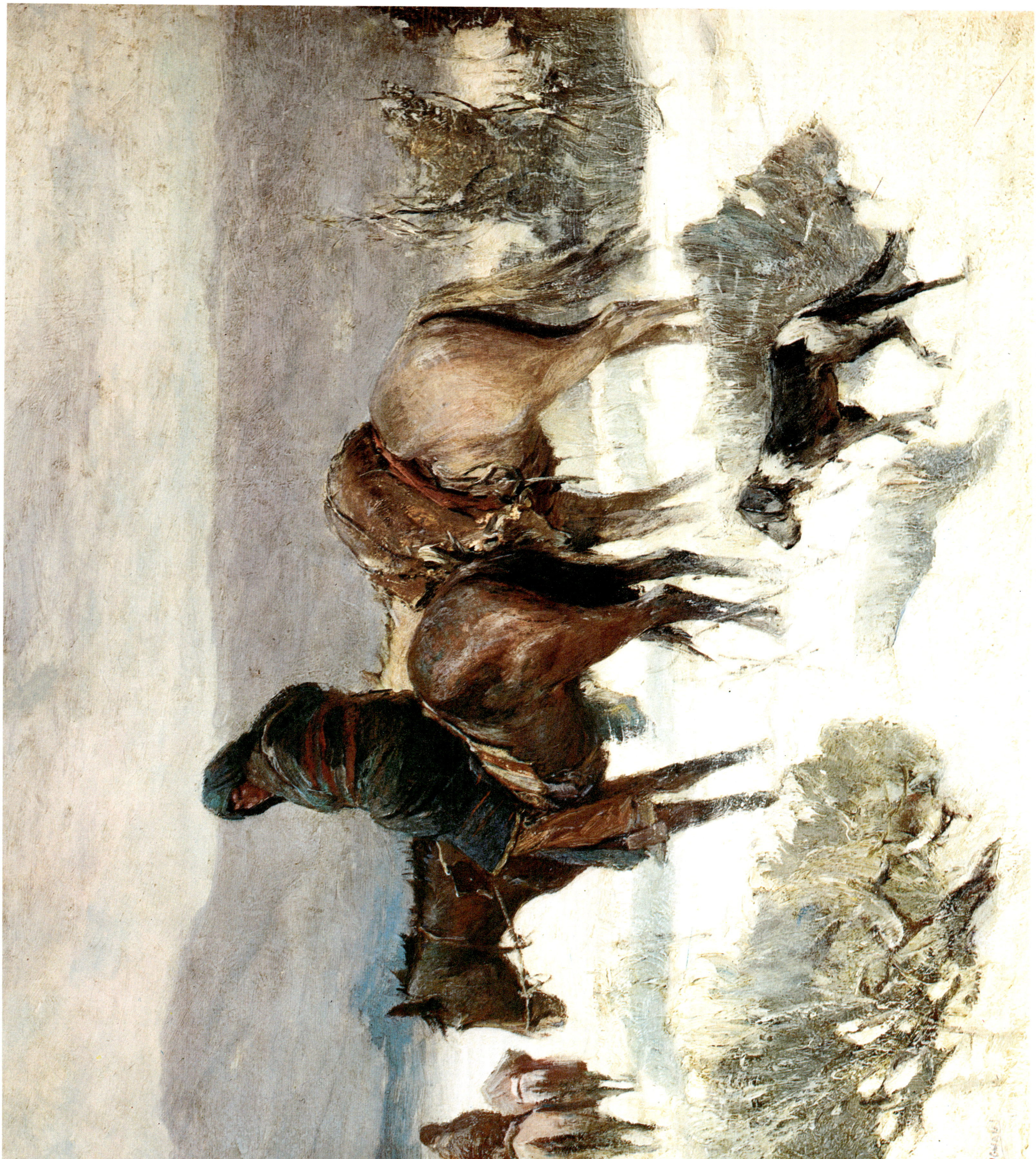

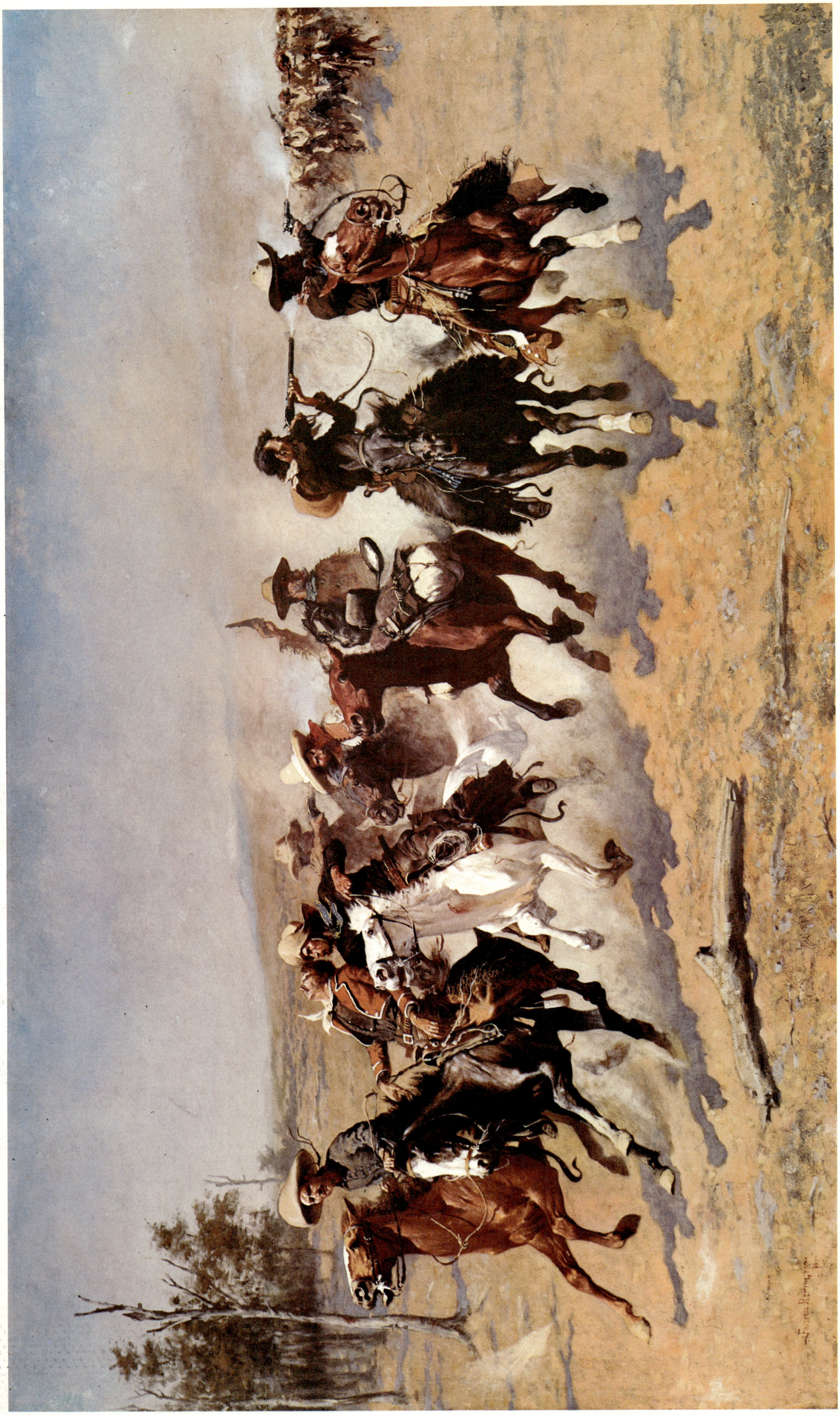

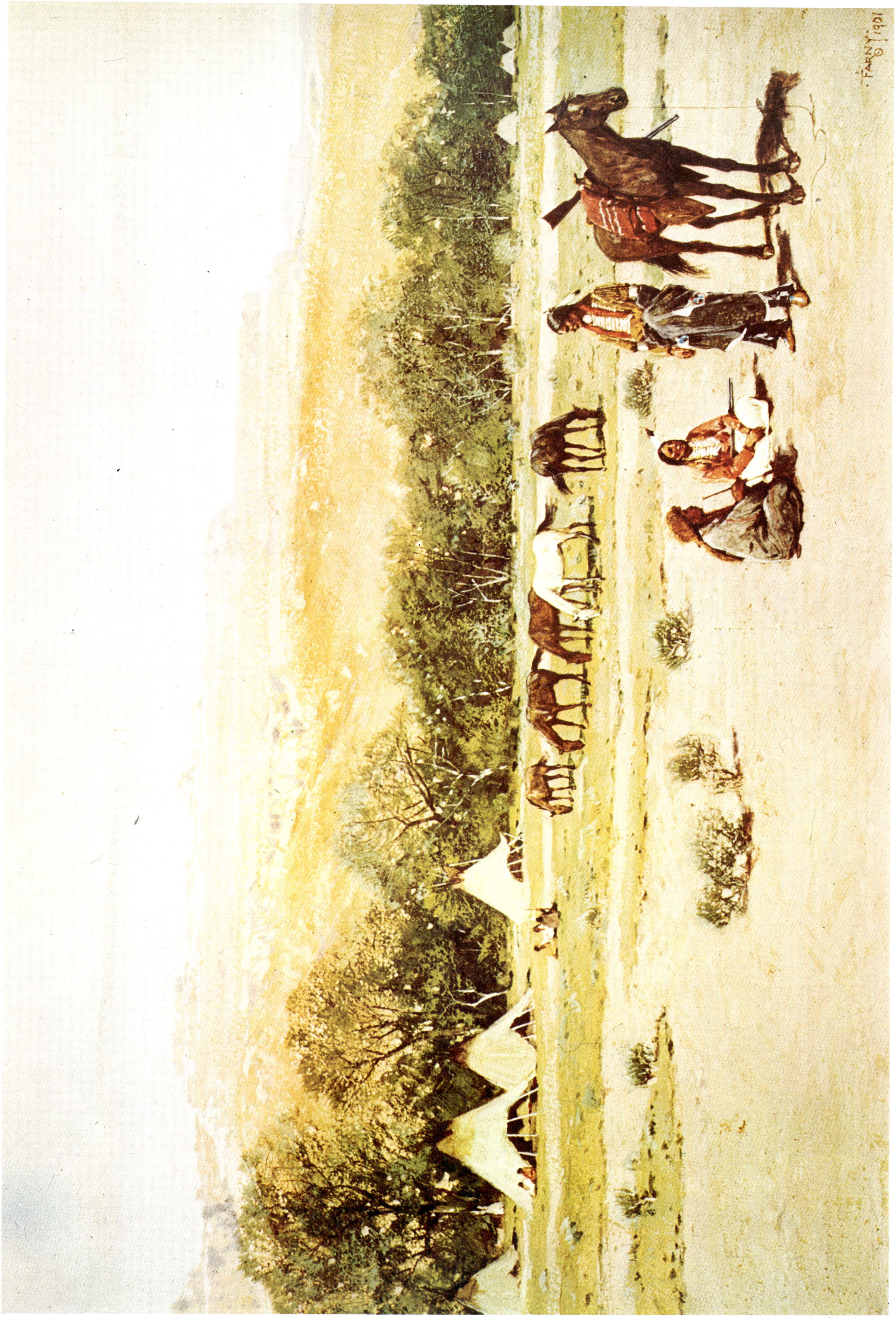
FARNY 1901

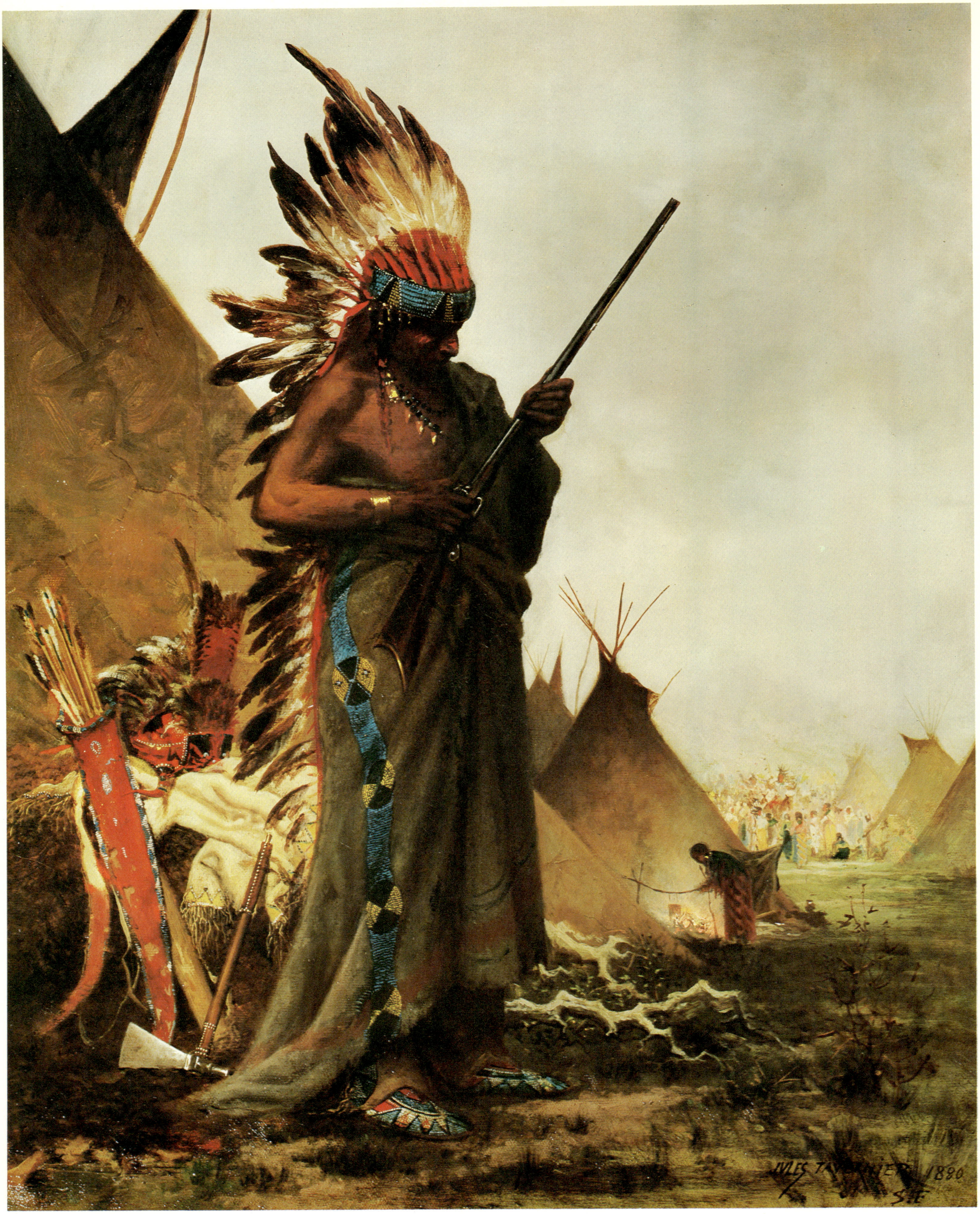
JULES TAVERNIER 1880
S.F.

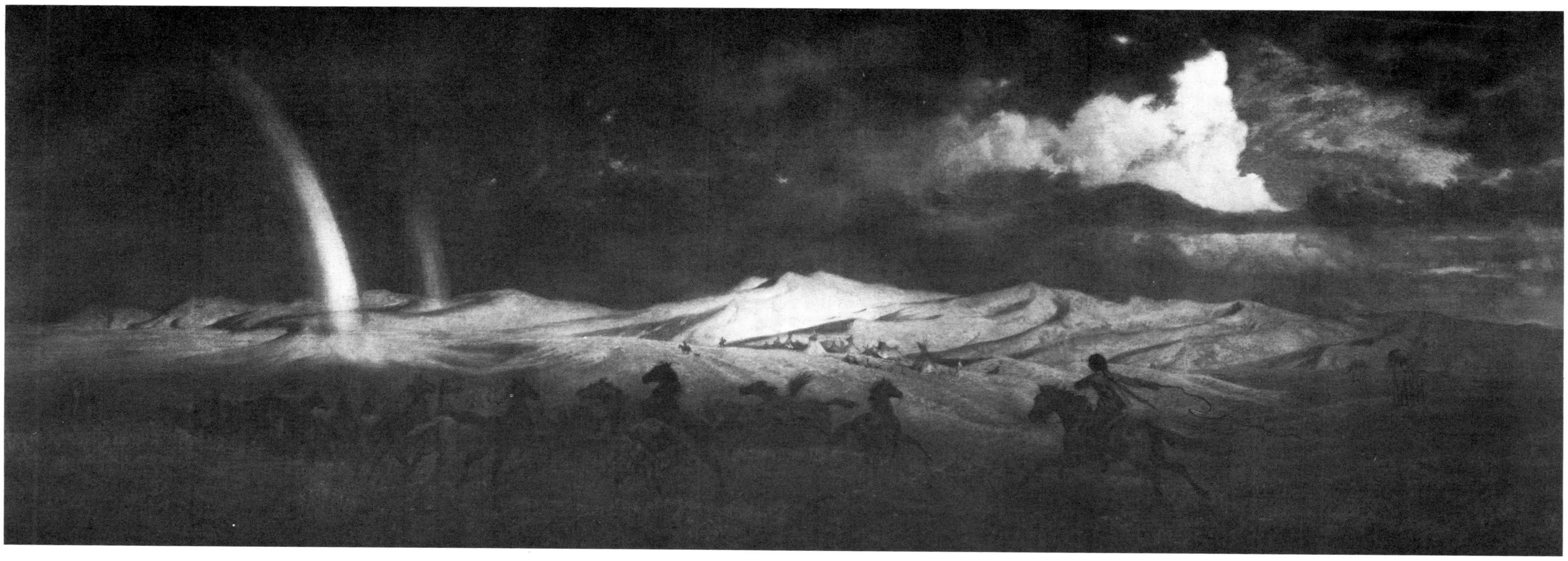

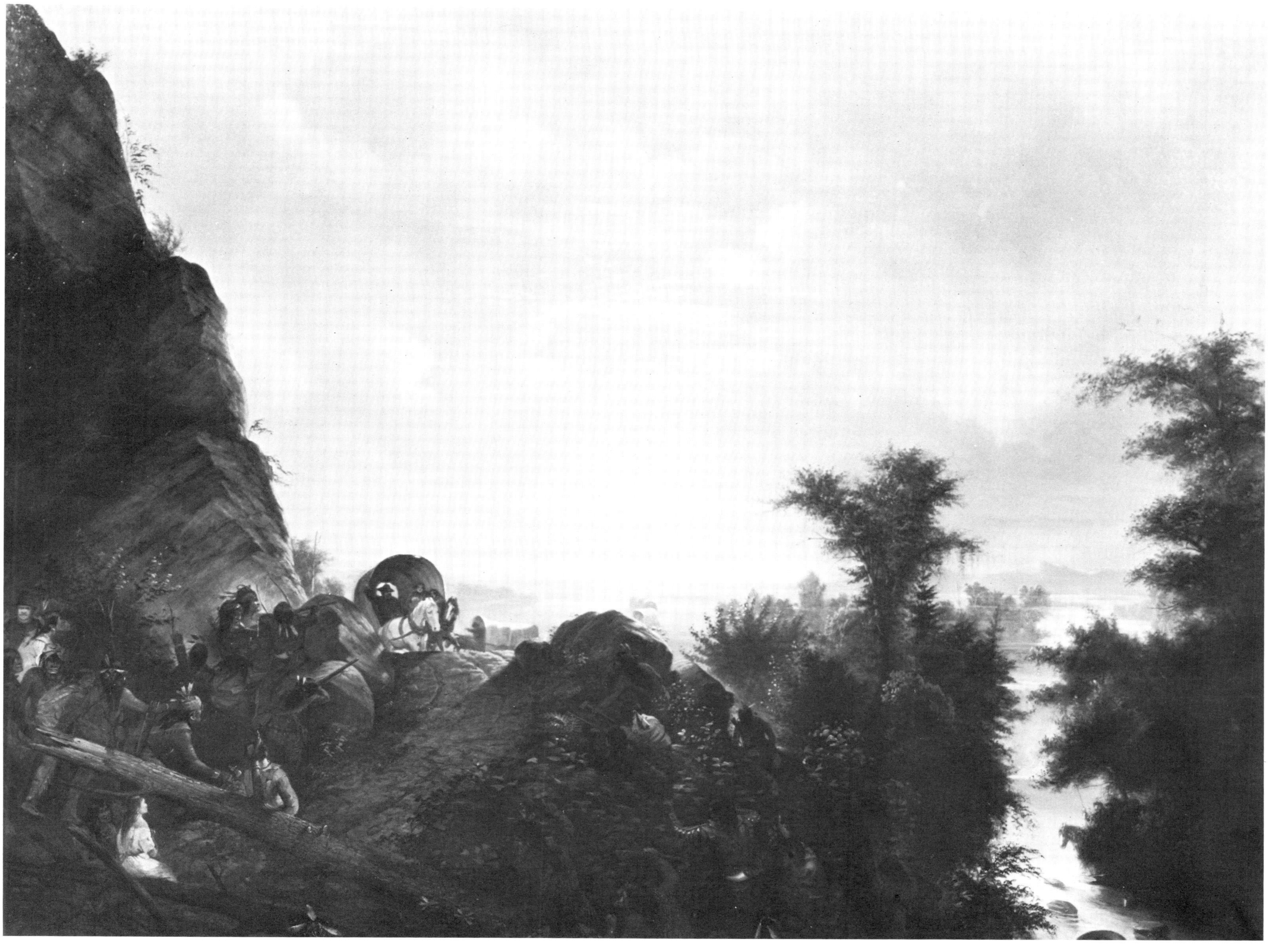

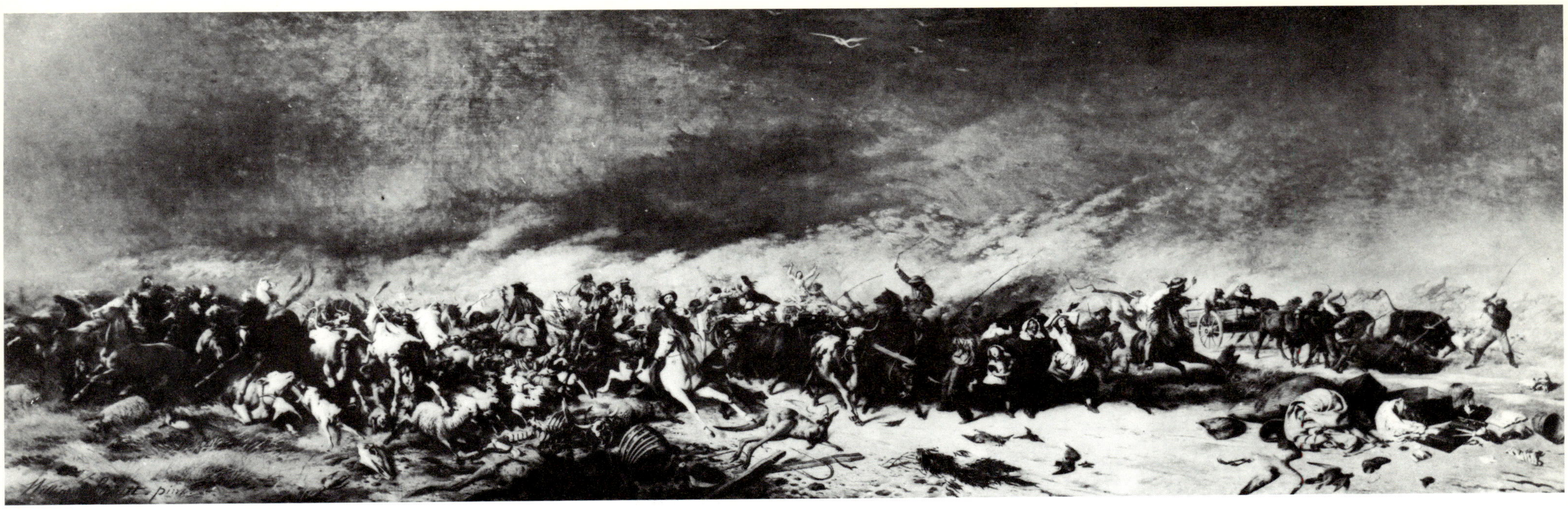

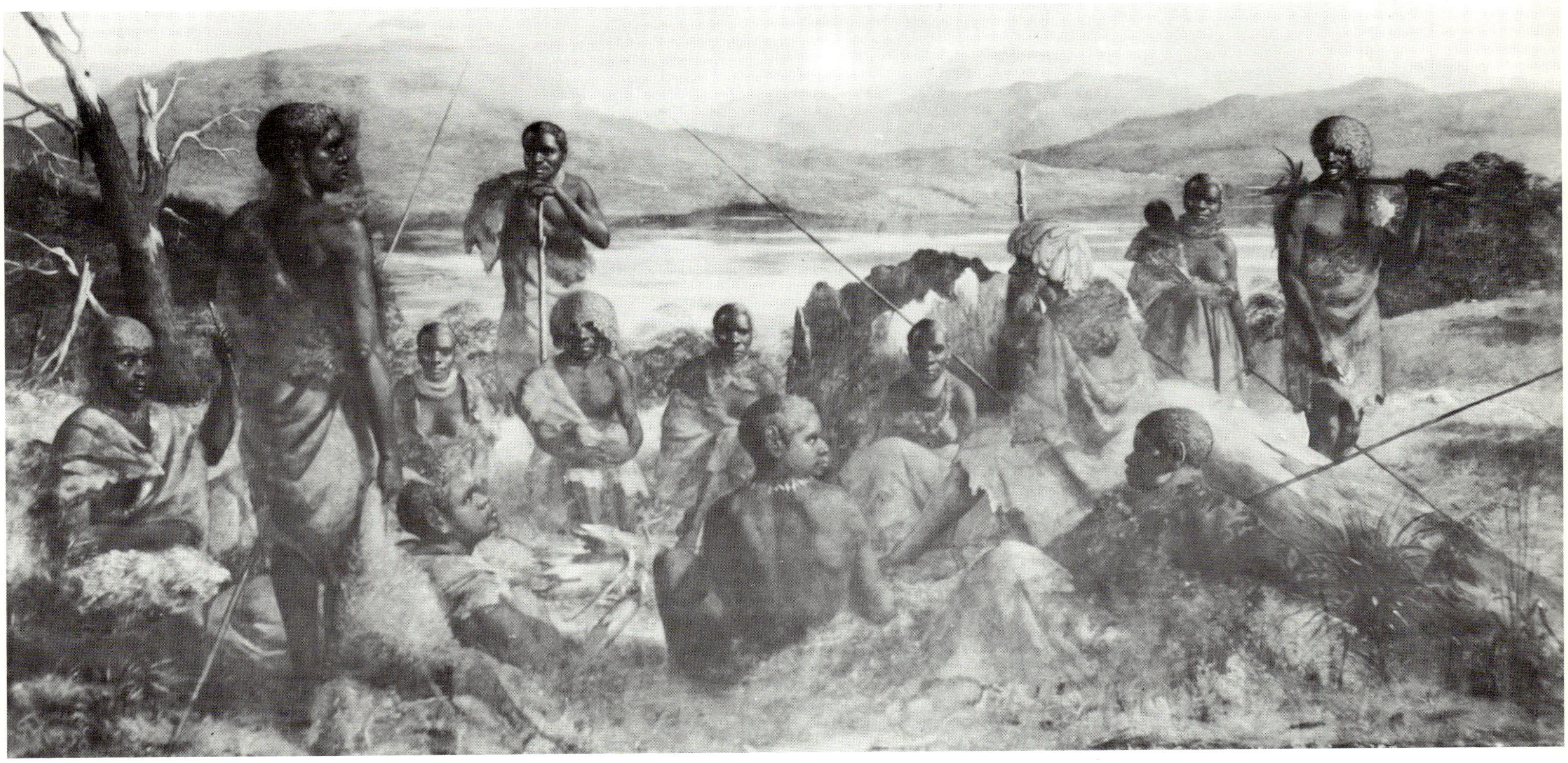

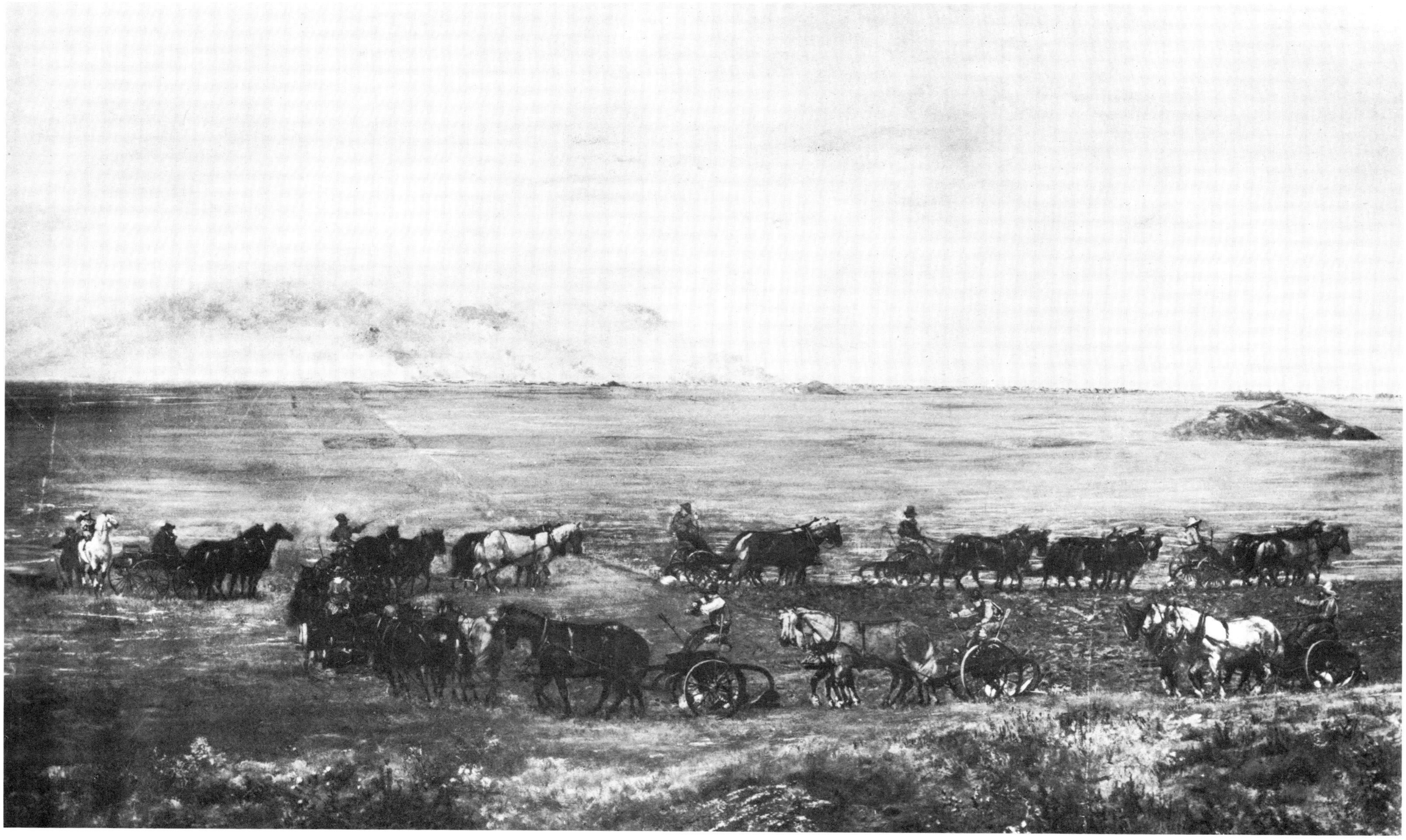

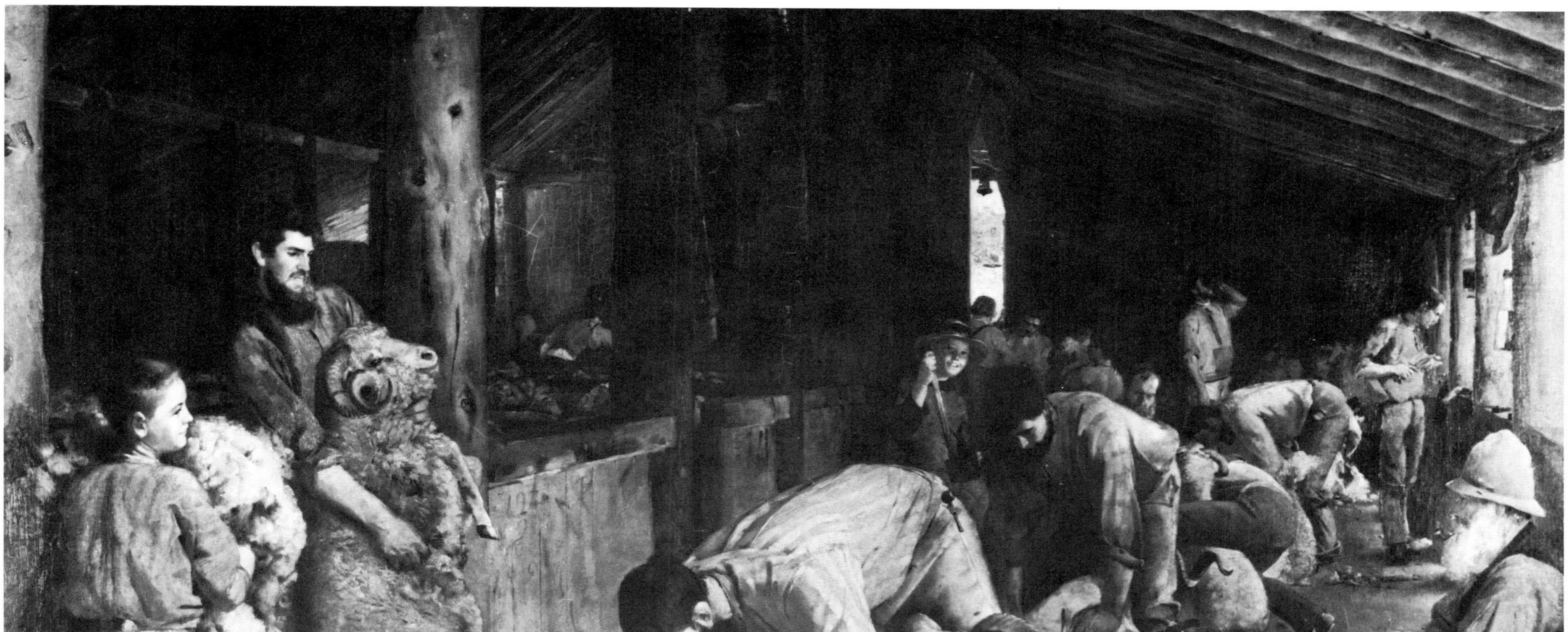
TOM ROBERTS

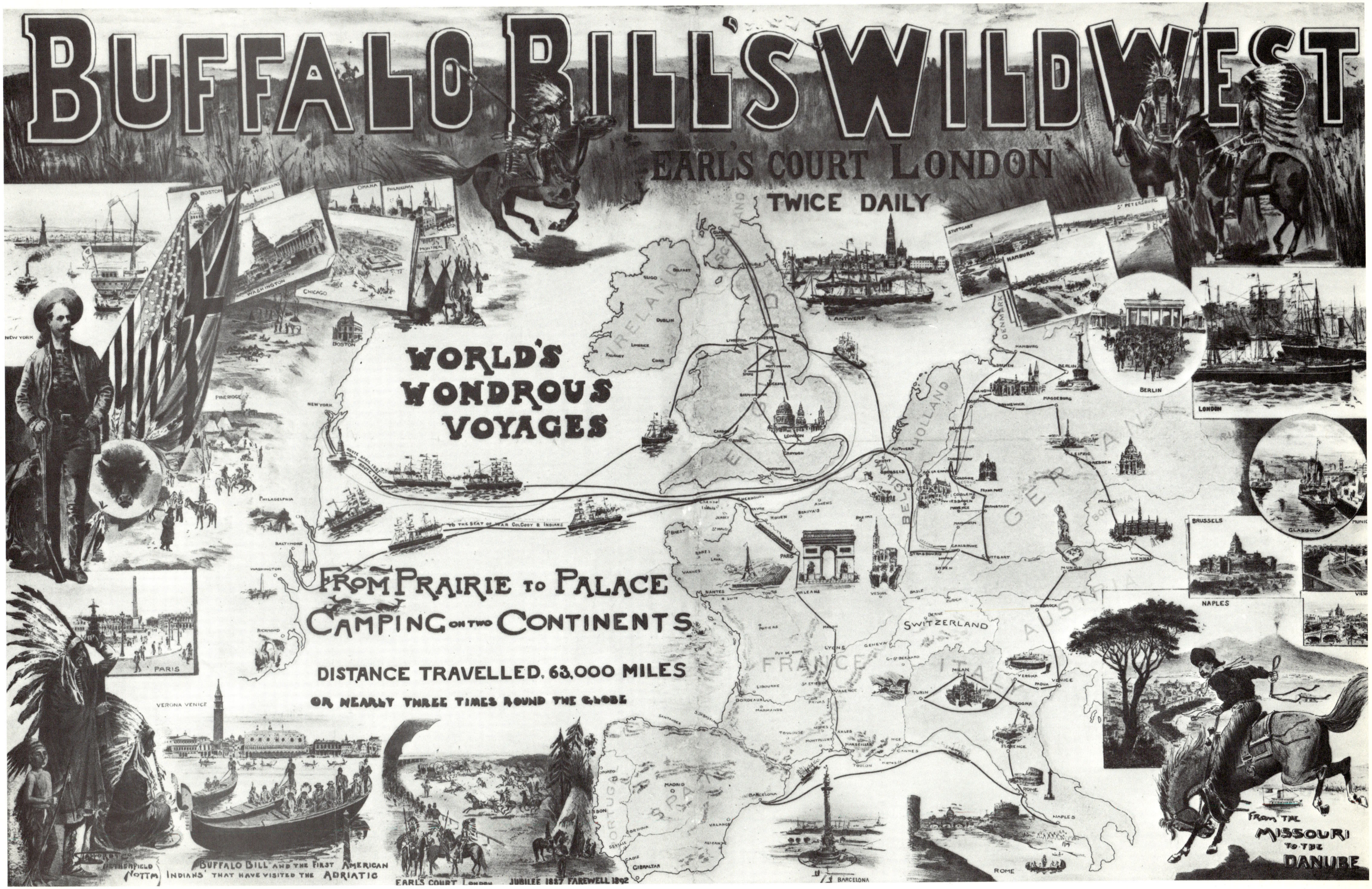
BUFFALO BILL'S WILD WEST
EARL'S COURT LONDON
TWICE DAILY
WORLD'S WONDROUS VOYAGES
FROM PRAIRIE TO PALACE
CAMPING ON TWO CONTINENTS
DISTANCE TRAVELLED, 63,000 MILES
OR NEARLY THREE TIMES ROUND THE GLOBE
BUFFALO BILL AND THE FIRST AMERICAN INDIANS THAT HAVE VISITED THE ADRIATIC
EARLS COURT LONDON JUBILEE 1887 FAREWELL 1892
FROM THE MISSOURI TO THE DANUBE

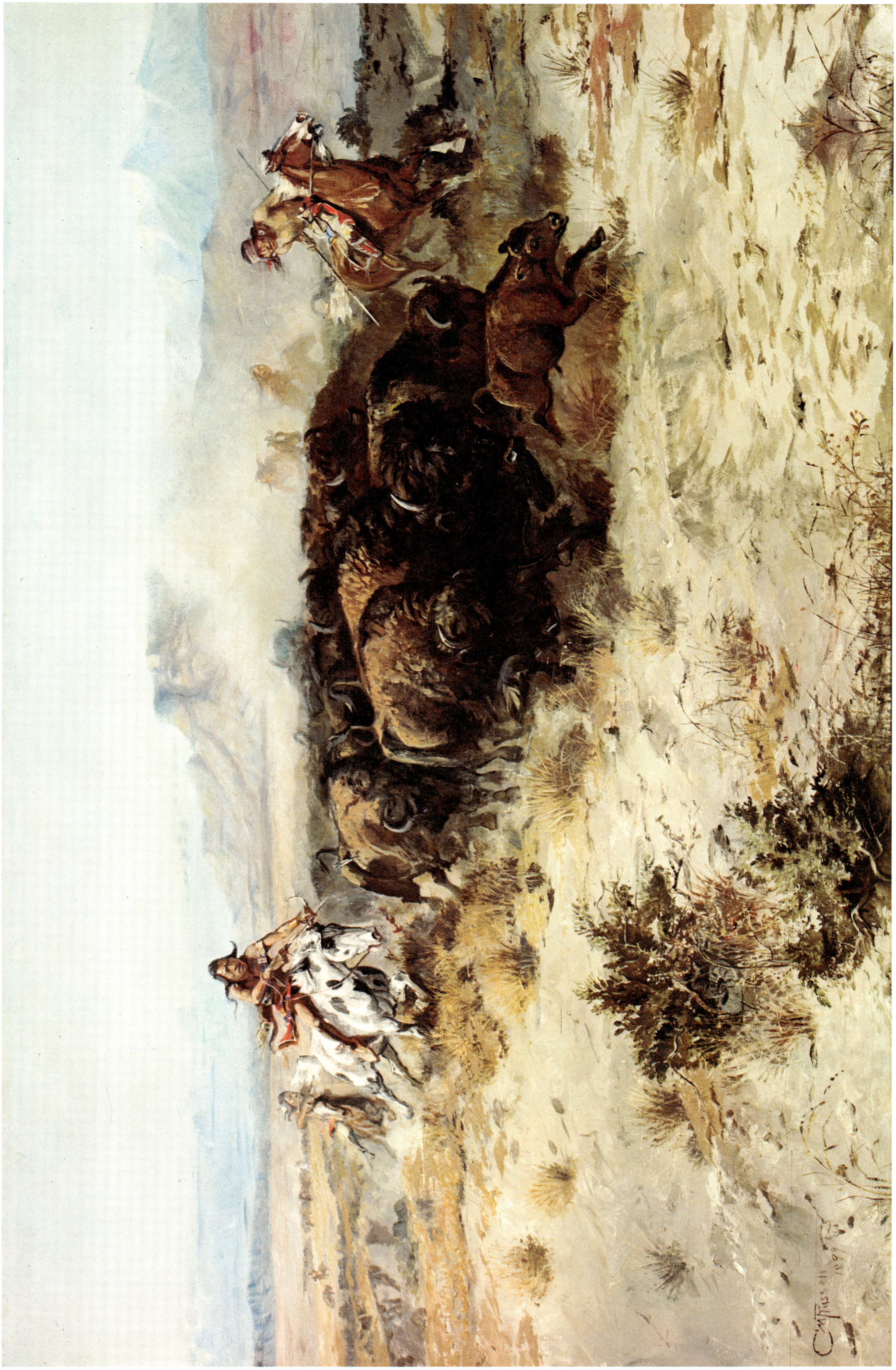

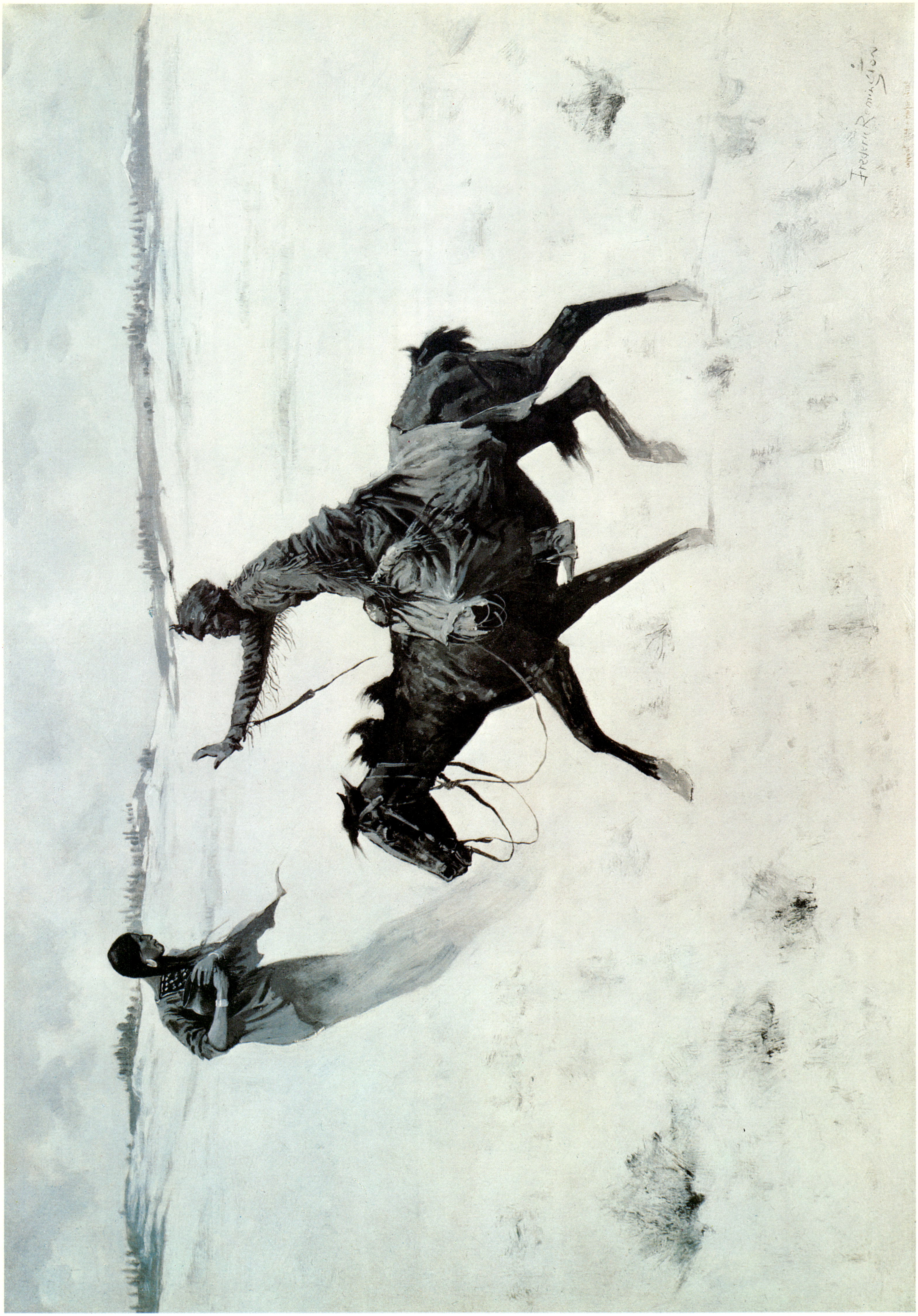
Frederic Remington

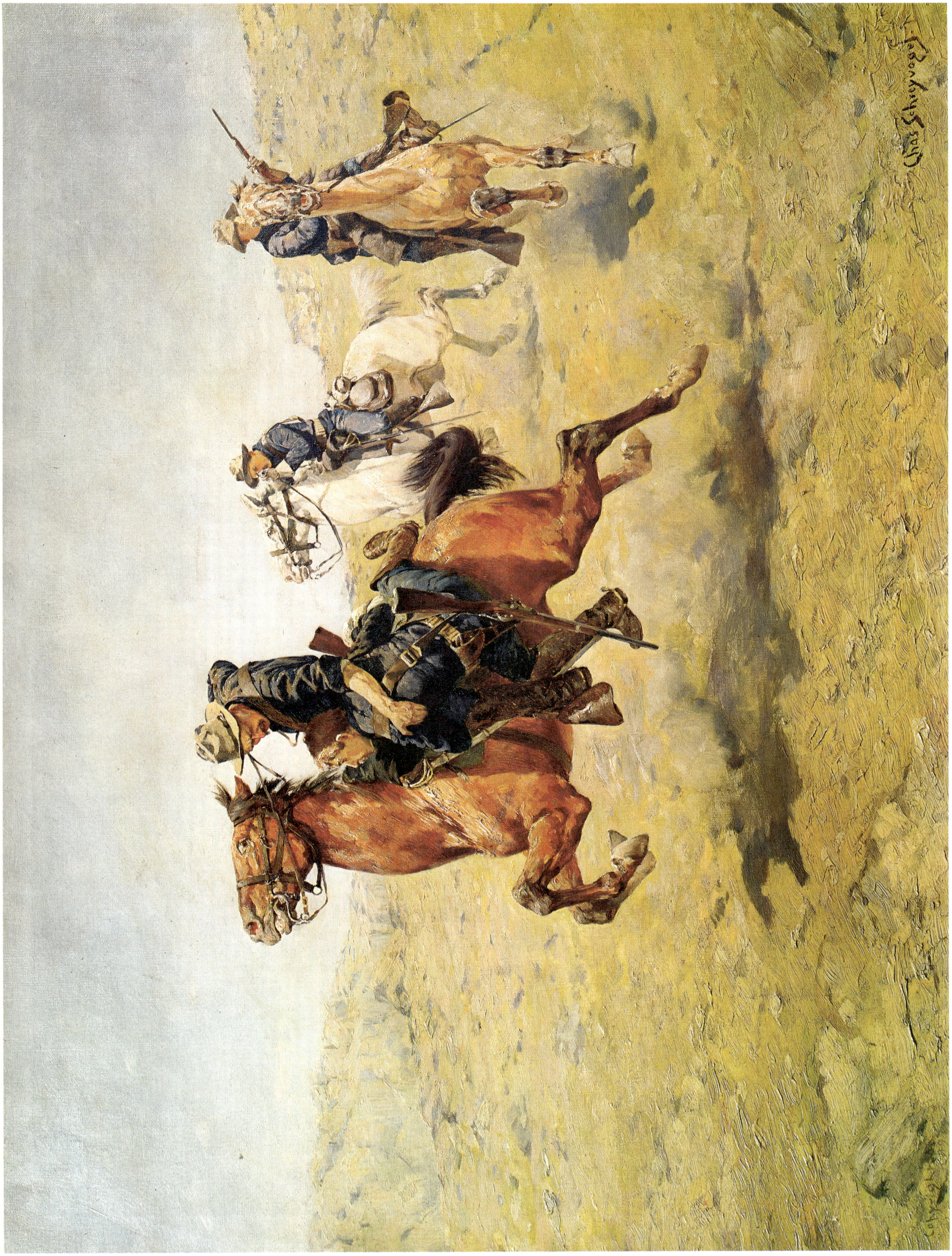

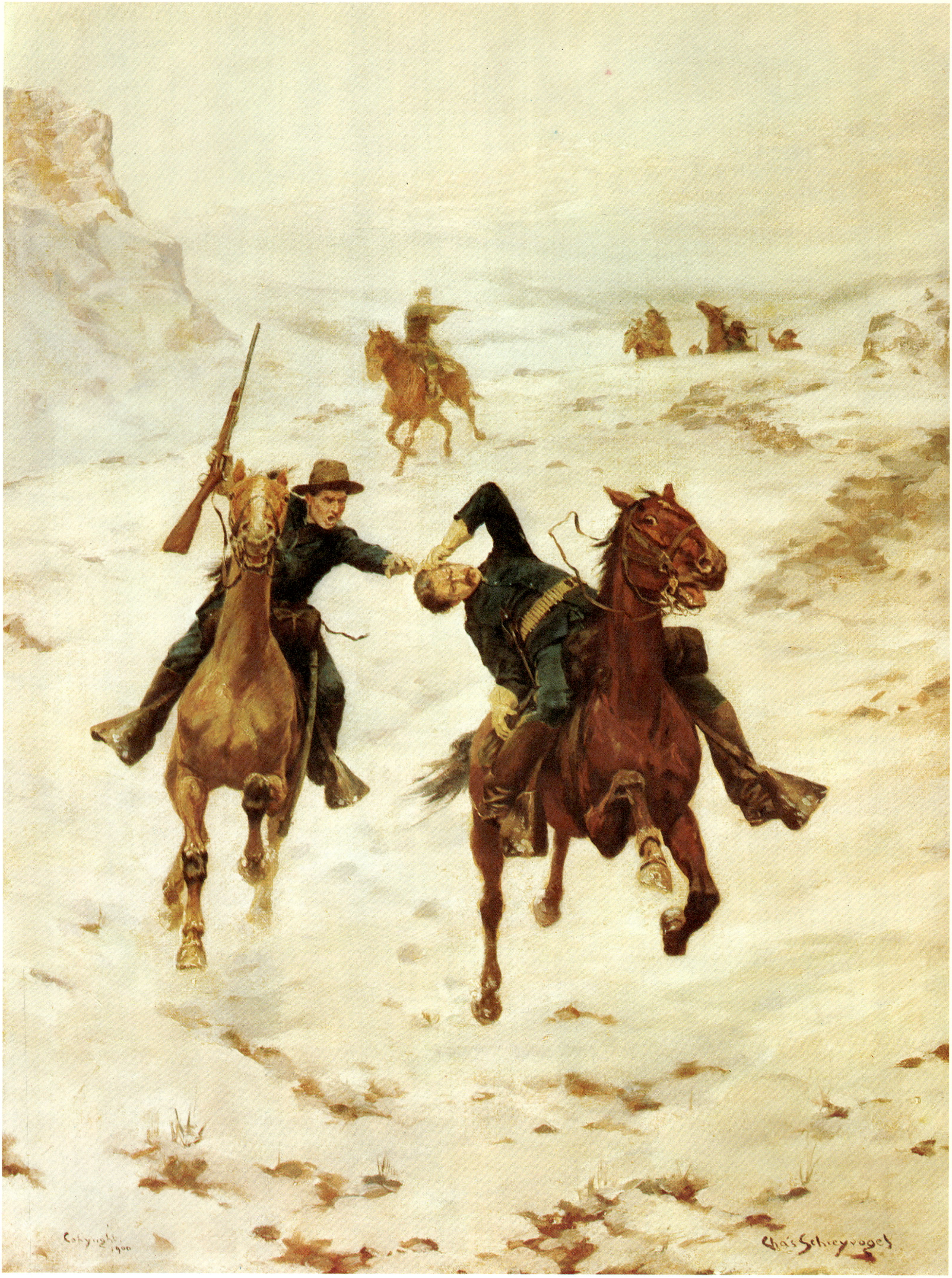

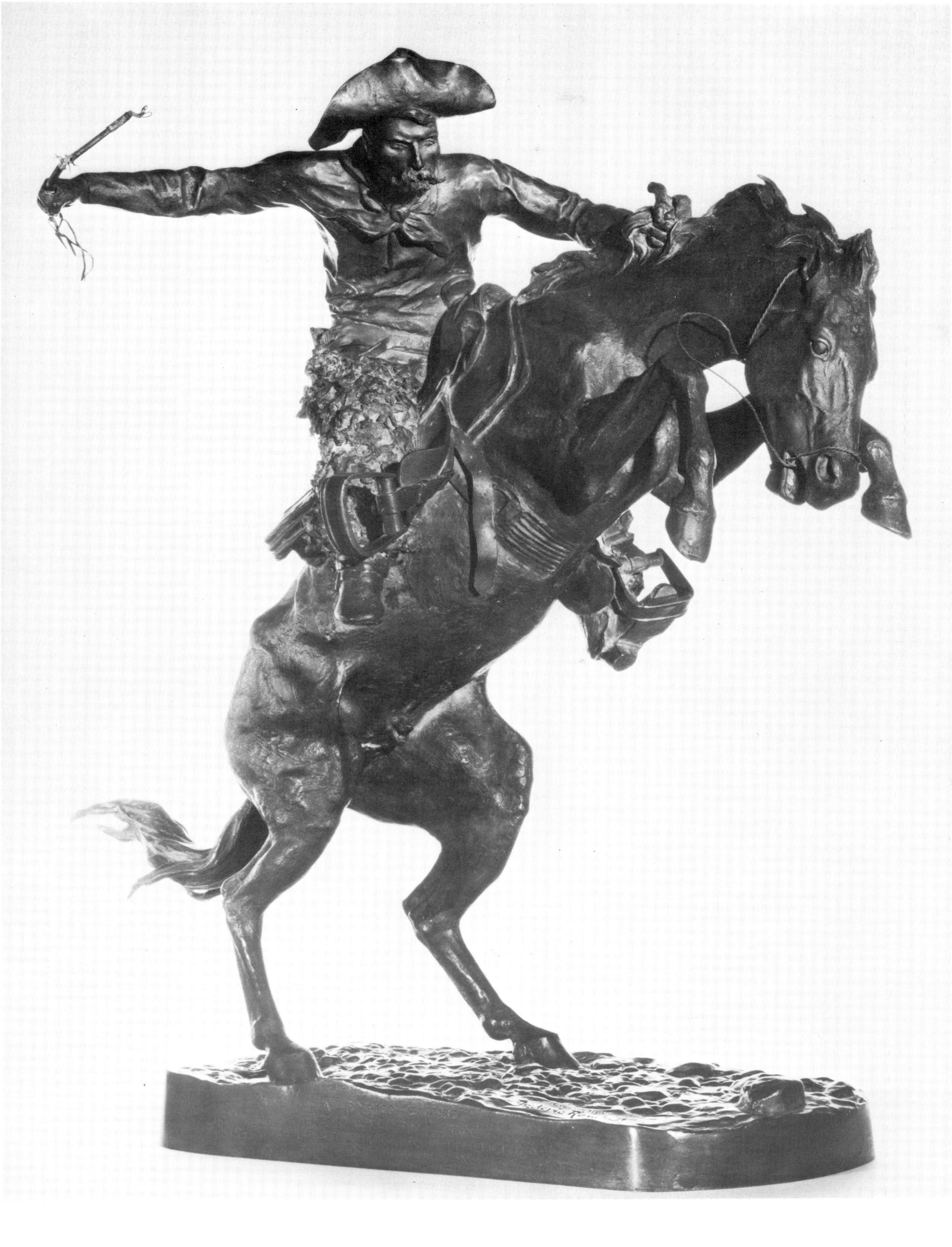

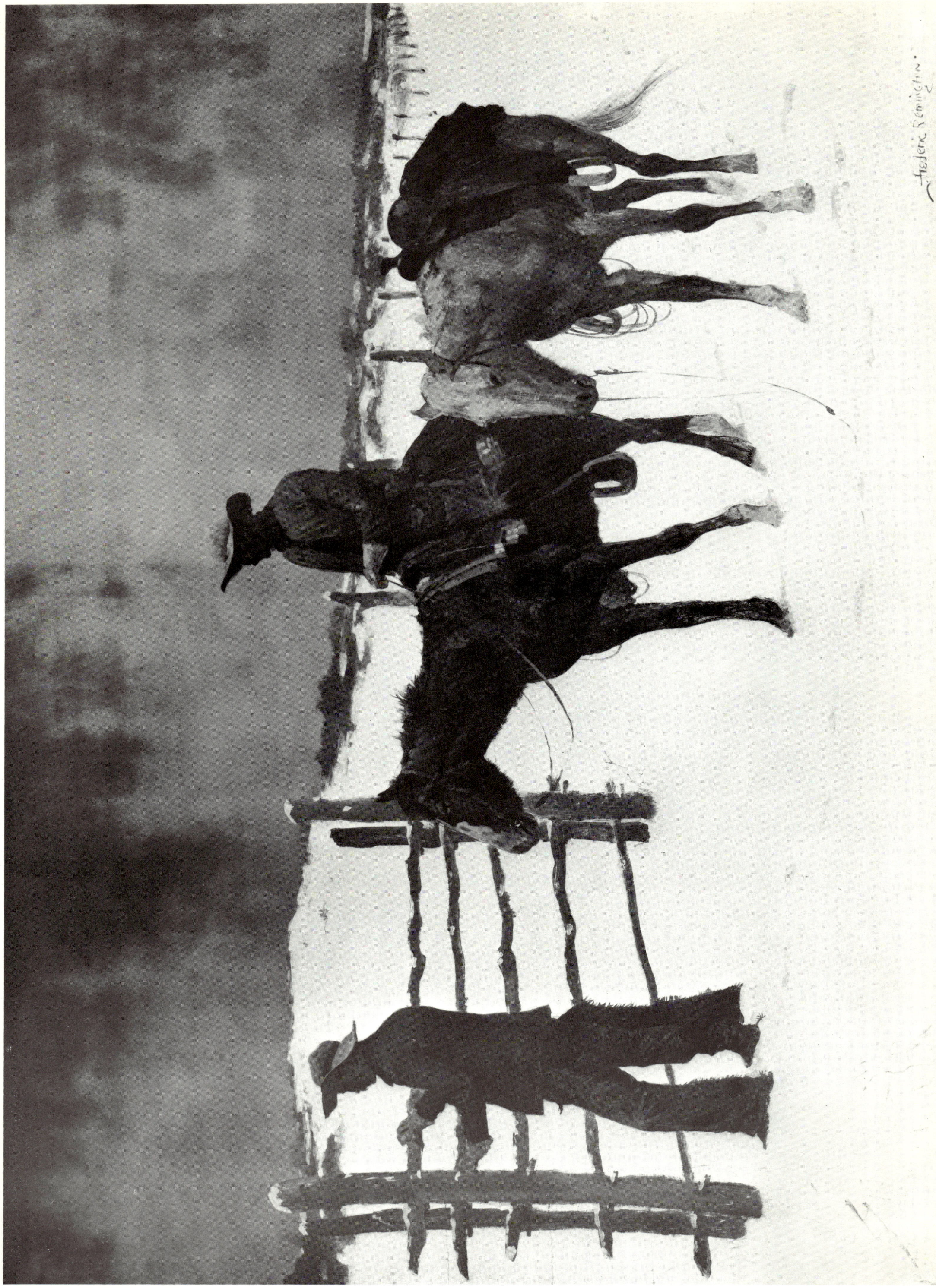
Frederic Remington

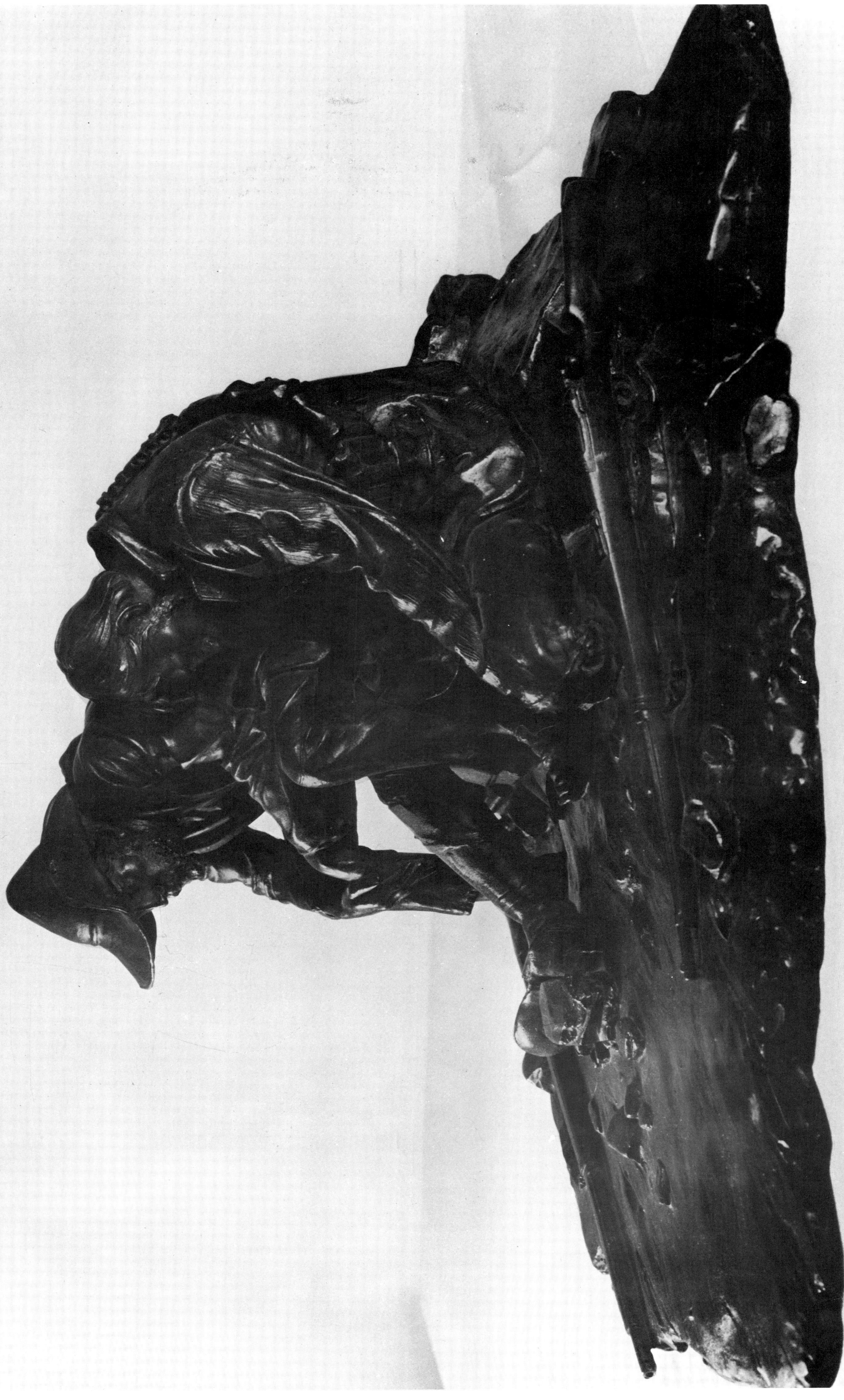

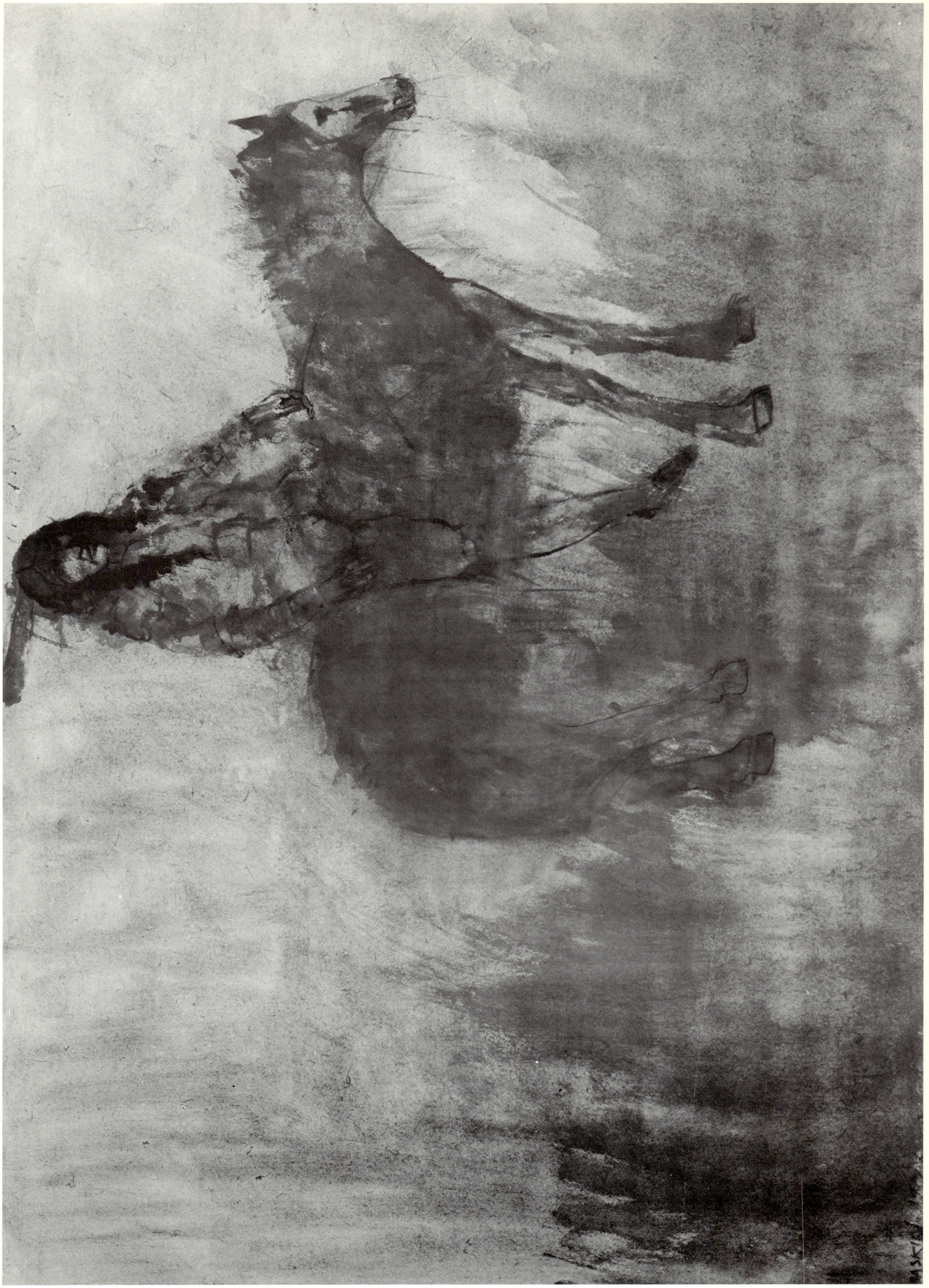

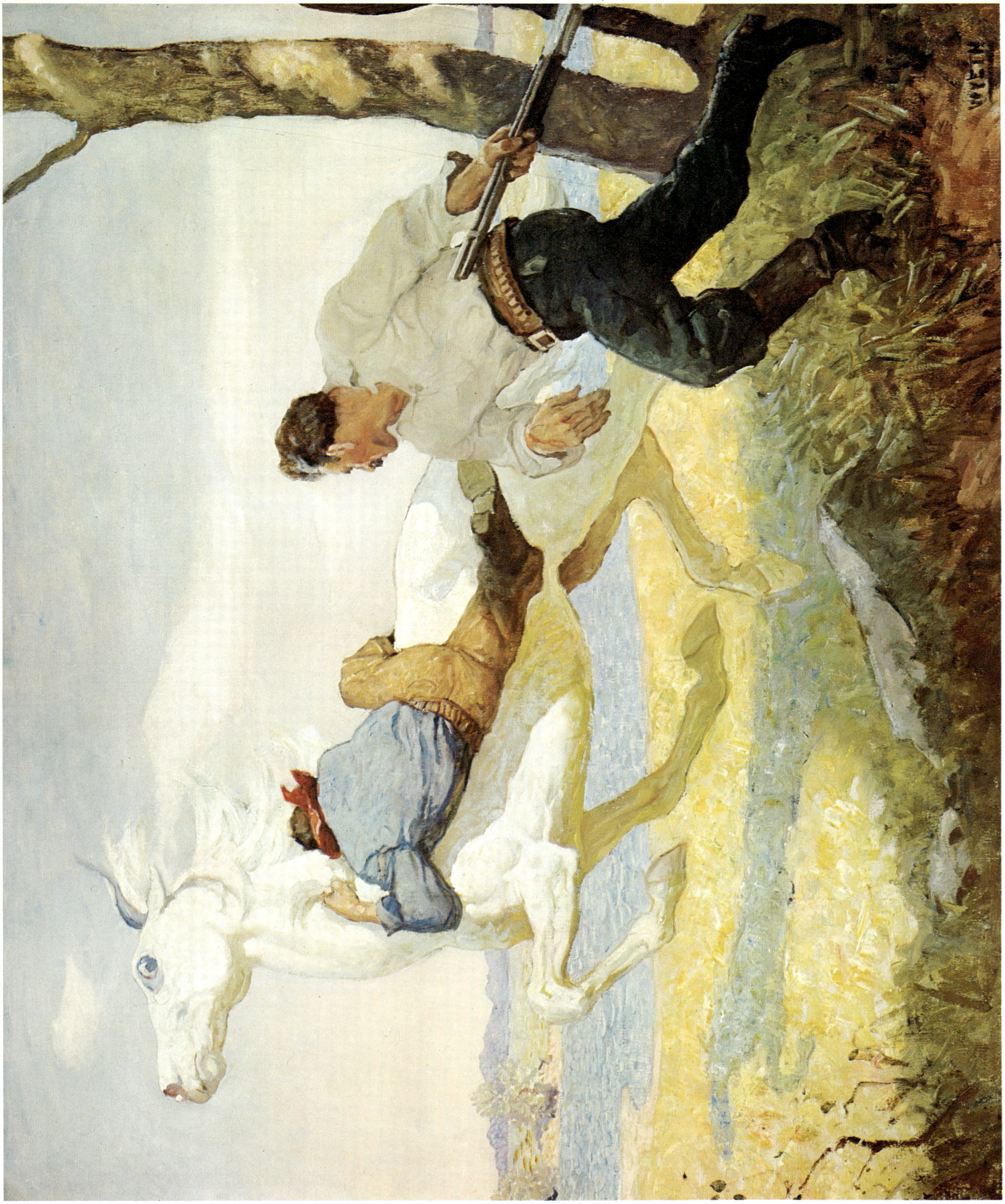

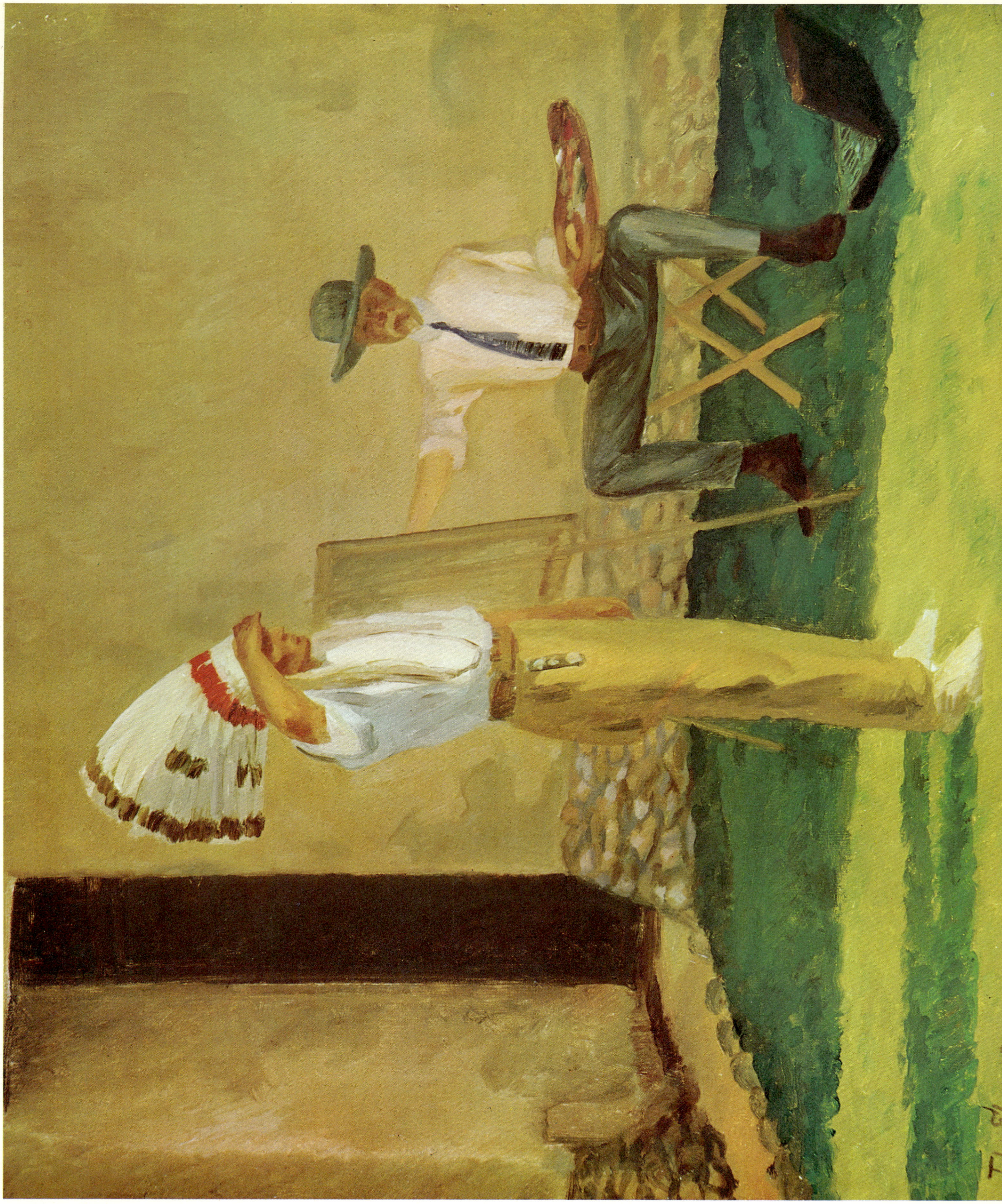
John Sloan-'20

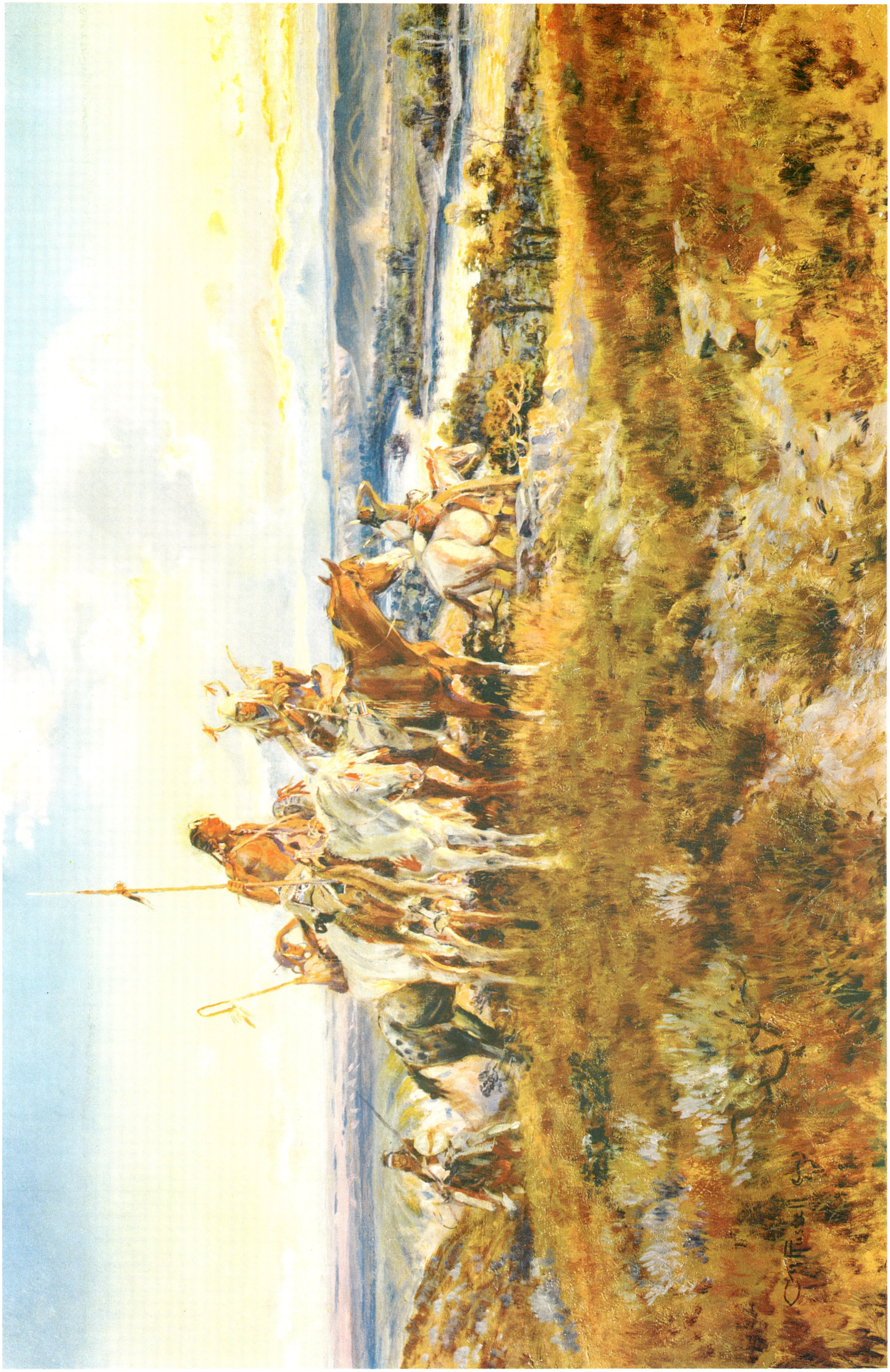

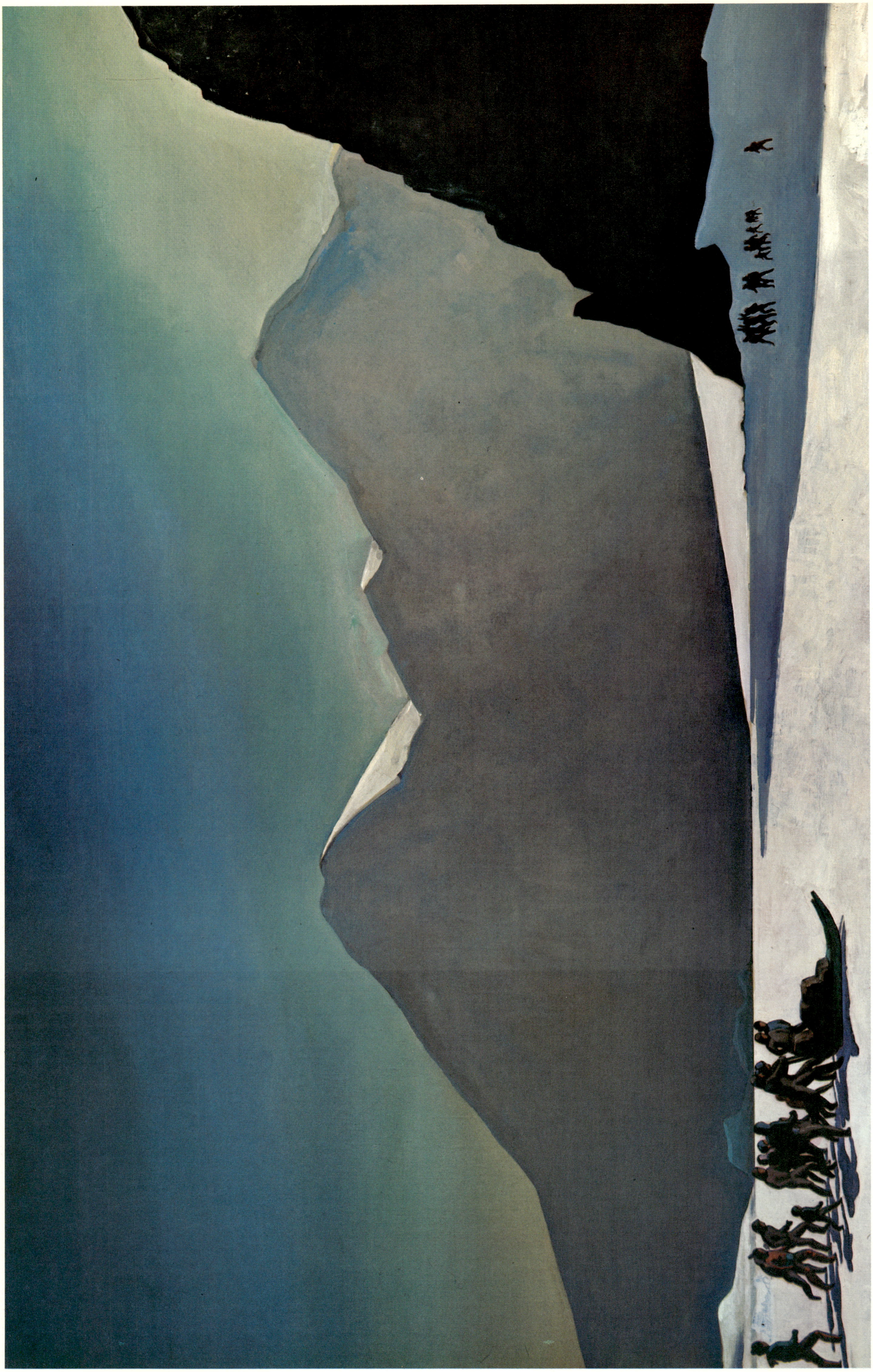

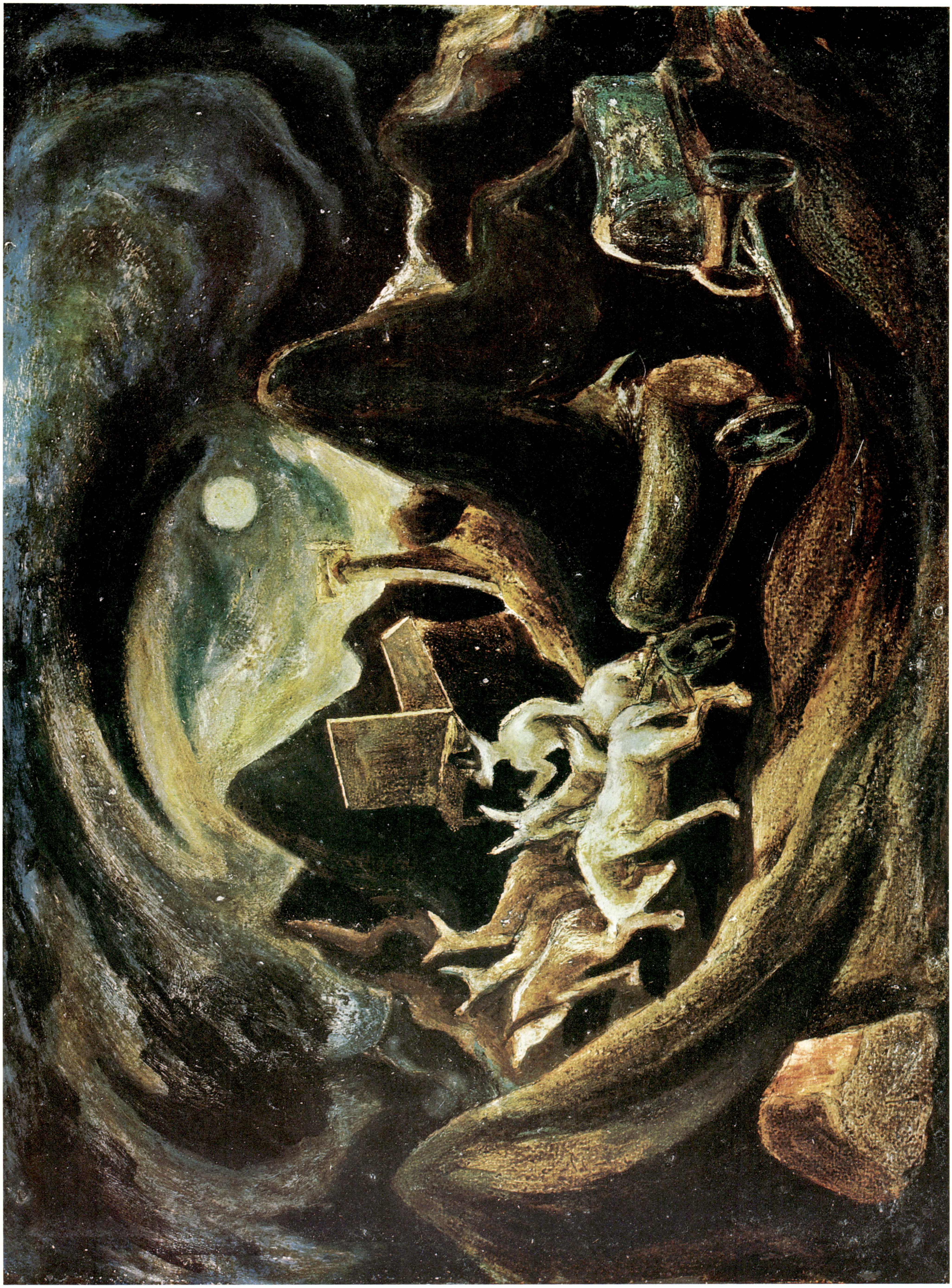

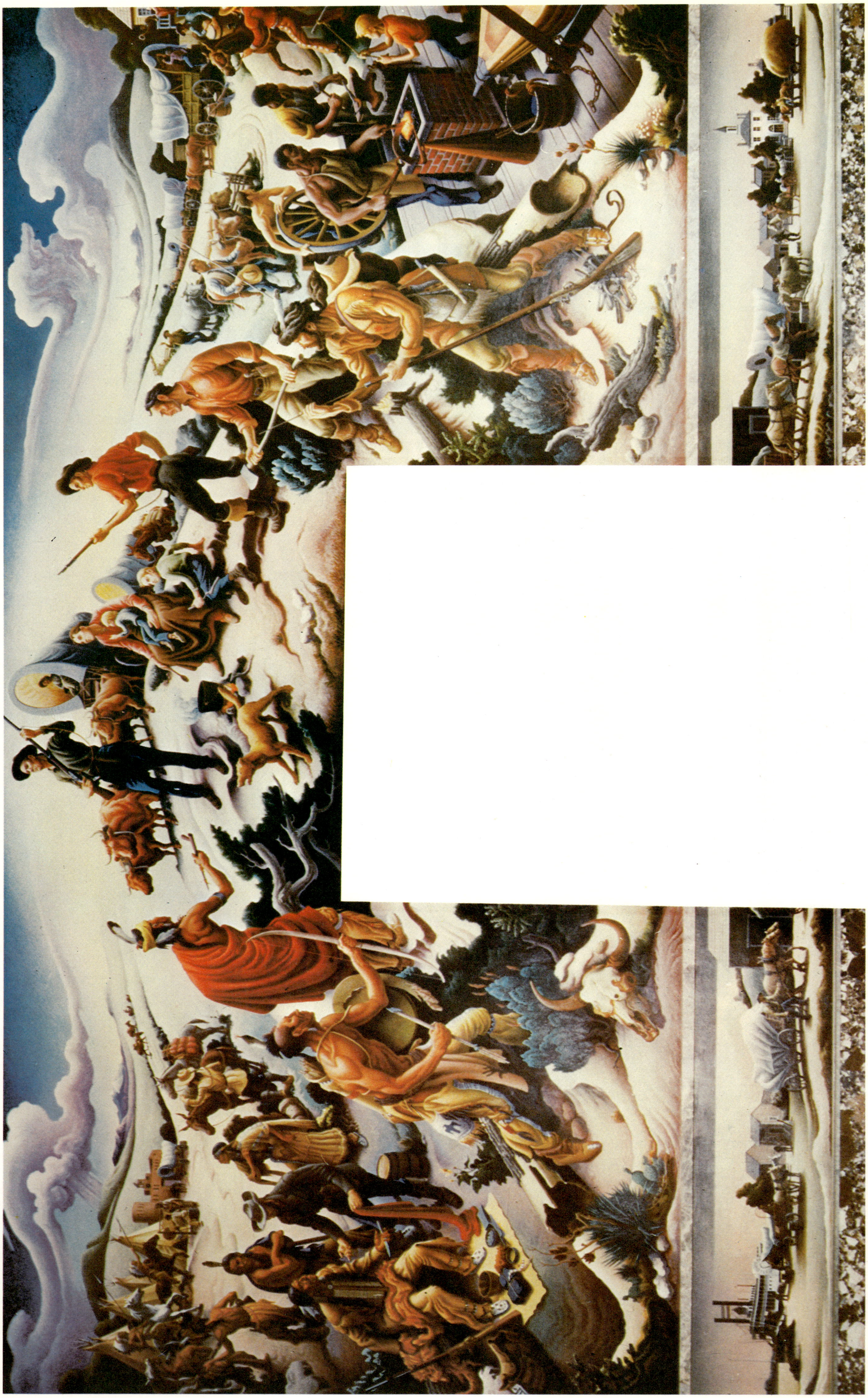

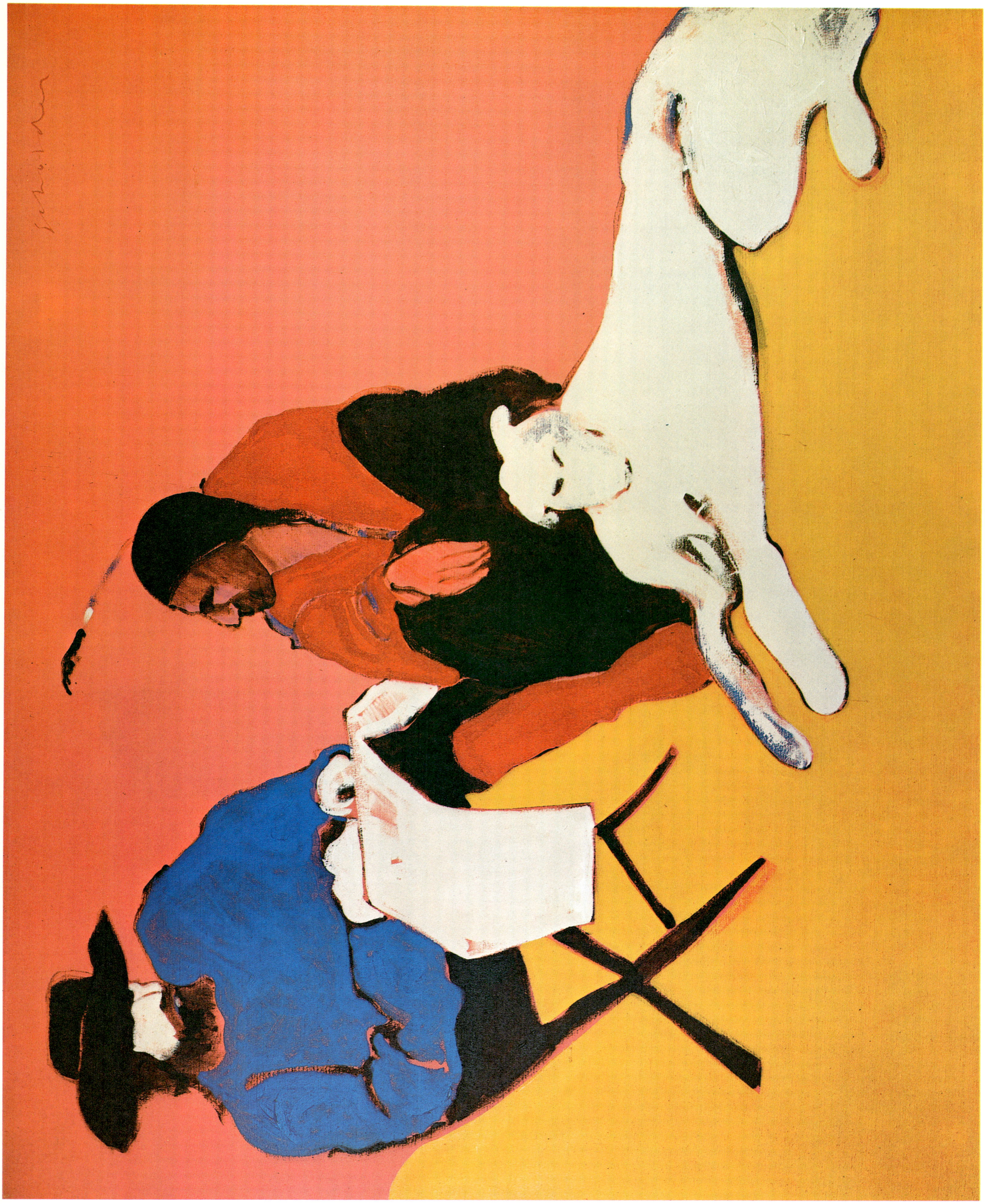

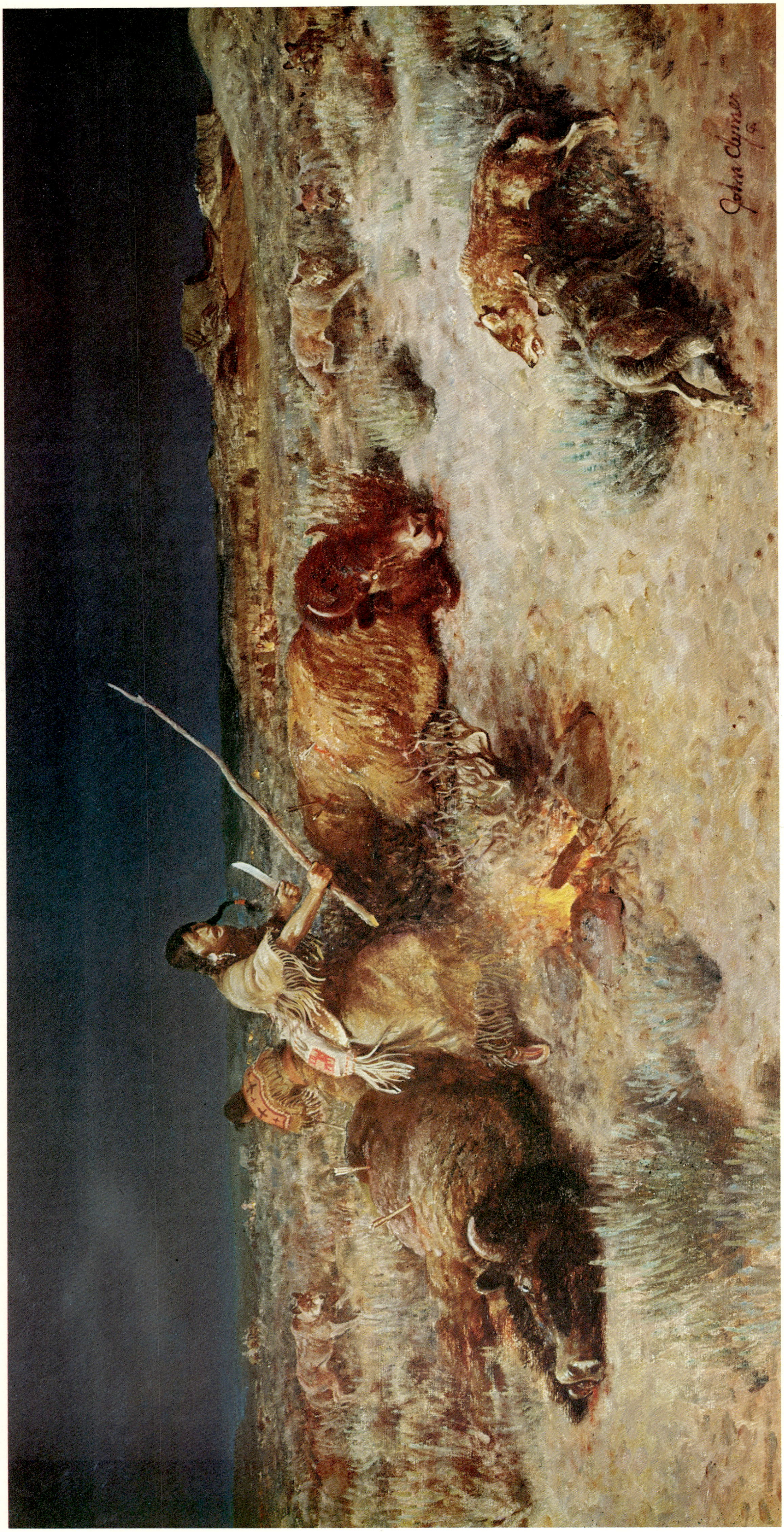
John Clymer

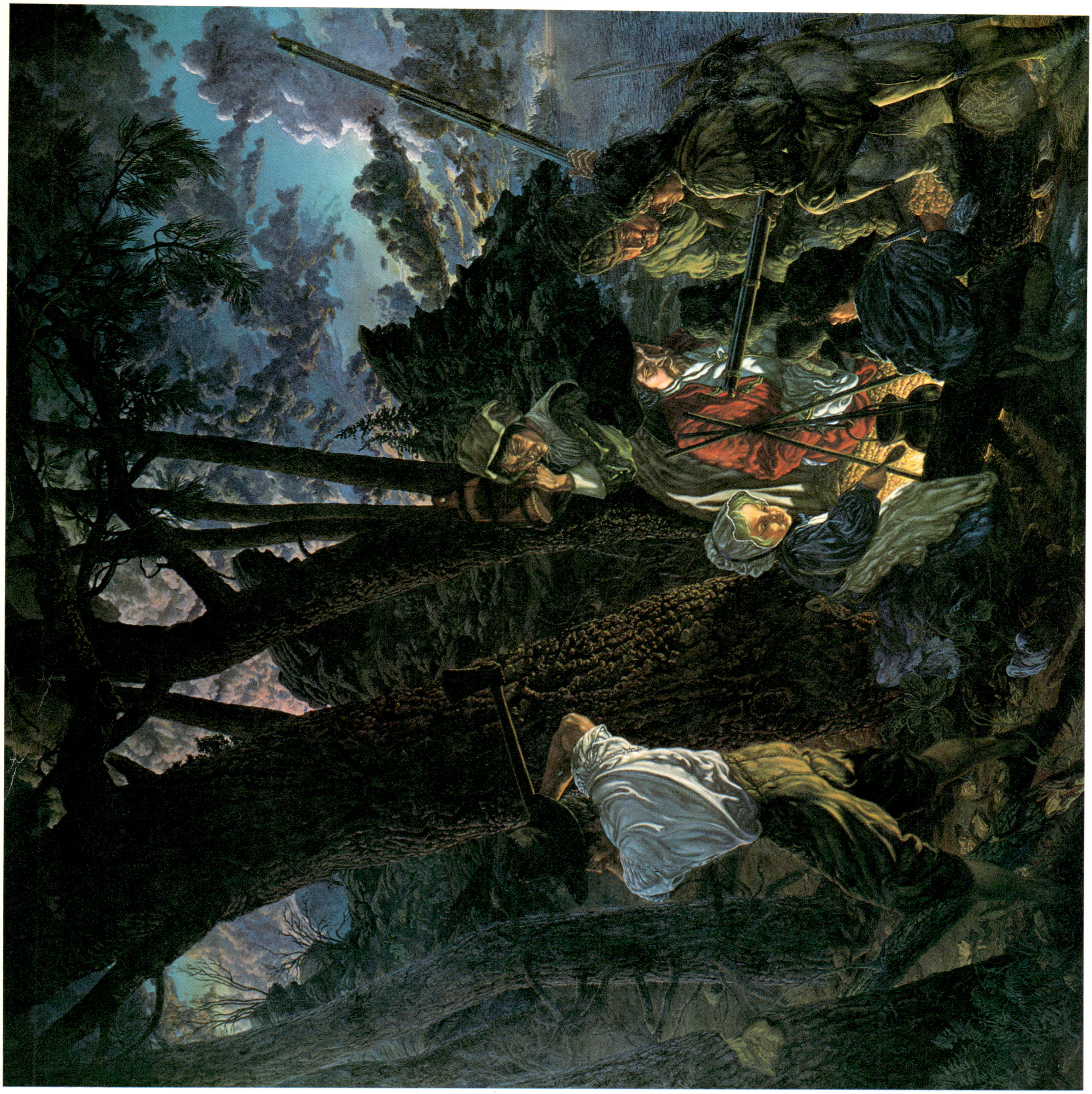

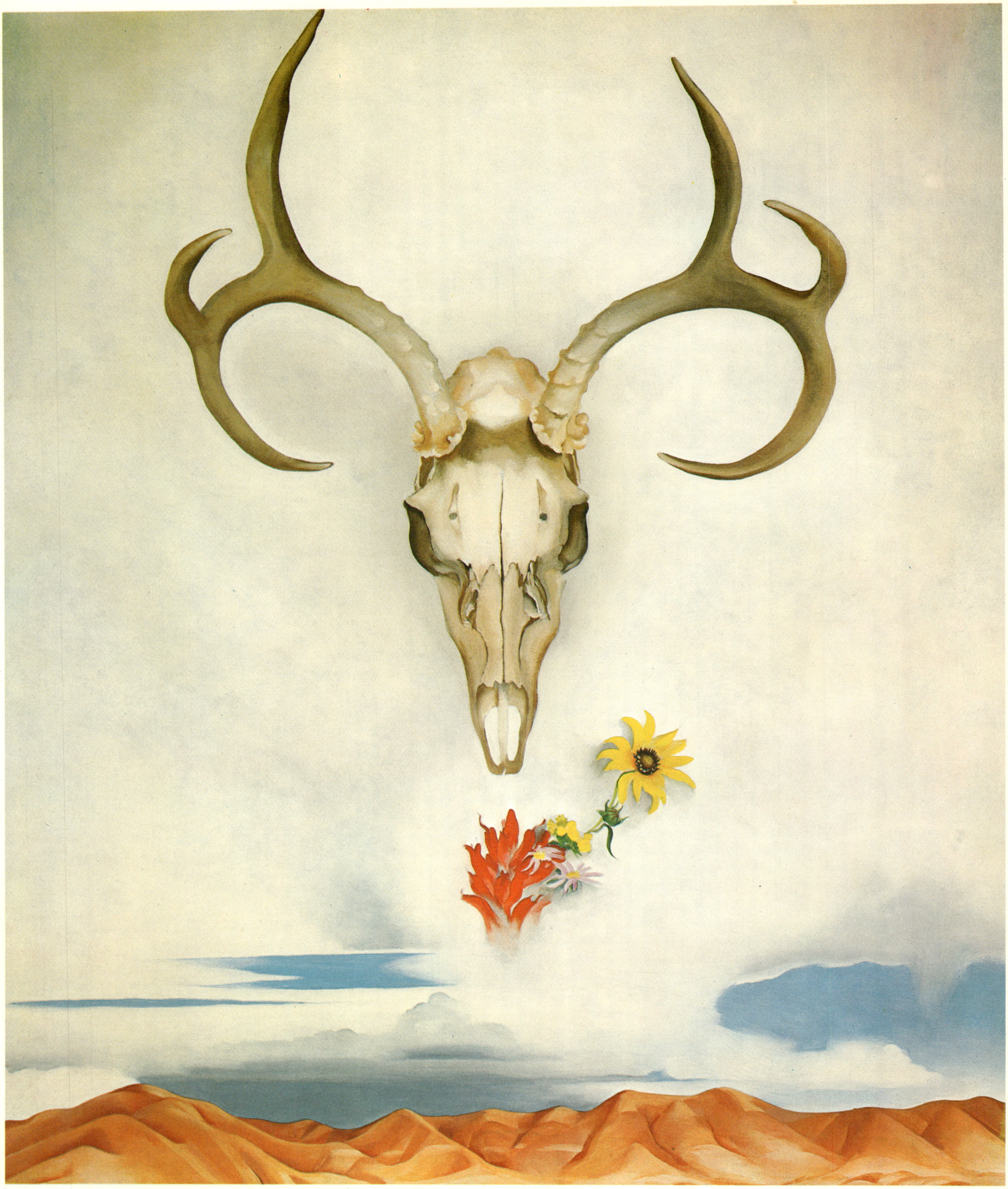